Systematic Urban Planning

Darwin G. Stuart

The Praeger Special Studies program—
utilizing the most modern and efficient book
production techniques and a selective
worldwide distribution network—makes
available to the academic, government, and
business communities significant, timely
research in U.S. and international economic, social, and political development.

Systematic Urban Planning

Praeger Publishers New York Washington London

PRAEGER SPECIAL STUDIES IN U.S. ECONOMIC, SOCIAL, AND POLITICAL ISSUES

Library of Congress Cataloging in Publication Data

Stuart, Darwin G
    Systematic urban planning.

    (Praeger special studies in U.S. economic,
social, and political issues)
    Includes bibliographical references.
    1. Cities and towns—Planning—1945–
2. Cities and towns—Planning—United States.
I. Title.
HT166.S78   309.2'62'0973   75–19825
ISBN 0–275–56060–0

PRAEGER PUBLISHERS
111 Fourth Avenue, New York, N.Y. 10003, U.S.A.

Published in the United States of America in 1976
by Praeger Publishers, Inc.

Printed in the United States of America

PREFACE

This book is based upon several years of both academic and consulting experience. It is derived from the author's work as a student, teacher, and consultant in urban planning and systems analysis.

Two chapters are based upon the author's doctoral dissertation, completed at Northwestern University in 1969. Three chapters are based upon research monographs prepared for the American Society of Planning Officials, from 1970 to 1972. Two additional chapters are based upon consulting assignments performed for the San Diego Region Comprehensive Planning Organization, from 1972 to 1974.

The final chapter (actually Chapter 1) provides an overview and perspective on each of the others. Over this time span of several years, 1969-75, the author's hopes and expectations for systematic planning methods have mellowed a bit. With the benefit of real-world experience, initial, somewhat "idealized" concepts of planning have evolved to be more pragmatic in nature. In particular, it has become the author's view that the quantitative mathematical models that have given rise to much of the "systems approach" in planning are no longer (and perhaps never were) the primary foundation around which our systematic planning techniques should be built. It is hoped that this evolution of thought is evident in the various chapters, which are reprinted without significant change from their original journal or monograph sources.

The book is primarily nontechnical in nature; the reader need not be versed in quantitative methods. It is written for urban planners, public administrators, engineers, elected officials, educators, students, environmentalists, and any others interested in improving urban planning methods. It is concerned with those methods of planning and evaluation that are relevant to the full range of urban issues— growth, development, redevelopment, social equity, economics, environmental conservation, public service systems, and transportation.

The four basic steps of the "systems approach" to urban planning are examined: identifying goals and objectives, formulating alternative plans and programs, predicting the effectiveness of alternatives, and evaluating those alternatives. Problems and prospects for this more rational approach to planning are reviewed. Case studies are used extensively. The roles of quantitative methods, computer processing, community participation, data and information systems, qualitative analysis, cost-effectiveness evaluation strategies, and other aspects are explored. It is concluded that judgmental elements—the "art" of systematic urban planning—may well represent the key to successful application of this approach.

It is the purpose of the book to demonstrate that systematic planning concepts still hold promise and relevance for improving the urban planning process—and that these concepts hold no real mysteries. Their judgmental or artful aspects tie them closely to less structured approaches to planning. While the many examples and literature references given are a part of demonstrating the utility and validity of the systems approach, a secondary purpose of the book is to indicate that there is no one "right" way to employ systematic planning methods. In this sense, the book is clearly introductory in nature. Within the broad four-step systems approach, many methodological variations are possible and desirable.

The author is indebted to several of his associates and colleagues, who reviewed the various chapters at different stages of their development. These include Rodney E. Engelen, Joseph L. Schofer, Martin Wachs, George L. Peterson, Franklin H. Beal, Frank S. So, Richard J. Huff, Stuart R. Shaffer, and Lee Johnston, as well as other colleagues, advisors, and contributors at Barton-Aschman Associates, Northwestern University, ASPO, and San Diego CPO. Their advice and assistance are gratefully acknowledged.

CONTENTS

LIST OF TABLES

LIST OF FIGURES

Systematic Urban Planning

OVERVIEW:
THE ART OF
SYSTEMATIC
PLANNING

This book is about urban planning methods. Even more, it is about the broader process of planning within which various methodologies are used. From several different perspectives each chapter stresses the need to be "systematic"—meaning simply the need to identify and analyze more carefully the multiple consequences of urban plans.

Since the first of these chapters was written, interest in (and the credibility of) the so-called systems approach to governmental problem solving, of which urban planning is, of course, one area, has risen and then waned to some extent. This rising and waning in the early 1970s can be tied to attempts to employ planning-programming-budgeting systems (PPBS) at various levels of government. The defunct Model Cities program is a case in point. There were few successes and many failures, especially at local and regional planning levels, in applying the systematic concepts of PPBS.

One premise of this book is, however, that it would be a mistake to dismiss these systematic concepts because PPBS and systems approach are no longer fashionable phrases. Somehow, the basic ideas and methodological approaches must be retained and strengthened, with much less reliance on jargon and its limitations. The need for more systematic planning—that is, the need for sounder urban and regional planning (and other governmental) decisions, based on a fuller understanding of impacts and consequences—grows more rather than less urgent.

If the basic concepts of systematic urban planning are sound, why have we so few successful applications of this approach? A primary reason probably lies in the overly high expectations for the role of computerized mathematical modeling on the part of both nontechnical users and model builders themselves. It has been found that mathematical models do not provide all the answers after all, and that there are large elements of uncertainty in the results they do provide. Many assumptions must be made explicit, and large doses of subjective judgment must still be applied. Mathematical models do not make our analysis tasks any easier; if anything, they probably make them harder. It is the disillusionment with the quantitative-analysis side of systematic urban planning that probably accounts for the lack of widespread popularity of the systems approach.

A second major premise of this book is consequently that the quantitative-analysis aspects of systematic urban planning are not, in the end, its most important elements. Instead, the driving force behind successful applications of more systematic approaches to planning must arise from its subjective and qualitative aspects. The success of planning methodologies should not be judged on their mathematical precision but rather on the degree to which nonmathematical factors have been explicitly dealt with. In many respects, these underlying qualitative aspects might be termed the "art" of systematic urban planning.

There are essentially four steps in the systems approach: (a) identifying goals and objectives, (b) formulating alternative plans and programs, (c) predicting the effectiveness of alternatives, and (d) evaluating those alternatives. Much emphasis in the past has been given to the use of quantitative forecasting tools, the need for objective, rigorous, quantitative data, and an overall feeling that the precision represented by computers is critical to effective systems analysis. In fact, however, this chapter stresses that the most important ingredients of systematic urban planning may well lie in its judgmental aspects. An attempt has been made to indicate, with examples, how creative, more sensitive, or "artistic" elements might be applied. It is concluded that systematic urban planning is probably more an art than a science, regardless of the extent to which computer models and similar quantitative analysis tools are used.

For example, in identifying goals and objectives, the art will lie in reaching community agreement and consensus and in expressing objectives meaningfully and consistently. In identifying alternative plans and programs, the art will lie in the imaginative design of alternatives. This is one of the least developed steps of the system approach. In general, a richer variety of alternatives appears to be needed. In predicting effectiveness, the art will lie in devising analytic methods that do not call for extensive mathematical modeling (particularly, new, large-scale models). Emphasis should be placed on the imaginative use and adaptation of existing, smaller-scale models. In the evaluation of alternatives the art will lie in successfully handling the goal-weighting problem and in accounting for qualitative objectives.

To help structure an examination and review of how these judgmental or more sensitive aspects of systematic planning are of special
importance, the remainder of this chapter is organized around a listing
of 17 problem or issue areas. Similar lists appear in several other
chapters, but the purpose of this particular listing is to emphasize the
"artistic" content of each issue area. This list subsumes those in other
chapters. The various problem or issue areas are further organized
around the four basic steps in the systems approach.

IDENTIFYING OBJECTIVES

This step in the planning process has sometimes been used as a
convenient focus for citizen-participation activities. Although there
are great dangers of superficiality, overabstraction, and even irrele-
vancy here, developing and identifying objectives can be a valid starting
point for strengthened community participation, an improvement that
is certainly needed at other points in the planning process. In fact,
one of the difficult issue areas, pervasive in all four steps of the systems approach, involves the different techniques by which increased
community participation can be made more effective.

In relation to identifying objectives, the effectiveness of many of
these participation techniques will center, in turn, upon how three
other problem areas are handled. The importance of these other areas
extends beyond community participation strategies to include better
structuring of the involvement of all "actors"—political decision
makers, professional planners and engineers, public administrators,
and the like. Included are the need for focusing more clearly on critical community problems (rather than on abstract goals), for explicitly
allowing for and managing disagreement and conflict over objectives,
and for identifying from the beginning the criteria and measures by
which goal achievement will be assessed.

Focusing on Critical Problems

Asking a group of citizens (or planners) to sit down and begin to
list all of a community's goals and objectives can be a laborious and
sometimes unrewarding, incomplete undertaking. It is usually much
easier and relevant to ask for an identification of problems—current
problems—a community and its residents are experiencing. Focusing
on these critical problems can also help guide other steps in the planning process, including the design of alternative programs for

alleviating problems, deciding what kinds of data would be useful for
measuring the extent of problems, and estimating the degree to which
alternative programs might be expected to work (further discussion is
given in Chapter 2). Community-problem formulation should also be
structured in terms of the community subgroups whose interests are
being considered. This can lead to a further focusing on significant
points of disagreement and conflict over the severity of problems,
discussed below.

The art in proper problem formulation—identifying real community
needs—probably lies most strongly with the techniques or procedures
of community participation. One such technique, the charrette or work-
shop, offers important potentials here.[1] Though as yet little used in
urban planning, charrettes are intensive workshops conducted on a
short-term basis (for example, over a weekend or on two or three
consecutive evenings). In a community-participation setting the emphasis is on problem formulation and the development of alternative
solutions. Experts (administrators, engineers, and planners) and citizens work together in a mutual learning atmosphere. The intensiveness
(for example, with all-day sessions) is an important element in stimulating a two-way flow of information.

It is important that neither community residents nor technical experts come to such workshops with preconceived plans and solutions.
Rather, the prevailing attitude should be one of a joint investigation of
local problems and ways for dealing with them. Community residents
can provide an intimate understanding of local attitudes and perceptions, while planners, engineers, administrators provide the technical
expertise needed to help identify feasible solutions. This kind of interaction can be quite useful in quickly developing "sketch-plan" alternatives that are directly responsive to community problems; a broad
range of such options should be pursued. Workshops of this type are
also useful for establishing a continuing two-way dialogue and, hopefully, for bringing out all relevant viewpoints.

Increasing Community Participation

The charrette technique is only one of many possible methods for
better structuring community participation. Offshoots of this highly
interactive approach could also involve the use of related, more specialized procedures, time and budget permitting. These procedures
would require the direct involvement of trained psychologists, anthropologists, or sociologists. They involve such formally and informally
structured devices as role playing, where citizens attempt to understand better the perceptions and values of the experts, and vice versa;

operational gaming, where conflict-type games, complete with rules
and playing materials, are used to educate participants in important
planning considerations; or group sensitivity-training sessions, where
a psychologist leads group discussions aimed at uncovering the most
basic goals and objectives of a community.

The use of such techniques could, of course, extend well beyond
the simple identification of problems and objectives. Other methods
for more effective community participation are under development and
application, particularly in urban transportation planning. [2] It should
be recognized that three commonly used "nontechniques" have serious
limitations because they neither facilitate a two-way interaction flow
nor provide a useful environment for "artfully" increasing community
inputs. [3] These nontechniques include public hearings and public meetings, whose formality and after-the-fact nature (plans having been
developed already) are serious drawbacks; citizen advisory committees,
which all too often have been superficial, inadequately representative
(or even biased), and perfunctory attempts to meet federal requirements for citizen participation; and community-attitude surveys, which
may represent a useful data source but clearly encourage only a one-
way flow of information.

Other more promising community interaction techniques include
the following: (a) advocacy planning, where local citizen organizations
(perhaps at governmental expense, rather than at their own) hire planning professionals specifically to pursue and "advocate" local planning
goals, in relation to broader urban planning programs; (b) the ombuds-
man, a sort of lobbyist who, like an advocate planner, could be hired
by a community organization to look over its full range of planning and
nonplanning interests in the governmental arena; (c) field offices,
which, as decentralized administration outposts, have a potential for
providing a permanent, continuing site available on a day-to-day basis,
where other, more structured participation techniques might be pursued; and (d) field work, which, perhaps in conjunction with a field
office, involves a sustained period of much closer contact with the
local community on the part of planners, engineers, and administrators, suggested by urban anthropologists and sociologists as the most
meaningful way to become familiar with local community values.

Managing Disagreement

Regardless of the type of community interaction technique used,
one measure of its success will be the degree to which disagreement
and conflict over local problems, and their solutions, are crystallized.
Unless such disagreements are brought out, there is a good chance

that the participation effort will be superficial and irrelevant. To stimulate these conflict realizations, it is probably essential that the identification of problems and objectives proceed hand-in-hand with the interactive development of possible solutions. The charrette technique is typically oriented in this way. Actual alternatives for problem resolution are necessary; moreover, detailed proposals (especially showing the geographic location of new facilities) are typically needed to help bring out potential conflicts. The problem of locating a highway route (with its displacement potential) has become a classic example, pointing to the necessity of identifying conflicts early in the planning process when there is a chance to pursue alternative solutions jointly with affected community groups.

Disagreement is consequently healthy, and it should be brought out quickly. "Managing" disagreement does not imply eliminating it. One of the most challenging features of the artistic side of systematic planning involves the structuring of community-participation activities so that consensus is not necessary, while still providing every avenue for some degree of reconciliation over disagreements among all participants. A focusing on disagreements and their elucidation should consequently be emphasized.[4]

Another community-participation technique, the Delphi technique, deals more directly with this management of disagreement problem.[5] The basic purpose of the Delphi technique is to permit the setting of priorities or relative rankings among a set of goals, issues, problems, or questions. This is accomplished by asking those involved, such as community residents, to participate in a series of sequential questionnaires. Two or three rounds may be conducted. During each successive round, the participants are given information and feedback on the results of the previous round, such as average rankings or reasons for extreme rankings. Disagreements are noted, but on an anonymous basis. Using this information, each participant is able to reconsider and refine his previous priorities. Each participant thereby becomes involved in a trade-off analysis, involving at least partial reconciliation of conflicts among a set of competing problems or objectives. Use of the Delphi technique is likely to generate both a majority consensus of opinion regarding some problems or goals and a series of clearly established minority opinions regarding the importance of other goals.

Identifying Suitable Criteria

Very often it is difficult to define exactly what is meant by a certain problem or objective, without indicating how it could be measured. There is consequently a strong link between goals and objectives and the quantitative or qualitative indicators of achievement that might be related to them. The identification of such indicators is not a simple process, since more than one measure will usually make sense, and since a certain amount of arbitrariness and merely partial coverage seems to be associated with selecting one indicator over others. The setting of possible minimum or maximum standards of achievement for particular goals and indicators, if desired, also seems to involve large doses of judgment. The development of urban indicators or goal-achievement criteria is still in its early stages, and is discussed in Chapter 5.

DEVELOPING ALTERNATIVES

Probably the development of alternatives ranks a close second behind their evaluation as the currently weakest step in systematic urban planning. Not only in land-use/transportation planning but also in the design of social, economic, and environmental programs there seems to be a tendency to try to develop the preferred plan too quickly. The assessment of many design options has too often been implicit and internal, rather than explicit, so participation in the evaluation of these options has been limited. On the other hand, it is no easy task to come up with several significantly different alternatives that appear promising in achieving a given set of urban objectives. Perhaps the development of alternatives calls for more artfulness and creativity than any other step in the systems approach. The pursuit of imaginative design is certainly one important issue area.

While a greater number of plan or program alternatives may be desirable, it is quite possible that too much information on these alternatives will be developed, at least in terms of the ability of decision makers to absorb and contrast the information. This danger is increased in light of a second important issue area, that of including more community-level characteristics as a feature of plan and program alternatives. In other words, we not only need more alternatives, we need to know more about each one. There are significant implications for facilitating trade-off analyses and for communicating differences of alternative plans (discussed below), when the rapidly expanding level of required evaluative effort must be made more manageable. In addition to expanding the range of options (an issue area in itself), a final problem area for the development of alternatives involves the pragmatic need for building existing systems and programs, to achieve imaginative solutions that are still evolutionary.

Pursuing Imaginative Design

One of the important conclusions that emerged from a recent review of metropolitan land-use/transportation planning in several regions was that the alternative policies tested were too conservative, too similar, and too generalized for differences to be obtained among the alternatives.[6] It was consequently recommended that for this level of urban planning, if alternative policies are to vary in any important way (that is, for significantly different levels of regional goal achievement), it will be necessary for significant, small- as well as large-scale variations to be made in proposed land-use development patterns and policies, including not only transportation but also sewer and water, open space, and the location and density of employment and population. This need for meaningful differences among a set of alternatives, once an evaluation oriented to relative levels of goal achievement has been completed, is not unique to the regional scale of planning; it also affects, for example, city-level planning and programming activities.

Presumably, "significant variation" among alternatives can be achieved through more creativity and imagination in the process of developing alternatives. By its very nature, imaginative design is not a process easily subject to a series of rules or guidelines. Multidisciplinary design teams have been advanced as one way to create at least more comprehensive—and, hopefully, more imaginative—alternatives, but these have not always worked well. At the transportation-corridor-planning level, if the implementation of transportation improvement strategies can be taken as any measure of success, such design teams have worked out too infrequently. In general, there does appear to be considerable potential for the injection of "fresh approaches" from persons trained in other disciplines.[7]

Including Community-Level Characteristics

In the review of metropolitan planning cited above it was also found that "the models and methods available were too blunt to produce differences in alternatives in response to the policies assumed" and that "the size of districts used for forecasting development of travel demand was probably too large to detect the assumed land-use and transportation interaction; the expected differences in spatial arrangements of activities and environmental quality may not exist at the aggregate district scale."[8] Without identifying the level of aggregation (zone size) that might be best, it was consequently recommended that the size of analysis districts for regional planning be sufficiently small to capture the kinds of differences anticipated to be of importance. In general, this recommendation calls for the specification of neighborhood and community-level characteristics and consequences of both local and regional plans.

The interrelationship between regional-level and land-use/transportation planning and the eventual community-level impacts, especially of major transportation capital investments, represent an important example here (these regional-local planning interfaces are discussed further in Chapter 4). In recent years the transportation-corridor level of planning has been the meeting ground within which many regional-local goal conflicts have been played out. System-level planning for urban transportation improvements has all too often shown that somewhat abstract system or network plans have meaning to the average citizen—and to the political decision maker—only when the local community or neighborhood-level consequences of new routes and facilities are spelled out. Consequences, such as residential and business displacement, noise and air pollution, esthetics, open-space land consumption, and related negative impacts, can have and have had great significance at the project decision-making level. Inadequate consideration of these community-level impacts has been a serious defect of too many system-level urban transportation plans—plans that have quickly become obsolete for lack of implementation of first-stage improvements.

Building on Existing Systems

Feasibility, both in cost/revenue and environmental impact terms, will continue to be a primary criterion of political decision makers in assessing public program alternatives. Determining whether a program will "work" and the public's ability to afford it will continue to be primary decision factors in the political arena. The need to blend the imaginative with the pragmatic makes the developing-alternatives step in systematic planning even more difficult. In general, the need here seems to be, in part, to make better use of existing facilities and to build upon those facilities to make both them and their incremental additions more efficient and functional.

To some extent, this problem area involves one of designing at least some plan and program alternatives to focus on better management of existing urban facilities and services, to increase "output" for minimum levels of additional "input" (especially capital investment in new facilities). The concept of "adaptive design" appears to have special merit here, where a clear understanding of behavioral factors appears to be important.[9] Such factors could involve, for example,

incentives and disincentives, economic or otherwise, that might affect
the use of existing facilities (for example, car-pooling incentives and
Central Business District [CBD]-parking disincentives), as well as
behavioral and functional aspects associated with the technical redesign
of existing facilities to increase capacity (for example, multiple-
occupancy vehicle lanes on freeways).

Expanding the Range of Options

Much of the problem in developing alternatives can be put quite
simple: We need more of them. However, the design of more plan or
program options that are sufficiently detailed at the community level
implies a considerable amount of additional work. When it is realized
that, in practice, it is difficult to separate the design of new alternatives from the evaluation of both new and old alternatives (discussed
further under cyclic redesigning of below), there seems significant
potential for various forms of computer data-processing assistance.
A number of innovative research efforts, more outside than within the
urban planning field, are currently exploring ways in which interactive
man-machine analysis methods can help to expand the range of options,
whatever the planning context. Two important features of this interactive computerized approach involve (a) assisting the user in quickly
generating new alternatives and (b) the high-speed identification of
significant impacts, in turn permitting more alternatives to be generated relatively quickly, in response to both the positive and negative
impacts analyzed.

One recent concept for greater interaction between man and the
computer has been termed "participatory online planning."[10] Under
this approach to man-computer synergism, remote computer terminals, possibly with graphic capabilities, could be used to allow for
immediate computer processing, feedback, additional user responses
and inputs, further processing, and so on. It is argued that, though
many problems can not be solved either by man or by computer working alone, the generation of ideas, alternatives, and solutions can be
further stimulated through man-computer interaction. In general, the
properly trained user, exercising judgment and decision making in
order to narrow down on important problem areas, can guide the computer to perform its high-speed mechanical tasks. Such interactive
systems should allow the user to explore a variety of "what if" questions, as a part of generating and investigating alternatives.

Recent efforts have been made to apply interactive man-computer
concepts in urban transportation planning.[11] A man-computer analysis
system was developed at the University of Washington, which also

enlisted the aid of a cathode ray tube (CRT) output device, similar to
a television screen, for displaying the results of analyzing alternatives. [12] These displays could involve maps, tables, graphs, or other
visual devices. Technical capabilities also exist for using the CRT
display screen for directly modifying alternatives by means of a light
pen. This urban transportation-analysis system (UTRANS) was developed and tested for the designing of alternative bus-transit systems
within a travel corridor in the Seattle region. Other research efforts
in applying this interactive graphics approach in the design of an expanded number of urban transportation alternatives, under other corridor and community service contexts, are also underway.

PREDICTING EFFECTIVENESS

Much time, effort, and money has gone into the development of
computerized mathematical models for urban systems analysis, particularly for urban-transportation systems, with extensive Federal
Highway Administration (FHWA) and Urban Mass Transportation Administration (UMTA) support, and secondarily in the area of urban-
development models. Other types of specialized models, for example,
in water and sewer system planning, and for housing-market allocation,
as well as for other urban subsystems, have also been developed. [13]
In recent years, these computer modeling efforts have come under
sharp criticism. [14] Many criticisms relate to the fact that such models
have come to have a life unto themselves, overshadowing their essentially supportive role as predictive techniques in the broader urban-
planning process. Such models have been costly and time-consuming
to operate, difficult to understand, and inflexible in meeting new analysis demands.

Many of these criticisms could be interpreted to mean that the art
of model design and application is underdeveloped. Here, particularly,
as with the other three steps in systematic planning, the need for artistry relates to the participatory and perceptual needs of nontechnical
users. These are the same users (political decision makers; community representatives; planners, engineers, and administrators, among
others), whose roles are important in other phases of the planning
process. Perhaps model builders, due to the complexity of the technical aspects of their work, have overlooked this continuing need for
relevance within the broader process of planning and decision making.
Consequently, four user-oriented issue areas can be identified: (a) increasing the understandability of modeling results, in layman terms,
(b) emphasizing the explicit inclusion of important policy variables
within urban-simulation models, so that the effects of policy variations

can be tested, (c) where appropriate, developing short-cut models that overcome current operational problems, and (d) where appropriate, developing specialized, problem- or function-oriented partial models.

Increasing Understandability of Results

A communications gap has always seemed to exist in the field of urban computer modeling, particularly with political decision makers and citizen groups, let alone with the nontechnical colleagues of modelers. Overcoming this gap is no small assignment, since the mathematical, computer programming, and data preparation intricacies of urban modeling do, in fact, require large amounts of energy. What is needed, however, with considerable skill and patience in communications (see below also), is an explanation of the logic of model structure (identifying the dependent and the independent variables), an exposition of any "theoretical" underpinnings (hypothesized causal relationships), and, most important, an explanation of the relevance, sensitivity, and uncertainty of modeling results (outputs) to the current land-use/transportation (or other) decision-making problems of an urban area. This last area is the key: Predictive models must be made more informative, understandable, and especially useful to decision makers and citizens.[15] Above all, modelers need the confidence of their ultimate clients, governmental decision makers.

Emphasizing Policy Variables

Models themselves need to be improved, of course. Experience has already shown that considerable artistry and judgment is involved in the development of quantitative urban models. One important area for strengthening urban models, and a guideline for developing new ones, is the emphasizing of the explicit representation of policy variables. In general, this means that as many independent variables in a model structure as possible should be defined so that they can be interpreted as factors subject to public policy control, as policy "levers" within the model. By increasing or decreasing the values of these levers (increasing or decreasing the level of investment in public policies and programs), we can analyze and predict the effects on other dependent model variables, generally representing the social, economic, and environmental performance of the urban area (see Chapter 6 for further discussion). Recent mandates to "be more relevant to policy issues, "[16] nearly all of which are short-range and immediate in nature, certainly have these kinds of implications for basic model structure.

A controversial but still intriguing modeling effort, the Forrester model, does possess as a virtue this explicit representation of policy levers.[17] Though this model, in its present form, cannot be used for urban-policy analyses (it requires considerable further development), it does permit public policies and programs, such as low-cost housing construction, job-creation programs for the underemployed, slum-housing demolition, low-income-housing construction subsidies, or the stimulation of new industrial development to be explicitly represented as policy options, with modeling outputs then defined in terms of changes in income levels, employment rates, housing vacancy rates, and other socioeconomic features of an urban area.

Critics of the Forrester model point out that it has not been calibrated or tested against real-world data (a serious shortcoming), that it has no spatial or geographic dimensions (an urban area is represented as a single point), that it is contradictory regarding the relationship between the sector of an urban area that is modeled and its surrounding environment, and that it confuses an experiment in model design with the premature and unsubstantiated use of the model for policy recommendations.[18] Nevertheless, this sort of model does represent a significant step in the direction of greater policy relevance, and, unlike most other urban models, it has attracted the attention of some governmental decision makers.

Developing Short-Cut Models

This and the following issue area were treated extensively at a recent conference on forecasting urban-travel demand.[19] At that conference it was observed that new and broader demands are now being made of travel-demand analysis procedures, with significant carryover implications for most other types of urban forecasting and analysis activities. In consonance with other issue areas described above, it was also observed that travel-demand models are now being asked to help evaluate a wider range of transportation options, including new technologies, low-cost capital options, and so-called no-build alternatives, as well as mixes of all of these in different transportation corridors. There is also a much greater need to examine the direct and indirect consequences of transportation alternatives more carefully, including issues of equity (who gains, who loses), and both regional and local social, economic, and environmental impacts. It was also concluded that a richer variety of travel-forecasting techniques is needed.

At the regional planning level, several serious operational problems in applying our current set of travel-demand analysis models have led to a call for more simplified "sketch-planning" models. Again, there is carryover here to urban development modeling and other urban public facilities systems analyses.[20] In general, too many existing regional system models are too time-consuming, too expensive, and too data-hungry to operate efficiently. Given that we wish to analyze a wider range of alternatives, analysis methods that reduce turnaround time (the time between deciding to analyze an alternative and getting usable output from a computer run) and cost must be developed. The short-cut, sketch-planning approach is one response that uses larger zones and coarser transportation networks, achieving these operational efficiencies at the expense of subarea detail.

For example, in the Los Angeles region a recent study employed a sketch-planning modeling package for rapidly exploring and analyzing a wide variety of regional transportation-control strategies.[21] Fifty-five different incentive/disincentive policies were tested, ranging from varying increases in parking price and supply to preferential treatment for multiple-occupancy vehicles to various kinds of transit service improvement. By comparison with previous, more conventional transportation-modeling packages utilized in the region, application of the sketch-planning package (covering trip generation, distribution, mode split, and assignment) proved to be much easier, faster, and less expensive. Turn-around times were greatly reduced and the study was conducted within a time span of only six months.

Developing Specialized Models

Because we need to know more about the impacts of more alternatives, it is also clear that additional, more specialized analysis and forecasting techniques will be necessary. Considerable artfulness and judgment will be necessary in the design of such techniques. Importantly, not all such techniques, and perhaps only a few of them, need to be based upon computerized modeling approaches. In many cases, all that may be needed are simple accounting procedures and algebraic equations (applied by hand) to keep track of different kinds of public-facility impacts (for example, acres of land required, by land-use type; the number of homes or businesses displaced; the number of jobs or families located within a specified distance). In fact, it has been argued that any further attempts to develop comprehensive, large-scale urban system models should be abandoned, and instead energies should be devoted to the development of explicitly partial modes, more manageable in nature, aimed at fairly specific policy questions.[22]

Such techniques appear especially needed at the corridor or community-planning level, both to deal with shorter-range impacts of many types, and with more locally-oriented, subarea impacts. The transportation-corridor planning context referred to earlier is a noteworthy example. It is important to remember that, even for short-range impacts, our analyses must still take the form of predictions. Because of this, for some impacts it will still be desirable to try to develop empirically derived forecasting models, establishing causal relationships between dependent and independent variables. For example, such models might deal with the rate and nature of land-use change in the vicinity of transit stations, or the change in land values stimulated by urban-redevelopment projects. Many such specialized techniques should also emphasize the behavioral aspects of facility or system usage. For example, considerable effort is now being devoted to disaggregate travel-demand analyses that emphasize the travel decision-making behavior of individual trip makers.

EVALUATING ALTERNATIVES

It should be remembered that the role of the analysis and modeling improvements that might be achieved under the preceding issue areas is a supportive one, to provide forecasts of impacts that will tell us something about the effectiveness of alternative plans. The outputs of urban modeling and analysis applications must be converted directly to measures (criteria) of goal achievement. There is consequently a strong linkage between identifying suitable criteria and emphasizing policy variables. Reasonable and reliable relationships must be established between policy alternatives (independent variables) and goal-achievement criteria (dependent variables).

In this section, several additional problem areas involving the evaluation of alternatives are reviewed. Again, successful handling of these problem areas appears to require considerable skill and judgment. Among others, the following improvements are: (a) strengthening the interplay between the design of alternatives and their evaluation, in some sort of iterative or cyclic way, (b) facilitating trade-off analyses, especially for citizens and decision makers, when goals and objectives may be in conflict, (c) developing techniques for communicating the significant differences among alternatives, again with an emphasis on citizen and decision-maker audiences, (d) explicitly

treating the variations, in relative importance or weight, that different
evaluation participants attach to different objectives, and (e) explicitly
treating and recognizing the role of uncertainty in the analysis and
evaluation of alternatives.

Cyclic Redesigning of Options

Experience has clearly shown that the division of the systematic
urban-planning process into the four steps around which this chapter
is organized is quite artificial in nature. In practice, these steps cannot be conducted in strict sequence, and, in fact, trying to undertake
them sequentially would probably be a serious mistake. Instead, as
discussed further in Chapter 3, there appears to be great benefit in
conducting many pieces of each step in both a concurrent and a cyclic
manner, in relation to each of the other steps. Determining the amount
of concurrency and the number of cycles is, again, part of the artistry
of all of this, and perhaps one of the most important parts. Certainly
the time span available, the budget assigned, and the composition,
background, and skills of the staff involved will influence, within any
given urban area, the way the various steps in the approach might be
carried out.
   One of the most important cycling dimensions to add to the process
is the provision of opportunities for the redesigning of alternatives
after at least some stages of impact analysis and evaluation have been
completed. In fact, it should be anticipated that such iteration between
design and evaluation will also lead to redefinitions of the objectives
and measures by which alternatives are assessed. An important learning component is involved in this design-evaluation-redesigning cycling,
as the two steps become more interdependent and iterative. Evaluation
activities should be organized so that they can structure the search for
further design solutions, as a part of mediating between the impacts
and objectives of locally- and regionally-oriented systems.[23] As part
of this iterative process, it is also desirable to screen alternatives to
reduce the number considered at each successive turn (only the most
promising should be retained). This might lead to eventual identification of a "best" recommended plan as a refinement and piecing together
of elements from a final number of alternatives.

Facilitating Trade-off Analyses

Inevitably, the analysis and evaluation of alternative urban plans and programs will reveal that some objectives are achieved at the expense of others. There will be both positive and negative impacts. Some groups and subareas will gain greater accessibility to work or recreation opportunities from a new urban freeway, for example, while other groups and subareas, especially those located near the facility, will be vulnerable to undesired air pollution, noise, dislocation, neighborhood disruption, esthetic, and other negative impacts. Suitable formats for comparing and trading off these pluses and minuses must be developed, oriented to the concerns and values of community participants and public decision makers.

As discussed further in Chapter 4, various goal-achievement and cost-effectiveness matrix approaches to this comparison format problem have been developed and applied. While such approaches may permit the calculation of summary index scores for each alternative (by adding up the rows or columns of a matrix), significant dangers of oversimplication exist in using summaries. It has been suggested that, instead, the evaluation process be kept open and detailed as long as possible.[24] Furthermore, an important part of trade-off analysis will be to maintain a disaggregated format for presenting impact data, so that distributional, localized effects can be taken into account by all participants in the evaluation.[25]

Communicating Significant Differences

In general, the goal-achievement and/or cost-effectiveness matrices that might be used in trade-off analyses cannot do the full communications job. Experience has shown that, even without expanding the number of alternatives and impacts considered, in the past too little attention has been given to a clear exposition of the differences among alternative plans and programs. Too often the lengthy process of analyzing by means of computer models such factors as travel demand, use of system supply, or various kinds of benefits and disbenefits has been left in the technical arena. As one critic has observed, "we think too much about the models and too little about the maps and charts and photos and common sense that sell particular planning strategies."[26]

A variety of communication devices—bar charts, pie charts, zone maps, network maps, line graphs, point graphs, color-coded tables, and so one—have great potential for meeting our rapidly expanding communication needs. The cognitive and perceptual capabilities of the average citizen and governmental decision maker should serve as primary constraints. Contrasting micro- versus macro-scale impacts should continue to receive emphasis. Development of such communication tools should certainly not be left as a last-minute exercise; sufficient time, budget, and manpower should be allocated to this increasingly demanding assignment.

In fact, this is perhaps one of the more important frontier areas in the development of more effective plan evaluation methodologies. Developing communication tools that transmit fairly large amounts of information in an efficient, understandable, and decision-facilitating way is a formidable task indeed. Another important judgmental element that must be addressed involves the everpresent need to sort out those differences among alternatives that are significant and those that are of lesser importance. Clearly, this sorting out must be related to goal-achievement/cost-effectiveness analyses. It is also essential to meet the typical demands of decision makers for "highlights" and "summaries" effectively; the dangers of oversimplification must be avoided.

Assigning Weights to Objectives

Specific community objectives will have more importance to some people than they will to others. In fact, within a set of goals and objectives, when there are significant conflicts and trade-offs, there are likely to be many different sets of relative weights among participants in an evaluation. Explicit recognition of goal weights consequently represents an important consideration in plan-evaluation strategies; it is a consideration that also involves many procedural choices (further discussion of these procedural aspects is provided in Chapter 2, 4, and 7). Goal-weighting exercises can be made a part of the different community-participation strategies discussed earlier, in which the identification and discussion of goals and objectives could also include their weighting.

In too many instances, goal weights have been assigned in the abstract. As discussed under the heading "Managing Disagreement," above, it is usually the case that community participants need concrete examples—preferably, actual plan or program alternatives—to help them decide which plan characteristics are important to them as objectives. The same applies, perhaps even more so, in the assignment of weights to objectives. Specific conflict or trade-off situations, in the form of plan, program, or project alternatives, appear to be essential to the focusing of this activity. In addition, not only the speci-

fication of alternatives but the analysis of their relative impacts should
desirably precede goal weighting. It is likely that the weight assigned
to a specific goal will vary with its level of achievement, according to
some sort of sliding scale of valuation. Varying marginal rates of
substitution among effects should not be overlooked. [27]

Recognizing Uncertainty

It is very likely that many participants in plan evaluation will either
change their goal weights as time passes or change them as new alternatives are presented or as more is learned about a given alternative.
The notion of "value-sensitivity analysis" has been proposed to deal
with these uncertainties, partly as a way to increase the credibility
and accountability of plan evaluation results. [28] Chapter 7 describes
a sensitivity-analysis technique for dealing with two other kinds of uncertainty involved in plan evaluation: uncertainties associated with
forecasted goal-achievement impacts (including computer modeling
outputs) and with cost forecasts.

An important additional thrust for sensitivity analyses regarding
forecasted impacts and costs would be the singling out of those variables to which evaluation results are most sensitive. If it is possible to
single out a smaller set of dependent and independent variables upon
which much of the relative performance of alternative plans hinges,
then these variables are the ones that should be emphasized in further
data-collection and analysis activities. Modeling refinements regarding
these variables might be pursued. Such an approach was suggested in
the experimental development of the Forrester model, in which it
seemed increasingly that some variables and parameters in the hypothetical model structure were much less crucial in influencing results
than others. [29] However, as noted earlier, empirical substantiation
of this particular model has not been accomplished.

SEQUENCE OF CHAPTERS

The remaining seven chapters of the book are organized in a
sequence that generally does the following:

1. Examines the basic concepts of systematic urban planning (the
    steps in the process)
2. Investigates a series of examples of applying these concepts, at
    different levels of planning

3. Reviews some of the key issues involved in plan evaluation method-
    ologies (an important component of systematic planning)
4. Highlights the critical role played by improved data and information
    in the form of "urban indicators"
5. Examines the potential of a promising quantitative analysis tool—
    mathematical programming—in a systematic planning context
6. Describes an experimental technique for explicitly dealing with the
    uncertainties inherent in the quantitative aspects of systematic
    planning
7. Provides a review of urban information systems, in support of
    strengthened urban and regional planning programs.

To provide a perspective on the remainder of the book, brief summaries of each of these chapters are given below.

Chapter 2 contrasts three different approaches to the urban-
planning process, each of which contains five or six basic steps. These
approaches are referred to as "strategy models" for urban planning,
in the sense that each addresses the fundamental question of how to go
about the process of planning. It is concluded that the first of these
approaches, the comprehensive goal-achievement model, faces very
serious implementation problems and is probably unworkable. A
second approach, on the other hand, termed the "successive limited
comparisons model," is more pragmatic in nature, but also appears
too conservative in its reliance on incremental improvements in existing institutional decision-making procedures. The third strategy,
recommended as a compromise, is defined as a "program-policy
trade-off model." This compromise approach is rational and systematic but noncomprehensive, and it attempts to blend the best from the
other two more extreme approaches. The key to this strategy lies in
its emphasis upon "process," a continuing series of successive plan
analyses and evaluations, concentrating on identifying the marginal
trade-offs and differences among alternatives. The result is a basic
conceptual approach to systematic urban planning.

Chapter 3 outlines a similar approach to a more systematic urban-
planning process. Using a more simplified, four-step version of the
systems approach (as compared to the three conceptual approaches
examined in Chapter 2), a series of case studies is examined. The
diversity of the case studies, and their characteristic lack of thoroughness, indicates the need for a more generalized "strategy model" as
a basis for comparison. Through the review and analysis of specific
examples, this chapter develops a two-pronged framework for more
systematic urban planning. The first dimension of the framework
centers on clarifying the different levels of planning at which systematic methods and concepts might be applied. Four different levels are

distinguished: overall planning processes, analysis of urban systems, analysis of urban problems, and improving governmental operations. The second dimension then centers on the four basic steps in analysis that have already been described above. The chapter concludes with the development of a series of guidelines for systems analysis that stress the operational problems involved, especially those in an urban-planning context.

Evaluation of alternative plans, frequently one of the least-developed steps in the urban-planning process, is the focus of Chapter 4. This chapter stresses that some of the most important impacts of regional plans occur at the community level, although, for many reasons, such local impacts are not often treated in regional planning. This problem is explored in general and is related to the state of the art of comprehensive plan-evaluation methods. An approach is suggested whereby comprehensive regional planning agencies can assess both the regional and local impacts of alternative plans. This approach structures the presentation of information about regional and local plan impacts, and provides a simple format for facilitating subjective assessment of such impacts by decision makers and community residents. This approach involves the construction of a comprehensive goals-achievement matrix.

In this fourth chapter the regional level of planning is used as an example to single out some of the key issues involved in plan evaluation methodologies. These issues, organized into five categories, have important implications for other planning levels and steps in the systems approach. The five elements include (a) the planning/evaluation process, (b) the application of criteria and measures, (c) the identification of goals and objectives, (d) the development of effective comparison formats, and (e) the opportunities for meaningful citizen participation. In the context of an actual case study Chapter 4 is more optimistic than Chapter 2 regarding our ability to operationalize goals and objectives, to measure their achievement in meaningful terms, and in the application of goal-weighting procedures. In contrast with Chapter 2, in which the technical difficulties of employing goals and goal weights are emphasized, here the overriding importance of more effective community participation, though perhaps technically imperfect, forms the primary justification for addressing these difficult steps. The emphasis shifts to ways in which community participation and related avenues for two-way communication can be better structured.

Chapter 5 departs somewhat from the basic concepts of systematic urban planning—the steps and methods in the planning process—to examine a crucial underlying theme. This underlying theme involves the development and use of data that document the extent of current

urban problems, as well as the efficiency or effectiveness of current
public plans or programs, and that support the analyses of interrelationships between these problems, plans, programs, and other environmental factors. Too often attempts to improve planning methodologies have suffered from a lack of necessary data or, even
worse, from a misuse of whatever data might be available. The concept of urban "indicators" involves a particular kind of "performance"
measure. In general, urban indicators involve data that show how well
any given set of goals and objectives is being achieved; they indicate
the general relative well-being of a city.

In this context, then, urban indicators represent a very important
kind of data needed to support the analysis and evaluation steps of systematic urban planning. In Chapter 5 it is stressed that urban indicators are in an early stage of development. Three different types of
urban indicators are defined: (a) social indicators, as related to
general community change, and related goals and problems, (b) impact
indicators, more specifically related to public agency effectiveness in
achieving goals and solving problems, and (c) performance indicators,
more administratively oriented in nature, relating to public agency
efficiency. Basic information resources available for the development
of urban indicators are reviewed. Potential uses of urban indicators,
particularly as related to systematic planning and programming, are
outlined. It is suggested that regional or local planning agencies might
assume responsibility for the development and use of urban indicators.

The remaining three chapters are somewhat more technical in
nature. However, for the most part they have been written for the nontechnical reader, with a minimum of mathematical jargon. They serve
to illustrate some of the ways in which computerized mathematical
modeling and information systems can be employed in support of
strengthened urban planning.

Chapter 6 investigates how one of the most intuitively powerful
mathematical analysis tools can match alternative plans and programs
against goals and objectives to identify those alternatives that might
achieve optimum levels of goal achievement. The chapter explores
the potential application of mathematical programming in the evaluation
of alternative urban plans and improvement programs. After a brief
review of past modeling efforts of this type, an examination of the
problems likely to be encountered in identifying and measuring specific
objectives and programs is presented. The Model Cities Program is
used as an example. A simple linear programming model is subsequently developed, built around a matrix of relative effectiveness coefficients, a set of performance standards, and appropriate program
budgets. Supporting analytic techniques and information systems are
also discussed. Finally, potential applications of the model are sur-

veyed, and examples presented of its use in testing and evaluating basic Model Cities Programs and objectives.

Much work remains to be done before viable urban improvement programming models can actually be developed. Chapter 6 consequently attempts to draw several basic guidelines for continuing research effort. First, the need for consistency and comparability in the selection of quantitative measures or index of goal achievement is examined. Second, the need is shown for expressing alternative programs and policies in terms of three essential characteristics: the objectives to which they are related, the impact or effectiveness that they will have in achieving each objective, and the costs associated with varying levels of effectiveness. Third, in order to permit comparisons and trade-offs among different programs and groups of programs, it is essential that a common measure of goal achievement be developed. One way to define such a common measure of goal achievement is to develop a programs-objectives matrix in which each coefficient represents the percentage of objective j, which can be achieved by each dollar invested in program i. Fourth, it must be understood that program-objective-effectiveness matrices of this type will require a prodigious amount of supporting research and analysis, if they are to predict the individual impacts of alternative programs and policies. Finally, the sensitivity analysis of all variables and parameters—standards, budgets, or programs—within a mathematical programming problem can provide a good deal of information on relative costs, effectiveness, and trade-offs.

Coupled with the need for more effective community participation and for improved communication devices for facilitating that participation (investigated earlier in Chapter 4) is a need for acknowledging the uncertainties associated with the forecasted consequences of any long-range plan or program. These three aspects of systematic planning—participation, communication, and uncertainty—are further addressed in Chapter 7. Urban transportation planning is used as an example, with implications for other levels and subject areas of planning as well. As in Chapter 4, the evaluation of alternatives step in the system approach is singled out for emphasis. The cost-effectiveness framework described earlier is used to structure the plan evaluation and sensitivity-analysis techniques employed in a specific case-study example. Special attention is given to identifying ways in which the results of computerized plan analyses can be reported to laymen and/or decision makers within a context of directly exploring some of the trade-offs, conflicts, and sensitivities among these alternatives, with various simple forms of interactive computer assistance.

An experimental technique for exploring the sensitivity of transportation-plan evaluations to forecasting and community-value uncertainties is described. Three kinds of uncertainty are included: goal-achievement impacts, costs, and goal-weights. Within a cost-effectiveness evaluation framework, an "online" capability for inter- actively and iteratively testing plan comparisons is outlined. A series of user-oriented computer instructions is developed to test plan- comparison outcomes according to a wide variety of user-selected changes in impact forecasts, goal weights, and cost forecasts. A sample, hypothetical application of the technique is described. Further refinements within a real-world applications context are recommended.

Chapter 8 is less closely related to the fundamentals of systematic urban planning than the previous chapters. Computerized urban infor- mation systems exist in many urban areas, and have been too often established with little regard for potential use by urban-planning agen- cies. The variety and scope of these urban-information systems is extensive, however, and there are some that do attempt to accommo- date urban-planning data requirements. This chapter attempts to show how such computerized information systems may be better applied in urban planning. The four-step systems approach is used as a frame- work for partially defining planning information needs.

Four specific interagency urban information systems—two from the Los Angeles region and two from the San Francisco metropolitan area—are reviewed. Several different types of system application for planning purposes are described, including data retrieval, report generation, statistical analysis, and computer graphics. Again using a case study example, metropolitan planning-data requirements are reviewed. The design and operation of urban information systems is summarized briefly, in terms of the four major phases of data collec- tion, organization, processing, and maintenance. A final section ad- dresses the need for greater coordination of both computerized and noncomputerized urban-information resources.

NOTES

1. Barclay M. Hudson, Martin Wachs, and Joseph L. Schofer, "Local Impact Evaluation in the Design of Large-Scale Systems," Journal of the American Institute of Planners (July 1974): 255-65.

2. Marvin L. Manheim, et al., Community Values in Highway Location and Design: A Procedural Guide, Report No. 71-4, final report of the National Cooperative Highway Research Program Project 8-8(3) (Cambridge, Mass.: MIT Press, September 1971).

3. Hans Bleiker, John H. Suhrbier, and Marvin L. Manheim, "Community Interaction as an Integral Part of the Highway Decision-Making Process, " Highway Research Record, no. 356 (Washington, D.C.: Highway Research Board, 1971), pp. 12-25.

4. Barclay et al., op. cit.

5. Margaret Skutsch and Joseph L. Schofer, "Goals-Delphis for Urban Planning: Concepts in their Design, " Socio-Economic Planning Sciences (June 1973), pp. 305-13.

6. David E. Boyce, Norman D. Day, and Chris McDonald, Metropolitan Plan Making: An Analysis of Experience with the Preparation and Evaluation of Alternative Land-Use and Transportation Plans (Philadelphia: Regional Science Research Institute, 1970).

7. Edward De Bono, Lateral Thinking: Creativity Step by Step (New York: Harper & Row, 1970).

8. Boyce et al., op. cit., p. 68.

9. Barclay et al., op. cit.

10. Harold Sackman and Ronald L. Citrenbaum, eds., Online Planning: Toward Creative Problem-Solving (Englewood Cliffs, N.J.: Prentice-Hall, 1972).

11. Jerry B. Schneider, Interactive Graphics in Transportation Systems Planning and Design (University of Washington, 1974).

12. Matthias H. Rapp, "Man-Machine Interactive Transit System Planning, " Socio-Economic Planning Sciences 6 (1972): 95-123; Matthias H. Rapp, "Transit System Planning: A Man-Computer Interactive Graphic Approach," Highway Research Record, no. 415 (Washington, D.C.: Highway Research Board, 1972), pp. 49-61; Jerry B. Schneider, Claus D. Gehner, and Dennis Porter, "Man-Computer Synergism: A Novel Approach to the Design of Multi-Objective, Multi-Modal Urban Transportation Systems, " paper presented at the International Conference on Transportation Research, Bruges, Belgium, June, 1973.

13. Donald A. Krueckeberg and Arthur L. Silvers, Urban Planning Analysis: Methods and Models (New York: Wiley, 1974); Jack W. Lapatra, Applying the Systems Approach to Urban Development (Stroudsburg, Pa.: Dowden, Hutchinson, and Ross, 1973); Benjamin Reif, Models in Urban and Regional Planning (New York: Intext, 1973); Alan W. Steiss, Models for the Analysis and Planning of Urban Systems (Lexington, Mass.: Lexington Books, 1975); Alan G. Wilson, Urban and Regional Models in Geography and Planning (New York: Wiley, 1974).

14. Daniel Brand and Marvin L. Manheim, eds., Urban Travel Demand Forecasting, Special Report 143 (Washington, D.C.: Highway Research Board, 1973); Douglass B. Lee, Jr., "Requiem for Large-Scale Models, " Journal of the American Institute of Planners (May 1973): 163-78.

15. Brand and Manheim, op. cit.

16. Ibid.

17. Jay W. Forrester, Urban Dynamics (Cambridge, Mass.: MIT Press, 1968).

18. Gregory K. Ingram, "Jay W. Forrester: Urban Dynamics" (book review), Journal of the American Institute of Planners (May 1970): 206-8.

19. Brand and Manheim, op. cit.

20. George C. Hemmens, ed., Urban Development Models, Special Report 97 (Washington, D.C.: Highway Research Board, 1968).

21. Southern California Association of Governments, An Analysis of Incentives and Disincentives for Automobile Management in the SCAG Region, (Draft) Los Angeles (October 1975).

22. Lee, op. cit.

23. Boyce et al., op. cit.; Barclay et al., op. cit.

24. Boyce et al., op. cit.

25. Christopher Nash, David Pearce, John Stanley, "Criteria for Evaluating Project Evaluation Techniques," Journal of the American Institute of Planners (March 1975): 83-9.

26. Richard J. Bouchard, "Relevance of Planning Techniques to Decision-Making," in Brand and Manheim, op. cit., p. 18.

27. Nash et al., op. cit.

28. Ibid.

29. Boyce et al., op. cit.

2

RATIONAL URBAN
PLANNING: PROBLEMS
AND PROSPECTS

In recent years, the need for a more systematic, rational approach to urban planning has received increasing emphasis. [1] According to the rational planning process, the most appropriate and direct means for evaluating alternative urban plans is through a comparison of their relative levels of goal achievement. That plan that contributes most to achieving the goals and values of a given urban area is preferable. Various forms of this process have been advanced, particularly in terms of systematic program budgeting. [2] Different strategies and techniques for comprehensive goal achievement analysis and planning have also been outlined. [3]

Six basic steps are involved in this rational process:

1. All community goals must be identified, and measurable indexes for the achievement of each goal (the outputs) must be developed.
2. All existing government programs and policies that affect each goal must be identified, and measurable indexes of the resources consumed by each program or policy (the inputs) must be developed.
3. The levels of goal achievement or effectiveness for various alternative sets or combinations of programs and policies must be measured and predicted. The number of alternatives to be tested will depend in part upon the degree of thoroughness desired. This step involves the bringing of inputs and outputs into basic analytic frameworks and mathematical models.

Reprinted from Urban Affairs Quarterly 5, no. 2 (December 1969): 151-82, by permission of the publisher, Sage Publications, Inc.

4. For each alternative, the relative level of goal achievement must
   be stratified according to affected economic activities, social
   groups, and spatial locations. Weights must be assigned to indicate the relative importance of these activities, groups, and locations within the entire urban area.
5. Weights also must be assigned to indicate the relative importance
   of each goal. Both kinds of weights must be derived so that in some
   manner they represent a consensus of opinion or value ranking for
   the entire community.
6. Finally, on the basis of predicted impacts and relative weights, the
   alternative with the highest level of overall goal achievement is selected, subject, however, to the application of one or more budget
   constraints.

    This chapter examines the efficacy of comprehensive rational plan-
ning as a strategy for dealing with complex urban problems. The implications of each of the six steps above, in terms of the practical
problems and tasks involved, are discussed in the following section.
Many difficulties and weaknesses are identified, particularly in association with the enormous informational requirements of the method.
In the second section a more pragmatic alternative to rational planning
is presented, drawn from the public administration literature. It emphasizes the strengthening of observed administrative processes and
decision-making behavior. In the final section, a compromise model
is developed, one that is rational but noncomprehensive, and that
stresses a continuing process of successive plan evaluations. Its
method is to identify the community impacts over which alternative
programs and policies differ, and to illustrate how trade-offs among
different impacts might be made. This conceptual strategy model is
described using the Model Cities Program as an example. It is recommended as a more workable alternative to comprehensive rational
planning.

LIMITATIONS OF GOAL-ACHIEVEMENT MODELS

    As outlined in a recent article, the implementation of planning-
programming budgeting systems (PPBS) and related techniques at the
local government level faces severe difficulties.[4] Once a series of
activities has been identified as an interrelated program group aimed
at one or more specific objectives, it is likely that such activities will
actually be scattered through several government agencies, bureaus,
or divisions. Attempts to bring these together into a single, coordinated program will meet strong institutional and bureaucratic resist-

ance. The potential reorganization of agency functions and activities
will constitute a threat to the existing hierarchical structure and familiar working relationships.

While administrative problems such as these are undoubtedly of
major importance, even more serious conceptual and operational difficulties can be anticipated. These deal with the practical problems
of trying to identify, measure, and weight the various programs, policies, impacts, and goals that make up goal-achievement matrices. The
following paragraphs discuss in some detail the kinds of difficulties to
be overcome in each of the six basic steps of comprehensive rational
planning and plan evaluation. So many problems are foreseen that in
subsequent sections, a less ambitious framework for decision making
is developed.

Identify Community Objectives

One of the first problems to be dealt with lies in deciding what
kinds of values, goals, and objectives are to be analyzed. More abstract and philosophical values, such as increased personal freedom
and greater dignity, should be avoided. These are notoriously difficult
to investigate quantitatively and can almost always be adequately expressed as a series of more specific goals and objectives.

The kinds of general goals that cities often set for themselves,
such as improving the residential environment, strengthening and di-
versifying the economy, or enlarging human opportunities, still suffer
from a certain ambiguity as to how they might best be measured. There
is also a considerable amount of overlap among such general goals.
The achievement of one will also help to achieve others, often through
very complex kinds of social and economic interdependence. It is extremely difficult to say how much each goal depends upon each of the
others.

Consequently, it is desirable to look for more detailed statements
of desired outcome, particularly those that seem to be somewhat independent of one another, and that are also amenable to quantitative
measurement. The development of specific planning objectives of this
type should, in fact, be directly accompanied by the design and exploration of indexes or measurable criteria by which to evaluate the
achievement of each objective. Objectives should normally be developed
in such functional areas as employment and family income, housing,
health and welfare, education, physical environment, and transportation.

Attempts to identify specific community objectives in this manner—
say four or five objectives within each functional area—must face at

least three important limitations or weaknesses. First, as we become
more specific in expressing desired ends, there is an increasing tendency to end up describing public programs and policies themselves.
For example, identifying the objective of providing higher educational
facilities for students who may not desire a full four-year curriculum
is practically the same as describing a program to improve and expand
junior college facilities. This phenomenon, an aspect of what is sometimes known as the "means-ends hierarchy," may make it quite difficult to compare objectives and programs in any meaningful, measurable
way.

Second, interdependencies among objectives still may present
serious problems, in that we are most often unable to determine to
what extent one objective will influence those that interact with it. The
determination is necessary so that we can examine how alternative
programs aimed at one objective will also help to achieve others. The
most obvious example lies in the better education, fuller employment,
higher family income cycle. If one of our educational objectives is to
provide maximum opportunities for increased schooling, then we should
have some grasp of its interrelationship with a family income objective
to ensure that all residents have adequate or minimum disposable incomes. In this way, we can compare how educational programs such
as vocational and technical training, Manpower Development and Training, Neighborhood Youth Corps, and adult education classes serve to
achieve both objectives.

Third, the decision to choose one objective over another, to express an objective in a slightly different way, or to settle on one criterion measure instead of another means that we must inevitably
overlook some potentially important aspects or features within a functional area. In order to have a workable set of overall objectives, together with measurable criteria of achievement that do not strain our
information resources, we will necessarily be forced to make such
decisions. Often these omitted features will be unusually hard to
measure. For instance, if one of our housing objectives is to expand
the supply of low- and moderate-income housing, and we choose as
our index simply the annual number of units of various types provided,
we may be overlooking important qualitative considerations as to esthetic design, tenant satisfaction, and/or project building density.
These aspects might not be adequately covered in other housing objectives.

Identify Programs and Policies

While it might seem a relatively easy task to identify governmental programs and policies in need of evaluation, since these programs and policies have themselves brought forth a need for a more rational planning, such is not the case. Effective rational planning requires that programs and policies be redefined in terms of the objectives they are intended to achieve. This step enables basic goal-achievement matrices to be constructed, with programs on one axis matched against objectives on the other. Several important difficulties are likely to occur when programs and policies are treated in this way.

For instance, it is usually preferable for similar programs within different agencies to be grouped together as a single, coordinated program; i.e., the recreation, park, and open-space programs of city park departments, county park agencies, state conservation departments, and various other public and private organizations should all be identified together. It is also often preferable for dissimilar programs that contribute, in part at least, to a common objective to be grouped together as a program package; i.e., the maintenance of attractive residential environments involves the coordination of code enforcement, street improvement, park expansion, school improvement, housing rehabilitation, urban renewal, urban beautification, and other programs.

Because such program groupings cut across agency lines, and because they may be structured and oriented differently within different agencies, it may sometimes be quite difficult to pull out and properly identify various common-objective programs. In addition, the same interdependency problems that may affect community objectives can also cause difficulty here. Different public programs may depend upon companion actions by other agencies for full implementation or effectiveness. The urban renewal program is an obvious example, requiring, within specific projects, the possible coordination of land clearance, relocation, redevelopment, street improvement, freeway construction, park development, sewer and water improvement, and other public and private programs.

At least three other kinds of problems can also be suggested. It is often necessary to try to split or allocate programs among several different objectives, and to determine relative emphases in achieving these ends. This can lead to severe measurement problems. For instance, how might we define the relative importance among objectives for the Job Corps program—reducing unemployment, increasing educational levels, providing adequate incomes, improving physical and mental health, reducing crime rates? In addition, how can we be sure that we have identified all the objectives to which a particular program pertains? Would the Job Corps program also significantly affect the demand for low-income housing and the maintenance of attractive residential environments?

Third, and perhaps more important, where does the design of new programs, the development of innovative alternatives, fit in? An apparent weakness of goal-achievement matrices lies in their structural and procedural emphasis upon existing public programs and policies. The main focus of attention can easily lie upon allocating total budgets among this array of programs, upon making incremental shifts among existing programs to better achieve our objectives. The large amount of conceptual and empirical work needed simply to analyze present policies and programs threatens to overshadow the crucial importance of searching for entirely new alternatives.

Predict Effectiveness Levels

Suppose that, in spite of these kinds of difficulties in identifying community objectives and public programs and policies, we are able to rough out a programs-objectives matrix that seems reasonably satisfactory. We will have had to spend considerable time and resources developing quantitative indexes that represent each objective and program and in developing objectives and programs that are themselves conceptually consistent. Hopefully, we will also have identified a number of new, innovative programs and policies we would like to evaluate. Our assignment is now to predict levels of goal achievement within the matrix, given different combinations and emphases among programs.

If programs are represented as rows, one of these rows might be housing and building code enforcement. Correspondingly, one of the objectives columns might be to ensure that all housing units are in adequate, sound condition. The number of building inspectors, the number of code-violations suits filed, or the number of buildings entering receivership might be the quantitative measures representing this program, while the proportion of repeat code violations or substandard conditions reported by social service agencies might serve as measurable criteria for achieving the objective. Minimum acceptable achievement levels or standards, such as a substandard housing rate no greater than the current vacancy rate, might be established for this objective as well as for others. What would be entered in the cell where this particular row and column intersect?

In general, we would like to enter the number of goal units achieved—reduction in substandard housing units, for the given level of program investment or commitment—number of building inspectors.

We would proceed to compare each program in the matrix against the full set of community objectives, in some cases selecting different goal-achievement criteria (for the same objective) where these seem more appropriate; we would note possible negative goal achievements—programs that actually detract from certain objectives. In some cases we would group programs together for a single matching against other objectives. Where possible, we would like to sum the overall column achievement for each objective within each given set of alternative programs to be tested, but we are more likely to rely upon program-by-program, objective-by-objective comparisons.

Two key activities must be undertaken in order to fill in each relevant cell within such a goal-achievement or programs-objectives matrix. First, analytic techniques and mathematical models must be developed to predict how program input variables, appropriate intervening variables and parameters, and output objective variables will interact. Many of these variables will be represented simply by the quantitative indexes for programs and objectives previously established, while others will have to be newly developed. A research program into urban socioeconomic interrelationships of some magnitude is implied. Second, appropriate and necessary information resources and data-collection programs must be developed. This implies as well a considerable investment in improved urban information systems.

Analysis and Model Building

Both of these topics have been the subject of growing attention in the planning and urban research literature. Reviews of model building by Lowry and by Steger provide us with many insights into the tasks and problems of building predictive models for comprehensive rational planning.[5] While many different research directions might be taken in developing new techniques for urban socioeconomic analysis, we will here be guided by the need to predict relative effectiveness levels for alternative public policies and programs. This gives us something of a pragmatic, action-oriented posture, dealing as best we can with cause-and-effect, input-output kinds of empirical relationships. Very often, but necessarily, we will use models that rely on computer assistance.

As Lowry notes, it is the very difficult job of the model builder to "perceive repetitive temporal patterns in the processes of urban life, fixed spatial relationships in the kaleidoscope of urban form."[6] If we are able to identify such stable relationships, then we attempt to express them in terms of mathematical equations and formulas. In general, we seek more than simple descriptive models, which are designed only to replicate static or existing conditions. Such models may be of value, however, in permitting reliable estimates to be made of hard-to-measure output variables from easy-to-measure input variables. More often, we are interested in predictive models that are built, in one way or another, around implied or observed causal sequences. Given a logical framework of interrelationships, we wish to be able to say that, for some future value of a particular input, program, or "cause," we may expect corresponding future values for relevant output, objective, or "effect" variables.

A number of practical considerations can easily make the model-building or prediction phase of plan evaluation a complicated, lengthy process. Unless these practical aspects can be properly handled, the usefulness of predicted effectiveness levels may be seriously threatened. One of these factors is choosing the most appropriate level of aggregation—families, census tracts, traffic zones, community areas. Another is the handling of time in different models—the expected time lags between inputs and outputs, the presence of equilibrium concepts, and the frequency with which a model should be used. A third is the choice of mathematical technique or solution algorithm for actually operating a model. These may include simple algebraic equations; multivariate statistical techniques (such as linear multiple regression and factor analysis); gravity, potential, and network flow models; and Monte Carlo or stochastic simulation models.

Many different models and submodels will be required to fill out all the appropriate cells in a program-objectives matrix. Some models may relate a single program to a single objective (perhaps community health center services and a reduction in key disease rates), while others might relate larger program packages to several interrelated objectives. For example, we might wish to develop a relatively large-scale socioeconomic stimulation or impact model for testing the effects of the Federal Office of Economic Opportunity (OEO) programs. Here we would be working with such programs as the Job Corps, Neighborhood Youth Corps, Manpower Development and Training, Older Workers Program, and Youth Opportunity Centers, and with community objectives in such areas as unemployment, family income, housing rehabilitation, juvenile delinquency, and school dropout rates. Hopefully, we would be able to vary each program within the model and observe how overall levels of goal achievement are changed.

Urban Information Systems

Improved information systems will be an essential and integral step in strengthening our model-building and analytic capabilities. A wide variety of problems may be anticipated in trying to coordinate the data files of administrative agencies, which operate with relative independence. Compatibility with federal censuses (population, housing, and others) must also be sought. Major differences in collection methods, timing and frequency, identification and coding techniques, and spatial disaggregation procedures are likely to cause great difficulty. Without basic agreement in these areas, we will be greatly handicapped in trying to build and test flexible analytic models that relate social and economic output variables to administrative input variables, the latter often cutting across agency lines. Many of these variables will, of course, have been previously identified in our work with measurable indexes for objectives, programs, and policies.

Effective analytic support of goal-achievement matrices is also quite likely to call for the development of new data sources from existing administrative records. Major problems will result in trying to encourage the reorganization of agency record-keeping and data-storage procedures. The various operating programs of both the federal government and local governments represent substantial sources of data most often unavailable on a spatially disaggregated basis—a particularly restrictive characteristic. Examples include local record systems for various welfare programs, the public schools, property taxes and assessments, state employment services, various licensing records, health and medical records, state sales taxes, and others. The growing use of computers to increase the operating effectiveness of such administrative records offers hope for concomitantly increasing their statistical or analytic usefulness.

The scale of commitment that might be required in developing adequate information resources is potentially enormous—so much so that, within a PPBS framework, the development of an information system for a single program can snowball into a major assignment. [7] In addition, of course, is the major research commitment that will surely be needed to develop an acceptable series of analytic models. Three additional factors emphasize the major problems and limitations of such large-scale efforts.

First, it is quite likely that problems both with data availability and with the need for modifications in analytic techniques will force us to reexamine our original quantitative indexes continually. We may often find it necessary to define new indexes and criteria, to look for surrogates, which might be less satisfactory conceptually, but which are required for operational purposes. At times we may also actually have to search for new objectives, or at least for redefinitions of old ones, for similar operational purposes. We may even be forced to rethink our original programs-objectives matrix, or parts of it, at the risk of redoing considerable amounts of completed work.

Second, there is the real uncertainty surrounding the validity and reliability of most of our models. We will usually not have sufficient past data to test their predictive power, even assuming that such tests would be adequate. We simply have no assurance that unanticipated forces and shifts among variables will not lead to large predictive

errors, especially for longer-range models. Significant errors can
also be introduced simply through data imperfections. [8] Third, and
partly as a result of these uncertainties, we must always maintain the
perspective that the results of our quantitative analyses and predictions,
whatever their merit, are only intended to sharpen the judgment of
political decision makers. The experiences and intuition of these decision makers, together with additional qualitative analyses, are vital,
final-stage decision components.

Stratify and Weight Effectiveness

We have spent many months, probably years, in research and experimentation, designing, testing, and redesigning those analytic
models needed to fill out our programs-objectives matrix, concurrently
working our way through the maze of problems and details involved in
locating, collecting, manipulating, and even generating needed data.
In short, we have finally predicted the effectiveness levels for some
given set of alternative programs. We now enter the most crucial stage
of the rational planning process: evaluating the results of our predictions. In general, two kinds of evaluations must be made. First, we
must determine the relative importance of the specific activities,
groups, and subareas for which programs will be effective. Second,
we must determine the relative importance of each community objective.

Only very rarely if ever will a government program have uniform
application across an entire urban area. Almost inevitably a program's
impacts, consequences, and benefits will fall upon particular segments
of the population or sections of the city. Impacts must consequently be
stratified and identified in terms of these incidence groups, and the
relative importance or magnitude of each group determined. For example, urban renewal programs are aimed at older central city neighborhoods, while OEO poverty programs serve low-income families.
These neighborhoods and families form only a certain proportion of
the city's developed area and population.

How important is one incidence group compared to others? How
important are those groups (other subareas, other socioeconomic
classes), that have been left out, upon whom various programs have
no effect? Should large-scale redevelopment of inner-city neighborhoods be given preference over large-scale rehabilitation of neighborhoods further out, or should we concentrate instead on strengthening
key industrial development districts? Clearly, for public programs
and policies to be in the best public interest, these kinds of weightings

must be arrived at through some sort of sensing of public opinion and community-wide valuations. Problems to be faced in weighting incidence groups are the same as those involved in weighting community objectives. They are considered together in the following paragraphs.

Weight Community Objectives

It is highly unlikely that general public opinion polls to determine community weightings would be feasible or even meaningful. Costs would be exorbitantly high and potential questionnaire structures complex enough to cloud the validity of results. We will usually be forced to turn to secondary and representative sources: politicians, administrators, community organizations, business and industry leaders, planners, educators, public hearings, and perhaps a few well-designed, limited-range public surveys. These kinds of investigations are of such critical importance that they can, in fact, serve as inputs to the first step in comprehensive rational planning—identifying community objectives themselves.

As Hill has observed:

> In practice, goals and their relative weights may have to
> be determined iteratively as a result of a complex process
> of interaction among elected officials, administrators,
> planners, and various formal and informal groups reacting
> to explicitly stated objectives and the alternative courses
> of action proposed to meet these objectives. The deter-
> mination of community objectives and their relative valua-
> tion by the community is thus no easy task and requires
> considerable research. [9]

Transportation Planning Examples

Two recent transportation planning studies clearly illustrate the depth of potential objective weighting problems. A Louisville report develops an approach to the evaluation of alternative design concepts using a single set of weighted community decision criteria. [10] A task force from the Mayor's Citizens Advisory Committee was used as a representative community decision-making group for criteria evaluation. Though it was assumed that such a group would eventually be involved in actually structuring a list of specific community objectives or decision criteria, the list of some 35 objectives actually evaluated was put together by local planners. The hope was also expressed that a more diversified evaluation group, including elected officials and influential businessmen, could eventually be used.

Each member of the Mayor's Committee was asked to weight each objective individually, using both a raw ranking and a rating-scale technique. In the first technique the general idea is to rank order all objectives from one to 35, then determine overall rankings by summing those of individual members. The second technique utilizes a zero-to-ten rating scale, and asks individual members to rate each objective as to those of individuals. The normalized results of the two methods are then combined to get an average ranking or utility value. The objective to preserve historic sites and areas of natural beauty, for example, received a utility weight of 0.0192 (average rank of 21), while the objective to provide adequate low-cost housing received a weight of 0.0240 (rank of 11).

A Spokane study attempted to measure the relative importance of nine transportation planning objectives, four tangible and five intangible. [11] The method was again developed in association with a Citizens Advisory Committee. Proceeding from the assumption that frequency of citizen preference for one objective or decision factor over another is directly related to the importance of that objective, each committee member was asked to work his way through a checklist of paired comparisons, matching each objective against each other objective. After summing the results and performing a series of normalizing operations, a relative-preference rating was assigned to each transportation-planning consideration. Accident costs received the highest rating of 6.00, travel time costs a rating of 1.32 (both tangible), and intangible social factors involving effects on surrounding neighborhoods a rating of 0.96.

Methodological Problems

These methods for weighting community objectives are quite crude, considering the crucial importance that this step holds within the rational planning process. Though admittedly they are only first steps, it is difficult to imagine significant methodological improvements that are not complicated enough to confuse those tested, exorbitantly expensive, or equally inconclusive in their results. It is unlikely that citizen advisors or any other small group adequately represent the city at large. Expanding the sample to include members from all socioeconomic groups has been suggested, [12] but, within reasonable survey budget limitations, we then face difficult decisions as to types and numbers of groups to sample, alternative questionnaire techniques, and the possible weighting of groups themselves.

The Spokane study found that rankings by different groups (civil service employees and college students) differed significantly. How should this eventuality be treated? The Louisville study found that results varied markedly by technique utilized (ranking or rating). Twelve of the 35 objectives received a rank difference position of ten or more, while ten varied by five-nine ranking positions. Which of several possible weighting techniques are to be preferred and why? These kinds of potential limitations and inconsistencies are serious enough to merit long and hard reflection before proceeding further. Results of this type do not inspire the confidence needed for meaningful application within comprehensive rational planning. Yet, as Hill has noted, the key to alternative plan evaluation by means of goal-achievement matrices lies in the weighting of objectives, activities, locations, groups, or sectors.[13]

In addition, both the Louisville and Spokane studies note that the objectives which were actually considered are too general to be really useful in plan evaluation contexts. They should be stratified into more detailed, more specific components. If this is done, what is the danger that objectives will then become too technical, too project specific, and too difficult to understand, both for citizen-advisors and other laymen? In fact, the Spokane report suggests that only a jury of experts would be qualified to assign relative values to a more detailed set of transportation planning objectives.[14] With such increases in detail and specificity, what survey methods would be able to manage a full set of community objectives effectively, say 100 or more in number? What test groups could meaningfully comprehend such a survey? In short, is a comprehensive weighted hierarchy of community objectives a realistic possibility?

Identify Preferred Alternatives

The final step in the rational planning process is the selection and recommendation of that alternative or set of alternatives that attains the highest level of goal achievement. In its simplest form, this step is quite straightforward, provided each of the other steps in the process has been carried out successfully. For instance, utilizing an effectiveness-matrix technique, we simply multiply the relative utility of each objective by the predicted level of effectiveness (normalized) that each alternative will have in achieving that objective. Then, for each alternative under consideration, we sum these products to get a total utility score. The alternative with the highest score is to be preferred.[15] Results of this technique might be summarized in terms of the specific plans, programs, policies, or projects under review. In Spokane, for example, a "roadway alternative evaluation table" was developed.

We gain added realism, however, when the costs of each alternative are balanced against its total utility score. Government policies and programs are, of course, enacted under very real budgetary limitations. The utilization of these budget constraints as a part of comprehensive rational planning can often be crucial in identifying the best feasible alternative. This general plan-evaluation technique is known as cost-effectiveness analysis. In general, there are two broad approaches possible in applying budgetary or cost constraints.[16] First, under the fixed utility approach, we choose that alternative that attains some specified minimum level of total utility at the lowest overall cost. Second, under the fixed budget approach, we choose that alternative that attains a maximum level of total utility for a given, fixed budget. In either case, we may be forced to pass over highly rated alternatives because they are too costly.

While normally we would think of costs only in dollar terms, complications can arise if we wish also to consider other resources consumed, opportunities foregone, or conflicting objectives unachieved. Hill has ambitiously proposed that all costs be represented as negative contributions to objectives, so that each quantifiable objective would have a cost benefit account in terms of the same measurable index.[17] Costs, like benefits, would fall upon specific incidence groups. While presumably one of these incidence groups would be the taxpayers who must pay for government programs, the notion of determining all unfavorable impacts upon particular groups is a challenging one. Another kind of important constraint might be the specification of minimum achievement levels or standards for particular objectives, regardless of their relative weighting, so that a certain portion of scarce resources (land, labor, capital) would be firmly committed.

The potential application of mathematical programming models in this final stage of plan selection should also be mentioned, though our experience and capability in this area is currently quite limited. In general, the idea is to define public investment alternatives or program policy variables in terms of a single input metric—probably dollars. Associated with each investment alternative might be an aggregate utility score representing all the community objectives to which it would contribute. Alternatively, associated with each objective might be a minimum performance standard that must be achieved. In the first instance, the objective of the model would be to maximize goal achievement, provided the total available budget is not exceeded. In the second, the objective would be to minimize the total budget spent, provided that minimum performance standards are met.

The great advantage of mathematical programming is that the technique itself generates a large number of alternative overall programs, considering many more combinations of program policy variables than we could put together by hand, and ends up selecting one combination that is optimal. This optimality, defined either in terms of maximum utility or minimum budget, will be subject to certain additional constraints—certain minimum expenditures for education, recreation, housing, and the like must be achieved; maximum expenditures in other areas cannot be exceeded.

The difficulties that stand in the way of effective development of this conceptually appealing kind of mathematical model are essentially those confronting the rational planning process itself—identifying, measuring, interrelating, and weighting objectives; measuring, predicting, stratifying, and weighting effectiveness. Because our capabilities in these areas are at present quite primitive, the development of public investment programming models is not far advanced. A recent application of integer programming in transit planning, for example, used only four objectives and one program policy variable (transit extensions), which were further limited to an all-or-nothing appearance in the solution.[18]

THE LINDBLOM STRATEGY

The questions and problems posed in preceding sections are clearly of monumental proportions. Our present ineptness in handling them suggests strongly that comprehensive rational planning is impractical and inappropriate as a strategy for evaluating alternative urban plans, programs, and policies. The method simply calls for much more knowledge than we are realistically able to bring to bear at any given point in time. There is small consolation in the admonition that though we may never be able to attain the ideal of rational planning, its systematic, comprehensive approach should nevertheless guide our thinking. The rational approach tends in practice to break down rather quickly.

Can other logical frameworks for planning and public decision making be devised, perhaps less ambitious, more pragmatic, and more attuned to observed administrative processes? Will such frameworks thereby be more useful as guidelines and evaluation schemes for urban planning? The weaknesses and limitations of rational planning are, in fact, so severe that other lines of thinking have been advanced that substantially reject this approach as a model for governmental decision making. Lindblom, in particular, develops a strategy that is in some respects a kind of polar or oppositely structured alternative. At one point called a method of "successive limited comparisons,"[19] and at another, a process of "disjointed incrementalism,"[20] this approach is essentially a behavioral model of governmental policy making.

The method of successive limited comparisons recognizes that, in practice, the selection of objectives, the structuring of programs and policies, and even the analysis of program policy effectiveness are not distinct activities, but are closely intertwined. As a result, the identification and evaluation of means and ends are carried on together, and ends are considered only in terms of how they are combined in specific program or policy alternatives. There is no separate classification and listing of goals and objectives. Such an abstract effort tends to overlook local conflicts and disagreement over objectives, calls forth the complex relative weighting problems mentioned above, and is likely to be little used when it comes to the actual evaluating of specific programs and policies.

Lindblom observes that the relative values of different objectives will often change when the circumstances under which they are being considered and compared change. He remarks:

> That one value is prefered to another in one decision situation does not mean that it will be preferred in another decision situation in which it can be had only at great sacrifice of another value. Attempts to rank or order values in general and abstract terms so that they do not shift from decision to decision end up by ignoring the relevant marginal preferences. Even if all administrators had at hand an agreed set of values, objectives, and constraints, their marginal values in actual choice situations would be impossible to formulate. [21]

Under the Lindblom method, objectives and policies are actually chosen at the same time. Alternative programs and policies are compared in terms of the objectives over which they differ, and these are considered only in terms of how they differ marginally or incrementally. For example, suppose alternative policies X and Y both offer the same level of attainment of objectives a, b, c, d, and e. However, X promises a somewhat higher level of f, while Y offers a higher level of g. Then the choice between the two policies becomes simply a trade-off of a marginal amount of f for a marginal amount of g. In making the choice of policy, we simultaneously choose its set of objectives. [22]

The method of successive limited comparisons is not without its own faults, however. Lindblom focuses upon systematically describing how policy decisions are actually made, in the hope that subsequent practice of the method can be conducted with greater skill. With this behavioral emphasis, there is a tendency to avoid looking for more rigorous or rational kinds of improvement in methodology. The most serious shortcoming lies in limiting policy and program alternatives to those that differ in relatively small degree from policies and programs presently in effect. This restriction is intended to simplify greatly the analysis required for evaluating alternatives by requiring that we examine only those incremental aspects in which a proposed alternative and its consequences differ from the status quo. However, it also forces us to overlook innovative, progressive policies simply because they may not be suggested by the present array of policies. Similarly, obsolete programs and policies may linger unnecessarily through a process of gradual phasing out. [23]

The most important feature of the Lindblom strategy, and the one that makes it especially attractive as an alternative to comprehensive rational planning, lies in its emphasis upon successive comparisons. The rational planning approach, in contrast, suggests that once we are able to construct an acceptable programs-objectives matrix (and develop needed analytic methods and information resources), we may then proceed to adjust programs and policies mechanically, as necessary. Eventually, with gradual refinement and adjustment, the method itself will become so powerful that the course of public investments and policies can be charted for years ahead at a time.

The Lindblom method, however, calls for a never-ending chain of successive policy choices and analyses. The method is repeated again and again, dealing with new problems and opportunities as they arise, continually adjusting past and present programs and policies, but never attempting or expecting to define a comprehensive, once-and-for-all set of policies. The method assumes that objectives will continuously be revised in the face of changing conditions, and that public policy making will constitute an endless process of successive partial approximations to changing objectives. [24]

A PROGRAM-POLICY TRADE-OFF MODEL

The remainder of this chapter proposes a third general model for governmental decision making, one designed especially to guide the formation and evaluation of alternative urban plans, programs, and policies. In general, it represents a middle-range compromise lying somewhere between the extremes of comprehensive rational planning and disjointed incrementalism. [25] The identification and weighting of community objectives, key phases of the rational process are left out, and the Lindblom method of simultaneously choosing objectives and policies is adopted in their place. On the other hand, the design of new programs and policies (essentially absent from both methods) is emphasized, and the central importance of being able to predict relative effectiveness levels meaningfully is maintained. The identification of marginal trade-offs among alternative programs and policies represents the final step in the method. The notion of continuing, successive applications to changing urban problems is emphasized.

This third approach is contrasted with each of the others in Figure 1. In addition to its emphasis upon repeated applications, it contains five basic phases:

1. Currently important community problems must be identified, as reported by local politicians, business leaders, public administrators, educators, the press, community organizations, minority groups, and others.
2. New programs and policies must be designed to aim directly at solving these problems, and measurable indexes of the resources consumed by each program or policy (the inputs) must be developed.
3. Major community impacts or consequences for each program or policy must be identified, and measurable indexes of each impact (the outputs) must be developed.
4. The levels of effectiveness for alternative programs and policies, in terms of the relative impacts achieved, must be measured and predicted. This step also involves the bringing together of inputs and outputs into basic analytic frameworks and mathematical models.
5. Marginal difference or trade-offs among alternatives, in terms of relative community impacts, must be identified, and appropriate budget constraints applied. These results are presented to decision makers for any assignment of relative weights.

To illustrate how such a program-policy trade-off model might have relevance and possible application to current urban planning activities, the following paragraphs discuss each step in the process in terms of the Model Cities Program. The federal legislation authorizing this urban improvement program seems, in fact, to anticipate and even implicitly employ the beginnings of this kind of model. For example, the Model Cities Program is (a) problem-oriented toward the needs of blighted and poverty-stricken urban ghettos, (b) action-oriented toward designing new programs and policies to meet these needs, and (c) effectiveness-oriented in calling for new techniques of evaluation and analysis, so that we may compare the results of different model neighborhood strategies.

Identify Community Problems

The first three steps in the process are closely related, and would in practice be carried out together. In general, the identification of

FIGURE 2.1

Strategy Models for Urban Planning

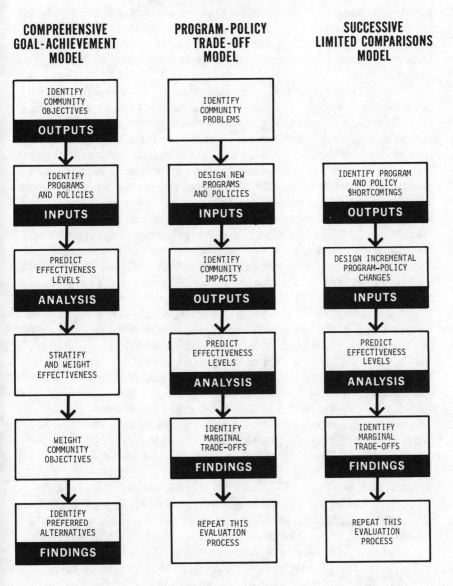

COMPREHENSIVE GOAL-ACHIEVEMENT MODEL

- IDENTIFY COMMUNITY OBJECTIVES — **OUTPUTS**
- IDENTIFY PROGRAMS AND POLICIES — **INPUTS**
- PREDICT EFFECTIVENESS LEVELS — **ANALYSIS**
- STRATIFY AND WEIGHT EFFECTIVENESS
- WEIGHT COMMUNITY OBJECTIVES
- IDENTIFY PREFERRED ALTERNATIVES — **FINDINGS**

PROGRAM-POLICY TRADE-OFF MODEL

- IDENTIFY COMMUNITY PROBLEMS
- DESIGN NEW PROGRAMS AND POLICIES — **INPUTS**
- IDENTIFY COMMUNITY IMPACTS — **OUTPUTS**
- PREDICT EFFECTIVENESS LEVELS — **ANALYSIS**
- IDENTIFY MARGINAL TRADE-OFFS — **FINDINGS**
- REPEAT THIS EVALUATION PROCESS

SUCCESSIVE LIMITED COMPARISONS MODEL

- IDENTIFY PROGRAM AND POLICY SHORTCOMINGS — **OUTPUTS**
- DESIGN INCREMENTAL PROGRAM-POLICY CHANGES — **INPUTS**
- PREDICT EFFECTIVENESS LEVELS — **ANALYSIS**
- IDENTIFY MARGINAL TRADE-OFFS — **FINDINGS**
- REPEAT THIS EVALUATION PROCESS

problems would in turn suggest new kinds of potential programs and policies for solving them, while the different impact groups that programs might affect would usually become apparent in working out problem-program relationships. There is no real starting or ending place here; the main point is that alternative systems of inputs and outputs must eventually be identified in quantifiable terms, preparatory to developing analytic techniques for predicting relative effectiveness levels.

A logical or conceptual beginning lies in identifying currently prominent community problems. These may be local issues that are given heavy press coverage, demands made by minority groups through demonstrations and other actions, problems outlined by civic and community organizations, improvements suggested by public administrator, and politicians, and problems and trends identified by educators and other urban researchers. No effort should be made, however, to identify all important community problems. Only those that are currently most pressing should be considered. By consistently applying the method in a series of repeated, continuing rounds of analysis, we gain assurance that all important problems will eventually be considered. No attempt is made to define problems in terms of measurable indexes. They serve simply as orientation points for public programs and policies.

The Model Cities legislation establishes just such a set of problems, though they remain to be redefined in somewhat more specific local terms. [26] This is not a full set of urban problems, of course, but only that subset dealing with slums and blight in older urban neighborhoods. Depending upon how they are expressed, such problems can serve equally well as broad goals for relevant public programs. This use as goals should not be confused with the role of more detailed, measurable objectives in the rational planning model. Here goals are general and nonoperational. The goals or problems toward which Model Cities Programs aim have been identified as follows:

> The purposes of this title are to provide additional financial and technical assistance to enable cities of all sizes (with equal regard to the problems of small as well as large cities) to plan, develop, and carry out locally prepared and scheduled comprehensive city demonstration programs containing new and imaginative proposals to rebuild or revitalize large slum and blighted areas; to expand housing, job, and income opportunities; to reduce dependence on welfare payments; to improve educational facilities and programs; to combat disease and ill health; to reduce the incidence of crime and delinquency; to enhance recreational and cultural opportunities; to establish better access between homes and jobs; and

generally to improve living conditions for the people who
live in such areas, and to accomplish these objectives
through the most effective and economical concentration
and coordination of federal, state, and local public and
private efforts to improve the quality of urban life. [27]

Design New Programs and Policies

The emphasis above on new and imaginative proposals is the key-
note for the second step in the process. One of the most promising
and important features of the Model Cities Program is that wide options
are left open for cities to design their own coordinated neighborhood
demonstration programs. In concept, at least, many different combinations and permutations of both old and new programs and policies
might be acceptable for federal supplementary funding. The chief requirement is that the overall program "is of sufficient magnitude to
make a substantial impact on the physical and social problems and to
remove or arrest blight and decay in entire sections or neighborhoods. . . ."[28]

The various projects and activities that might make up such a program will draw upon many ongoing programs and existing agencies. For
example, in developing broad standards for ensuring that Model Cities
Programs will be comprehensive and coordinated, a number of familiar
program components have been suggested. [29] The exact approach and
emphasis appropriate for interrelating these typical components will
depend on the nature of local social, economic, and physical problems,
and the size and circumstances of particular cities. Such components
include the physical improvement of neighborhood environments, housing for low- and moderate-income families, transportation and access
to employment, educational facilities and services, manpower training
and economic development, recreational and cultural facilities, crime
prevention, health facilities and services, and social services and public assistance. Each of these is, of course, already the general responsibility of existing local agencies.

The importance of this second step lies in the potential for breaking
up present agency programs into smaller, individual parts, and recombining and regrouping these parts into coordinated packages that are
more relevant to actual needs and problems. These new packages
would be quite likely to cut across current agency lines. New program
elements, not now in existence, might be needed to fill gaps in overall
service. The main purpose served would be an analytic one, restructuring programs according to their effects upon community problems.
Actual administrative reorganization would not necessarily be implied,

though in some cases more efficient relationships could become evident. The implementation problems associated with comprehensive goal achievement and PPBS models would not be quite as serious here.

Though the emphasis in this phase is upon designing new programs, so that the key role of innovation and experimentation in solving urban problems will be prominent, in practice we will often be dealing with existing programs and policies. As shown in this Model Cities example, we will look for new ways to structure such programs, examine their interrelationships with other programs, and in general attempt to define and discuss existing programs in terms of how they can and cannot meet current needs. This orientation toward problem solving will provide a basic framework for systematically considering many different potential wide-ranging possible improvements, not limited, of course, to simple incremental shifts among budget catagories. However, we will not deal with all government programs and policies, simply because many (such as sewers, water supply, and streets) provide standard kinds of services not aimed at particular problems.

Identify Community Impacts

As in the rational planning method, programs and policies must be expressed in measurable terms, representing the inputs for analysis and evaluation. Similarly, a set of measurable outputs must also be identified. Though these may often be related to the problems and goals of step 1, this is not a necessary requirement. Through the practice of carrying out the first three phases of the method together, the outputs will be identified and grouped together in terms of the groups and locations affected. These may be intentional or unintentional consequences and outcomes. Because goals, objectives, programs, policies, and impacts will often be indistinct from one another, defined in the same general terms, impacts will be discerned and singled out in an informal kind of way.

This step will be a counterpart to the identification of objectives in the rational method, but without any rigorous listing or classification. Outputs will be measured in terms of incidence groups and locations only, which may or may not be associated with objectives in the rational approach. No attempt will be made to identify all possible impacts. Only those impacts and consequences that occur to us during the intertwined examination of problems, programs, and policies will be considered, and then only the most significant ones. The analysis of outputs will not be comprehensive; in fact, it will be greatly simplified in comparison to the rational method. What if neglected impacts turn out to be of critical importance? This is the key value of stressing the notion of process in applying the overall method—the chances are high that all important impacts will eventually become known through repeated, successive rounds of evaluation.

In general, the impacts of the Model Cities Program will be more specific reflections of the physical, social, and economic goals cited earlier. By definition, the location of most physical impacts will be within the model neighborhoods under study, while most social and economic impacts will be felt by low- and moderate-income families living within those neighborhoods. Thus, though the scope of the program is a full one in terms of potential projects and activities, its effects will be felt by a relatively small proportion of a city's area or population. Outside impacts might be felt, however, by absentee landlords, mortgage-lending institutions, commercial home builders, industrial areas in other sections of the city, as a result of major transportation system improvements, in response to open housing practices, or in other ways.

Though such physical impacts as changes in the number of substandard housing units, in the number of rehabilitation building permits issued, in the proportion of aged and low-income persons living under adequate conditions, in commercial vacancy rates, and in other kinds of physical indexes will be important, social and economic impacts will generally be more far-reaching and crucial. They will often be much harder to assess. Included here will be impacts involving unemployment and underemployment rates, welfare caseloads, the proportion of families above poverty income levels, infant mortality rates, various disease rates, juvenile delinquency and other crime rates, the number of new jobs provided, successful job-training placements, housing relocation loads and records, school dropout rates, levels of citizen participation, and longer-range follow-ups on Head Start, Upward Bound, adult education, and other special educational programs.

Predict Effectiveness Levels

Any systematic procedure for evaluating public programs and policies must rely heavily on analytic techniques for predicting expected outcomes. There must be come sort of method for estimating and anticipating the relative effectiveness levels of alternative program packages. As a result, the same sort of programs and tasks involved in developing mathematical equations and models mentioned earlier will also be present in working with a program-policy trade-off approach. However, because we will deal with a much smaller and more

manageable set of inputs and outputs, the amount of research and analytic effort required for model building will be correspondingly greatly
reduced.

What kinds of impact or effectiveness models seem appropriate for
the Model Cities Program? The fact of the matter is that very few if
any usable, proven models are currently available. Very little systematic analysis of the relationships between the kinds of programs
and impacts mentioned above has previously been conducted. Because
the Model Cities Program is one calling for immediate action, as well
as for significant progress in alleviating problems within a relatively
short time (presumably five years or less), we are actually forced to
proceed with new projects and activities without prior estimates of
effectiveness. This is the experimental or demonstration aspect of the
program; we are really testing alternative solutions at the same time
that we implement them.

The resulting implications for specific model neighborhood programs are that three key, interrelated directions of analysis and research should be pursued. First, an information-gathering capability
must be organized, so that relevant data regarding program inputs and
outputs will be available. Such an information system must be internally consistent, relatively complete, and maintained on a continuing
basis. It should be a top-priority program assignment so that from
the beginning we will have data resources sufficient to evaluate program performance. Where possible, relevant data for previous periods
should also be collected. Flexibility to revise data formats and to add
or delete new data items continually should be assured.

Second, the information system can be used to monitor the ongoing
performance of certain program components (mainly those for which
data is reported on a monthly basis, such as employment and welfare
activities). By examining the short-term or the month-by-month variation in important impact or output indicators, we can decide whether
a particular project or activity is as effective as we had originally
hoped, and can increase or decrease program inputs accordingly. In
this way, we will attempt to review rather quickly the appropriateness
of program components inaugurated without any explicit knowledge of
what their effect would be.

Third, the information system and the results of the monitoring
studies should be used to develop predictive models, for evaluating
alternative future courses and strategies for the program. As Model
Cities projects and activities develop and stabilize, and we begin to
consider their possible continuation, acceleration, or deceleration,
we should also begin to construct and apply the kinds of predictive
models we would have liked to employ from the very outset. We may
wish to predict effectiveness levels for continuation in present model
neighborhoods, for application in other areas of the city or, if our

results have been especially encouraging, for application to model
neighborhoods in other cities. We will particularly want to examine
alternative stresses and emphases among program components. Though
the analytic workload will be much more realistic and manageable than
under a comprehensive rational planning approach, it will still be a
heavy one. In particular, we will want to conduct supporting research
into basic input-output relationships, possibly utilize the results of research conducted elsewhere, and we are quite likely to discover unmet
data needs.

Identify Marginal Trade-offs

Assume that we have been able to develop a reasonably adequate
set of predictive models. As with the rational planning approach, many
different kinds of mathematical equations and statistical relationships
might be used. Though a substantial amount of research and analysis
will be required, it will be considerably less than that called for in the
comprehensive rational method. Inputs have been limited to programs
and policies that promise to solve current urban problems. Outputs
have been defined only in terms of the major impacts and consequences
anticipated for these programs and policies. Our evaluation strategy
is to examine these problem-solving inputs and outputs through continuing, successive rounds of analysis, predicting and repredicting
their expected interrelationships under changing urban conditions.

How will we utilize these predictions for evaluating alternative
combinations of programs and policies? In contrast to the rational
approach, we will not attempt to identify or select preferred alternatives; this is a task left for local decision makers. Our role will be
simply to communicate effectively the results of analysis. Broadly,
we will focus on two kinds of information: (a) identifying impacts that
are the same for each alternative, and comparing these with costs,
and (b) identifying impacts that are marginally different, and comparing
these with costs. Costs will be monetary only, those incurred in implementing various programs and policies. In terms of solving community problems, impacts may be either positive or negative. The only
assignment of relative weights involved will be those employed, either
implicity or explicitly, by decision makers in their final choice among
alternatives.

In communicating the results of analysis in this manner, several
basic steps are likely to be important. First, we will want to know
whether impacts not varying by alternative are at acceptable levels.
Assuming that only generally feasible alternatives have been included
for evaluation, we will want to locate satisfactory impact levels

involving minimum costs. Second, for those impacts that do vary, we will also want to know how each stands in relation to acceptable output levels. In assisting decision makers to make subsequent trade-offs among these incremental differences, we will again want to know where minimum costs lie. The use of minimum and maximum performance standards for certain impacts will thus enter here, accompanying a systematic kind of search for minimum cost alternatives.

We will probably be asked to conduct further analyses, raising or lowering the inputs and outputs associated with some projects and activities while holding others fixed, enabling decision makers to clarify how costs and impacts are related. Our predicitive models will have had to capture sufficiently the interdependencies among various programs to permit this step. In general, in making basic analyses of this type, we will be conducting a series of marginal trade-offs among under- and overachieved impacts, among less and more costly alternative programs, juggling individual components in search of more productive combinations. We will proceed informally, without any set method for successive marginal analyses, until decision makers are satisfied that enough information is at hand for their final choices and trade-offs.

In applying this final step to the Model Cities Program, we will, of course, first need a workable collection of predictive models. We may well be able to apply such a trade-off technique in a partial way, as a means for analyzing selected program packages, before other analytic work is fully completed. For example, we may wish to examine different methods for reducing current unemployment: job training and retraining programs, personnel recruitment programs, on-the-job training, industrial relocation, industrial development programs. After a sufficient period of experimentation, data gathering, and monitoring, the results of pursuing different alternatives can be compared and analyzed, identifying costs, positive impacts, and negative impacts. Appropriate marginal comparisons can be made, including the application of such standards as minimum successful job placements or new jobs created, and such cost constraints as federal OEO funds available. We will predict the future performance of alternative programs, and decision makers, applying whatever relative weights among impacts they choose, will perform appropriate trade-offs and select a final program combination.

CONCLUSIONS

The purpose of this chapter has been to identify some of the many operational difficulties associated with comprehensive rational planning.

The prospects of this strategy for urban plan evaluation are not, in any practical sense, encouraging. Its requirements for systematic, comprehensive levels of analysis are overwhelming. However, other logical, more limited frameworks and strategies for governmental policy making have been advanced. Within an urban planning context, the development of new strategy models, combining some features of both rational and other more pragmatic methods, appears to be especially desirable. One such model has been suggested here. This program-policy trade-off approach essentially attempts to identity the most important impacts over which alternative plans, programs, and policies differ, and to illustrate for decision makers just what these differences or trade-offs are.

A program-policy trade-off model is recommended as an alternative to the comprehensive goal-achievement model of rational planning. Its potential advantages fall in the following basic areas.

Inputs. Comprehensive rational planning calls for the stratification of all existing government programs and policies according to the previously established goals and objectives to which they contribute. A more limited program-policy trade-off approach requires only the identification and design of new programs and policies, in terms of their potential application to currently important community problems. Many of these new programs and policies will actually be improved versions of existing activities. Problems in the stratification and measurement of program-policy inputs will still remain, but at a more manageable level.

Outputs. The outputs of comprehensive goal-achievement models are defined in terms of a community's goals and objectives. Problems in measuring the achievement of often abstract objectives are abundant. A program-policy trade-off model would focus only upon the most important measureable impacts and consequences expected for program and policy inputs. These impacts would be informally related to previously identified community problems but would not be tied to a formal set of goals and objectives. Some important impacts may be overlooked, while the measurement of others will continue to cause difficulty.

Analysis. Both strategy models call for a heavy commitment of research funds and staff to the development of analytic techniques for predicting expected outcomes. This will require extensive work with various mathematical models and statistical techniques, as well as the establishment of improved and ongoing urban information systems. The development of programs-objectives matrices under the rational planning approach would permit a systematic comparison of relative

effectiveness levels for various program-policy alternatives. While
such a matrix could also have relevance under a program-policy trade-
off approach, it would be much smaller in scale, and would relate programs to expected impacts. The level of research and analytic effort
required would be large, but not nearly as great as that implied by
comprehensive rational planning.

Findings. Comprehensive goal-achievement models are usually ambitious regarding the recommendations to be made to governmental
decision makers. It is assumed that methods can be developed for
weighting both community objectives and program impacts upon different groups and locations. Such weightings will allow aggregate scores
for alternative plans, programs, and policies to be computed, so that
a single preferred or optimal alternative can be recommended. However, attempts to devise such weighting techniques have revealed very
serious operational and conceptual problems. A program-policy trade-
off model ignores the assignment of relative weights, and leaves this
difficult and essentially subjective task to political decision makers.
The method attempts only to identify the marginal differences or trade-
offs among the impacts of alternative plans, programs, and policies.
Basic characteristics of these impact trade-offs, such as appropriate
performance standards, sensitivities, and costs, are presented to
decision makers for their final evaluation.

Process. The notion of process within comprehensive rational planning
is not clearly defined. Goal-achievement models appear to be advanced
primarily as ends in themselves. They are granted such potentially
great powers that continuing planning and analysis activities seem assigned a secondary role of filling in the cells of some final programs-
objectives matrix. A systematic process of continuing analysis is, on
the other hand, fundamental to a program-policy trade-off model. No
final recommendations are sought, and an inability to deal fully with
all significant impacts is acknowledged. Findings will continually be
revised and analyses conducted in a never-ending chain of successive
comparisons. In particular, the basic steps in the method—identifying
and analyzing problems, programs, policies, and impacts—are not
carried out individually but in practice are concurrently and closely
interrelated.
    Both comprehensive goal-achievement models and program-policy
trade-off models are, of course, logical or rational in approach. In
fact, in some respects they are not distinct alternatives, but differ
mainly in terms of relative emphasis. Both center upon being able to
predict relative effectiveness levels, but the program-policy trade-off
approach recognized the practical limitations on research capability.

It admits that we must proceed on the basis of partial information, and that we must continually revise our predictions and analyses. It emphasized the development of a systematic but noncomprehensive process for compensating for past errors and new insights. In contrast, comprehensive rational planning appears to depend less upon an explicit process than upon an essentially overrational or overly optimistic model for evaluating and weighting goal achievement. A program-policy trade-off model appears to offer a more realistic and useful strategy for structuring the rational planning process needed within our urban areas.

NOTES

1. See R. L. Ackoff, "Toward Quantitative Evaluation of Urban Services," in Public Expenditure Decisions in the Urban Community, H.G. Shaller, ed. (Washington, D.C.: Resources for the Future, 1963), pp. 91-117; R. S. Bolan, "Emerging Views of Planning," AIP Journal (July 1968): 233-45; D. N. Michael, "Urban Policy in the Rationalized Society," AIP Journal (May 1965): 158-66; I. M. Robinson, "Beyond the Middle-Range Planning Bridge," AIP Journal (November 1965): 304-12.

2. See H. P. Hatry and J. F. Cotton, Program Planning for State County City (Washington, D.C.: George Washington University, 1967); W. Z. Hirsch, "State and Local Program Budgeting," Papers, Regional Science Association 18 (1966): 147-63; D. A. Page, "The Federal Planning-Programming-Budgeting System," AIP Journal (July 1967): 256-59; State Local Finances Project, Implementing PPB in State, City, and County (Washington, D.C.: George Washington University, 1969): State Local Finances Project, PPB Pilot Project Reports from the Participating 5 States, 5 Counties, and 5 Cities (Washington, D.C.: George Washington University, 1969); S. Mushkin, "PPB in Cities," Public Administration Review (March/April 1969): 167-77.

3. See G. H. Fisher, "The Role of Cost Utility Analysis in Program Budgeting," in Program Budgeting, D. Novick, ed. (Washington, D.C.: Government Printing Office, 1965), pp. 33-48; M. Hill, "A Goals-Achievement Matrix for Evaluating Alternative Plans," AIP Journal (January 1968): 19-24; E. S. Quade, "Systems Analysis Techniques for Planning-Programming-Budgeting," in Planning Programming Budgeting: A Systems Approach to Management, F. J. Lyden and E. G. Miller, eds. (Chicago: Markham, 1967), pp. 292-312; W. A. Steger and T. R. Lakshmanan, "Plan Evaluation Methodologies:

Some Aspects of Decision Requirements and Analytical Response," in Urban Development Models, Special Report 97, G. C. Hemmens, ed. (Washington, D.C.: Highway Research Board, 1968), pp. 33-72; M. B. Tietz, "Cost Effectiveness: A Systems Approach to Analysis of Urban Services," AIP Journal (September 1968): 303-11.

4. R. E. Millward, "PPBS: Problems of Implementation," AIP Journal (March 1968): 88-94.

5. I. S. Lowery, "A Short Course in Model Design," AIP Journal (May 1965): 158-66; W. A. Steger, "Review of Analytic Techniques for the CRP," AIP Journal (May 1965): 166-72. See also W. B. Hansen, "Quantitative Methods in Urban Planning," in Principles and Practice of Urban Planning, W. I. Goodman and E. C. Freund, eds. (Washington, D.C.: International City Managers' Association, 1968); pp. 277-94.

9. Hill, op. cit., p. 21.

10. See C. G. Schimpeler and W. L. Grecco, "Systems Evaluation: An Approach Based on Community Structure and Values," Highway Research Record, no. 238 (Washington, D.C.: Highway Research Board, 1968), pp. 128-52.

11. See E. L. Falk, "Measurement of Community Values: The Spokane Experiment," Highway Research Record, no. 229 (Washington, D.C.: Highway Research Board, 1968), pp. 53-64.

12. Schimpeler and Grecco, op. cit., p. 134.

13. Hill, op. cit.

14. Falk, op. cit., p. 59.

15. See Schimpeler and Grecco, op. cit., pp. 131-33.

16. See Fisher, op. cit., p. 42.

17. Hill, op. cit., p. 23.

18. See W. Jessiman, D. Brand, A. Tumminia, and C. R. Brussee, "A Rational Decision-making Technique for Transportation Planning," Highway Research Record, no. 180 (Washington, D.C.: Highway Research Board, 1967), pp. 71-80.

19. See C. Lindblom, "The Science of 'Muddling Through,'" Public Administration Review (Spring 1959): 79-88.

20. D. Braybrooke and C. Lindblom, A Strategy of Decision: Policy Evaluation as a Social Process (New York: Free Press, 1963).

21. Lindblom, op. cit., p. 82.

22. Ibid., pp. 82-83.

23. Ibid., pp. 87-88.

24. Ibid., pp. 86-87.

25. See Y. Dror, Public Policy-making Reexamined (San Francisco: Chandler, 1968); Y. Dror, "Muddling Through—'Science' or Inertia?" Public Administration Review (September 1964): 153-57; A. Etzioni, The Active Society: A Theory of Societal and Political

Processes (New York: Free Press, 1968); A. Etzioni, "Mixed-Scanning: A 'Third' Approach to Decision-making," Public Administration Review (December 1967): 385-92.

26. See U.S. Department of Housing and Urban Development, Improving the Quality of Urban Life: A Program Guide to Model Neighborhoods in Demonstration Cities (Washington, D.C.: Government Printing Office, 1966).

27. Public Law 89-754, Title I: Comprehensive City Demonstration Programs, Sect. 101.

28. Ibid., Sect. 103 (a)(2).

29. HUD, op. cit., pp. 8-10.

3

THE SYSTEMS APPROACH IN URBAN PLANNING

Systems analysis, PPBS, cost-effectiveness, program budgeting, systems engineering, operations research, the systems approach—these are all terms that are occurring with increasing frequency in the practice and the literature of urban planning. Often, a good deal of confusion has come to be associated with them. This is largely due to the fact that much of the conceptual and methodological development associated with these terms has occurred outside of urban planning. In the fields of economics, business administration, industrial engineering, public administration, civil engineering, management science, and military and defense analysis, different versions and applications of these basic ideas have been advanced. Though the interrelationships and overlaps among such concepts are strong, each field has tended to develop its own particular terminology and frame of reference.

Consequently, when urban planners have tried to reinterpret these systems concepts in terms of urban problems, needs, and issues, certain inconsistencies or ambiguities have resulted. "Borrowing" from these other contexts has usually been selective and partial. It has been difficult to move from general statements concerning the need for and the benefits of systems analysis to actual proposals for innovation and change in the urban planning process. There has been no clear delineation of possible broad areas of application in urban planning. Instead, a number of individualized techniques for applying the systems approach to a particular phase or aspect of urban planning have been developed. On the surface, most of these applications seem to have little in com-

Reprinted with permission from American Society of Planning Officials, Planning Advisory Service Report No. 253, January 1970.

mon. They have varied widely in terms of the approach, organization, content, and techniques of analysis that were used. Many have not been particularly successful or at least have fallen short of original expectations.

This chapter is primarily concerned with examples of these scattered attempts to apply the systems approach in urban planning. The term "systems approach" is interpreted broadly and is intended to more or less include each of the other concepts mentioned above. Through a review and analysis of specific examples, the chapter attempts to accomplish the following objectives:

1. Outline a framework or strategy for utilizing the systems approach. Four basic types or levels of urban-oriented systems analysis are identified: improving the planning process, analyzing urban systems, analyzing urban problems, and improving governmental operations.
2. Identify the steps or phases of analysis that are fundamental to the systems approach. Four basic steps in systems analysis, applicable at each level, are distinguished: identifying objectives, identifying programs, predicting effectiveness, and evaluating alternatives.
3. Develop guidelines that stress the operational problems of the systems approach. On the basis of the experience and results of each of the examples reviewed, a series of cautionary guidelines for each of the basic steps in analysis is presented.

Overall, the chapter outlines an approach or way of looking at the subject of systems analysis. Its aim is to make sense, through the use of specific examples, of a subject that has been violently condemned, outrageously praised, and almost always shrouded in technical jargon. Most important, it is intended for the use of both the smaller urban planning agency, unable to hire a staff of systems analysts and technical experts, as well as the larger planning agency, wishing to make the most of its systems personnel and specialized consultants. The report will show that much of the systems approach is not the special province of technical experts, but rather the proper concern of a planning agency's regular staff.

APPLYING THE SYSTEMS APPROACH

What exactly does the systems approach mean? What steps are involved? How should a local planning agency try to use the systems approach? Where should it be applied? When? There are no simple

answers to these questions. There are also no universally accepted
definitions of "systems analysis" or the "systems approach." In fact,
each new reference or example, particularly if drawn from a different
discipline, tends to define systems analysis slightly differently.

There may be variations in methodology, conceptual background,
reasons for using such an approach, or the end-products that are envisioned. Importantly, many such differences are largely superficial
and due mainly to the varying literary styles, semantic preferences,
writing skills, and educational backgrounds of the individuals involved.
Because systems analysis has lent itself to considerable and often
lengthy verbal exposition, drifting perhaps too much toward abstrac-
tions and broad generalizations, its basic elements have often seemed
rather elusive.

In this chapter an attempt is made to distill from among the many
varying definitions of systems analysis those basic steps or phases that
seem to be most fundamental. This is not to suggest that variations or
modifications of a basic systems approach are not desirable or even
essential. On the contrary, as the examples presented later in the
chapter will illustrate, any specific context for applying the systems
approach seems to demand unique treatment. Moreover, there is no
one "right" way to conduct a systems analysis—innumerable variations
in technique are possible, depending in part upon the agencies and the
individuals involved. A spelling out of the basic steps involved is
needed, however, to show where the common ground lies.

Basic Steps in Analysis

Four primary phases or activities are involved in applying the
systems approach within decision making, problem solving, or planning and analysis processes—including those of urban planning. These
need not necessarily be conducted in order, and in practice are often
conducted simultaneously or in some overlapping fashion. In any given
example, they may be referred to somewhat differently, and each may
be given different levels of relative emphasis. However, for any particular research study, analysis effort, or planning activity to qualify
as a fully developed systems analysis, each step must be present.
These four phases of the systems approach, illustrated in Figure 3.1,
are as follows:

Step 1. Identifying Objectives. The goals and objectives that are being
        sought must be explicitly identified. In general, it must be
        determined what the process, system, problem, or agency
        under investigation is intended to achieve. In the context of

FIGURE 3.1

Basic Steps in Systems Analysis

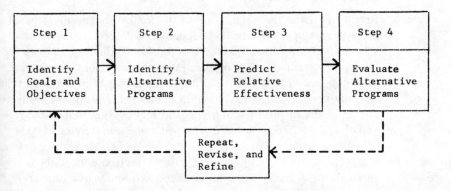

Step 1	Step 2	Step 3	Step 4
Identify Goals and Objectives	Identify Alternative Programs	Predict Relative Effectiveness	Evaluate Alternative Programs

Repeat, Revise, and Refine

urban planning, this centers upon the identification of all the important and relevant community objectives that may be involved. In many instances, such objectives will be straightforward and generally accepted (reduce crime rates, preserve adequate open space), while in others they may be somewhat controversial (reduce inner city-suburban school disparities, promote industrial development in area x). Most important, wherever possible, objectives must be expressed in some measurable, quantitative way, so that their relative levels of achievement can be compared.

Step 2. Identifying Programs. Given a specific set of objectives, alternative means of realizing them must be identified. In some instances, alternative plans, programs, or projects may be advanced before objectives are actually identified; in other cases, they may be designed directly to achieve previously stated ends. Most often, however, programs and objectives are identified and developed together, with both direct and indirect interconnections and feedback. Sometimes the dividing line between an "objective" and a "program" is thin and largely a matter of semantics or interpretation (e.g., provide public housing for low-income families, which could conceivably be either an objective or a program). Most important, programs must be expressed in some measurable, quantitative way, such that their contributions toward achieving pertinent objectives can be compared. Programs must be identified and expressed in terms of objectives.

Step 3. Predicting Effectiveness. One of the major characteristics of the systems approach is its emphasis upon the development of a systematic, well-organized method for evaluating alternative plans, programs, and projects. Perhaps the most crucial step in the approach lies in predicting the relative effectiveness that alternative programs will have in achieving objectives. This is normally the phase in which specific forecasting methodologies or related procedures are developed and used—various types of mathematical models, statistical analyses, program review and monitoring techniques, and data collection procedures. In general, in order to zero in on suspected or hypothesized program-objective interrelationships, it is necessary for both programs and objectives to be fairly specific and expressed in some detail. Often data on additional variables or factors will be required.

Though the data-collection and mathematical-analysis aspects of this step can assume large proportions, calling for electronic computer assistance, this is by no means inevitable. In fact, experience has shown that overcomplexity is a real danger during this third phase, threatening the success of the entire effort, and shortening the time available for the other phases of analysis. Nevertheless, the prediction of effectiveness is undoubtedly the thorniest and most difficult step in the entire systems approach.

Step 4. Evaluating Alternatives. In some systems-analysis applications, the evaluation of alternatives may be quite straightforward. Given an acceptable set of effectiveness predictions for a group of alternative programs, that program (or programs) should be preferred that is most effective in achieving objectives. For example, if limited resources are available, a budget constraint may be applied, and the program (or programs) most effective within that budget will be preferred. The cost-effectiveness of that alternative will be rated highest, since it will be expected to achieve the most for a given cost. Where multiple objectives are involved, it may become necessary to assign numerical weights to different objectives, using a subjective rating scheme to derive such weights.

In most cases, the final evaluation of alternatives will of necessity be subjective, open to the judgments of politicians, administrators, planners, and other decision makers. Steps

3 and 4 of the systems approach can provide selected quantitative estimates of impact and effectiveness and can possibly suggest techniques for weighting or trading off these impacts. However, the decision as to which forecasted result is best is in the end essentially a judgmental one. Very often, qualitative objectives must also be considered, in addition to those that could be treated quantitatively.

Basic Levels of Analysis

This basic four-step systems approach can be applied by urban planners along any of four broad levels of analysis. The examples that follow have themselves suggested this four-level categorization of potential applications, and each example offers a different, somewhat unique illustration of what might be accomplished within each level. In general, each example is described in terms of how it handled each of the four basic steps of systems analysis. In some cases, these steps were only partially completed. The imagination and diversity of approach shown by these case studies is, overall, impressive, strongly suggesting that there is much room for experimentation, innovation, and progress in applying the systems approach in urban planning.

The four basic levels of urban-oriented systems analysis provide the framework around which the rest of the chapter is organized:

Level 1. Improving the Planning Process. In the following two sections of this chapter, examples of applying the systems approach at its broadest level of potential use are considered. First, the orientation of the Model Cities Program toward basic systems thinking is examined. The relationship of federal guidelines and program requirements to the four steps of systems analysis is discussed, and some of the implications of each of these steps are reviewed. Second, the application of systems analysis within four other basic urban planning processes—capital improvement programming, the Community Renewal Program, land-use/transportation planning, and comprehensive city planning—is considered. Specific examples are reviewed and analyzed.

Level 2. Analyzing Urban Systems. Within different planning processes, it is common for individual planning components or subject areas to be singled out for detailed study. Frequently, in keeping with the traditional land-use orientation of urban planning, these subject areas are defined as

functional, physical, or spatial "systems." Each such system is comprised of a series of facilities or land uses, each
with its own particular location. Later in this chapter,
application of the systems approach in the study of three
physically or spatially oriented systems—residential land
use, parks and recreation, and health facilities and
services—is examined. Specific examples are again reviewed and analyzed.

Level 3. Analyzing Urban Problems. Recent trends toward the
broadening of urban planning to include the consideration of
social and economic problems suggest another potential level
for applying the systems approach. In general, it appears
best to focus upon social-economic-cultural problems, rather
than upon the broader social and economic "systems" or
"processes" of which they are a part. Analysis of social
and economic phenomena has proven to be extremely difficult. In a later section, aspects of the systems analysis of
urban problems are discussed, and a partial example is reviewed.

Level 4. Improving Governmental Operations. Concurrent with the
growing interest in the systems approach applied to urban
planning has been an even stronger and more widespread
interest in its application in urban public administration.
In fact, much of the literature and experience in systems
analysis has been generated by the application of PPBS to
governmental budgeting and decision-making, particularly
at the federal level. Though application of the systems approach in improving governmental operations is largely the
responsibility of municipal and other local governmental
agencies, there appears to be an indirect or partial role
open to local planning agencies. This role is discussed
later in the chapter, where an example concerned with fire
station location is presented.

    Utilizing this basic characterization of "steps in analysis" and
"levels of application," it is possible to examine comparatively any
number of widely varying examples of urban systems analysis. The
examples that follow are presented with two purposes in mind. First,
an attempt is made to note their similarities and differences. Summary
comparison tables are prepared to depict the major features and the
contrasts of the examples given in the sections, "Other Planning Processes," and "Analyzing Urban Systems." Second, each example is
discussed in terms of the four steps of the systems approach. Suffici-

ent details on methodology are included to give an indication of the
scope and flavor of each example. In the sections mentioned, each of
the basic steps of analysis is highlighted (via underlining) to provide
for continuity and ease of comparison.

IMPROVING THE PLANNING PROCESS:
THE MODEL CITIES PROGRAM

One of the most fruitful uses of the systems approach in urban
planning lies in structuring and organizing the planning process itself.
This is the broadest level of application, since it most often implies
or includes systems analyses that may be developed at more specific
levels—involving urban systems, problems, or governmental operations. At this broad level, planning agencies find themselves asking
such basic questions as: What is the purpose of this agency? What
community objectives should its activities and programs seek to advance? How should it attempt to influence the course of events in daily
urban life? What advice should it give to other governmental agencies
and departments? What priorities should be given to different objectives and to different public programs or actions? What is good or bad
about alternative public or private programs or actions for urban
changes?

The systems approach enables planning agencies to examine and
explore the answers to questions such as these more carefully. It does
not, of course, automatically provide the answers—these will always
require a good deal of judgment and interpretation. The systems approach offers a method for systematically organizing the study of these
fundamental questions of purpose and direction. In so doing, it also
offers a basic method for organizing or structuring the ongoing processes of urban planning. One relatively new urban planning process,
that brought forth by the Model Cities Program, has from the start
been firmly committed to the systems approach. Early Model Cities
efforts at developing this approach are discussed in the following paragraphs.

Federal guidelines for the Model Cities Program call upon City
Demonstration Agencies (CDAs), the local planning and administering
agencies, to identify specific goals, objectives, and program approaches for their overall program. [1] Requirements for the initial
Comprehensive Model Cities Program call for a document that is divided into three parts. The first section should contain (a) an analysis
of local social, economic, and physical problems affecting model
neighborhood residents, (b) a statement of the city's long-range goals

for overcoming these problems, (c) for each basic goal the identification of multiple program approaches or proposed governmental actions for helping to achieve that goal, and (d) an overall strategy for coordinating program approaches, one which identifies interrelationships among problems, establishes priorities among different goals, and indicates linkages or sequential ties between different program approaches.

The second section of the Program develops a five-year plan and program, and represents the key stage in the application of a systems-approach methodology. It is here that the city's broad goals must be restated in terms of more specific five-year and one-year objectives, expressed in quantifiable or measurable terms wherever possible. Each program approach, together with the specific projects and activities it implies, must be directly matched with an objective (or objectives), and the expected contributions that approach will make toward achieving goals and objectives must be measurably shown. It is essential that all significant projects and activities, whether public or private, new or existing, and regardless of eligibility for federal financing, be identified. To the extent possible, all the alternatives and options that are likely to have some impact upon achieving model neighborhood goals and objectives must be made known.

The principal vehicle for making these comparisons of objectives and programs is the required Five-Year Objectives Table, probably the single most important element within any individual Model Cities Program. Here each goal and objective is listed in order, together with the quantified achievement targets for each (where possible) for the first year, second year, and third through fifth years of the projected Model Cities Program. Under each objective are listed those program approaches, projects, and activities that are relevant, together with their expected contributions to each achievement target. If appropriate, these contributions should be measured in the same terms as the target objective. If this is not possible, other meaningful quantifiable estimates of impact should be made, and explanations given of their relationship to objectives.

The Five-Year Objectives Table essentially illustrates expected progress toward the achievement of model neighborhood objectives over a five-year period. It is supplemented by a Five-Year Fiscal Needs Table that assigns estimated costs to all the programs, projects, and activities shown or implied previously—those that are existing (both unchanged and proposed for improvement) and those that are proposed. Included in this table is the First-Year Action Program, which is subsequently developed in more detail as the third major section of the Model Cities document.

The systematic development and use of programs-objectives tables for more rigorously formulating and evaluating alternative governmental programs represents a significant advance in urban planning methodology. Cities involved in the Model Cities Program are, in fact, currently at the vanguard in developing innovative and potentially far-reaching systems approaches to planning—primarily through their treatment of the Five-Year Objectives Table and the various analyses and interpretations which support it.

Critical to this new approach is the ability to identify measurable indexes, or social and economic indicators (data), that will adequately reflect the achievement of a stated goal or objective. Our expertise in this area is not at all far advanced, and considerable experimentation should be anticipated.[2] Consequently, the Five-Year Plan and Objectives Table that individual CDAs develop is clearly intended as only the initial statement in an ongoing planning process subject to continuing revision and refinement as problems change, objectives shift, new measurable indexes become available, and new program approaches are designed. The basic systems framework, however (the use of programs-objectives comparison tables), remains the same.

As is typical of other attempts to more systematically structure broad urban planning processes, Model Cities Programs in particular cities have not advanced far beyond the first two basic steps in the systems approach: identifying objectives and identifying programs. First-round cities (those that, in general, completed their Comprehensive Program documents sometime in 1969) are just now beginning to grapple with the second two steps: predicting effectiveness and evaluating alternatives. They are undertaking the crucial continuing planning and evaluation segments of their First-Year Action Programs. Much can be learned about the problems and difficulties of attempting to apply the systems approach, not only for Model Cities but for urban planning processes in general, by examining specific goals, objectives, performance measures, program approaches, and projects from particular cities. A review of initial strategies for continuing planning and evaluation can also prove instructive.

Identifying Objectives and Programs

Tables 3.1 and 3.2 present the objectives and program approaches identified for housing and for education by the Chicago Model Cities Program. They provide an example of how one city has attempted to more systematically define its needs and resources in these two basic planning areas. Most of the objectives appear in fact to address fundamental issues and problems of inner-city life. While other cities might phrase such objectives differently, and perhaps organize them differently as well, it seems likely that nearly every American city with blighted neighborhood and slum-ghetto problems calling for Model Cities-type action should advance similar statements of desired

TABLE 3.1

Objectives and Program Approaches for Housing: Chicago Model Cities Program

Objective	Achievement Measure	Five-Year Achievement Target	Program Approach	Programs Included	Expected Five-Year Impact
1. Increase the proportion of sound housing units	Percent of total	80 percent	A. Improve the existing housing supply	1. DUR—conservation 2. Neighborhood Service Program	4,500 deficient units rehabilitated 4,000 sound units renovated
2. Replace substandard housing units	Number	3,000 units		3. Chicago Dwellings Association 4. Building Department	3,000 substandard units removed
3. Develop new housing units	Number	5,000 units	B. Develop new housing resources	1. DUR—redevelopment 2. CHA—public housing 3. CDA—conventional and modular 4. Private development 5. New-Town/In-Town	1,500 public-housing units 4,000 moderate-income units
4. Reduce the proportion of overcrowded units	Percent of total	10 percent			
5. Increase the proportion of owner-occupied units	Percent of total	30 percent	C. Increase housing opportunities for individual residents	1. Additional home owners	4,500 families
6. Reduce the proportion of families paying in excess of 25 percent of income for rent	Percent of total	30 percent		2. Renters assisted	4,500 families

Note: Achievement targets are for the West Model Neighborhood, one of four in Chicago.
Source: City of Chicago, Model Cities Program, Part II: Five-Year Forecast (1969).

improvement. (These particular issues do not, of course, necessarily represent a full picture of all possible objectives and problems.)

Tables 3.1 and 3.2 illustrate some of the problems associated with the need to quantify objectives. For example, because housing problems and programs deal primarily with discrete physical facilities (individual housing units), it is considerably easier to express housing objectives quantitatively. Goal-achievement measures can be expressed simply as the numbers of housing units that should be rehabilitated, replaced, or newly developed. Goal-achievement targets simply specify when each objective should be attained. (As noted above, cumulative targets are actually specified, for the first year, second year, and third through fifth years of the Chicago Model Cities Program.)

Educational objectives, on the other hand, deal mainly with persons and with human behavior, rather than with physical facilities. While persons can be counted (college-bound high-school graduates, adults enrolled in night school), many educational objectives are quite difficult to quantify. For example, the basic objective of preschool education programs is typically to better prepare youngsters for the normal schooling process. However, measuring whether this objective is actually achieved is not easy. Psychological tests, educational achievement tests, control-group comparisons, and sufficient passage of time may all be necessary in order to see whether students have in fact been better prepared.

As a result, while each of the housing objectives in Table 3.1 deals directly with the status of the model neighborhood housing supply (the problem), many of the educational objectives in Table 3.2 deal more with programs themselves than with the problems and deficiencies these programs are intended to resolve. For example, it is proposed to extend preschool education on a year-round basis, rather than to increase the level and pace of educational attainment for grade-school children. It is proposed to reduce the teacher-pupil ratio, rather than to improve the educational performance of students within each classroom.

The need for measurable indexes of goal-achievement has, at this initial and early stage of Model Cities planning, forced the frequent use of program-related indexes, rather than objective-related ones. It is assumed that programs will achieve implied objectives, and that measures of program inputs can serve as temporary surrogates for measures of program outputs. Thus, programs themselves become objectives, because we do not have adequate methods of measuring educational betterment. Eventually, however, given the time, data, and analytic skills required, and as more knowledge is gained about the functions and processes of educational services themselves, it will be possible to state educational objectives more directly.

TABLE 3.2

Objectives and Program Approaches for Education: Chicago Model Cities Program

Objective	Achievement Measure	Five-Year Achievement Target	Program Approach	Programs Included	Expected Five-Year Impact
1. Increase proportion of high-school graduates going on to college or other post secondary schools	Percent of total	75 percent	A. Curriculum and methods improvement	1. Cooperatively planned urban schools (CO-PLUS schools)	9 schools
2. Provide for extension of preschool education on a year-round basis	Number of children affected	1,200 children		2. Child-parent centers (preschool education)	9 schools
3. Have students in area in all levels have textbooks or supplementary materials relevant to their environment	Number of schools affected	9 schools		3. Teacher team leaders (additional teaching staff)	20-25 percent staff increase
				4. Resident teacher aides	One per teacher
				5. Provide needed instructional materials	$1,500 per classroom
4. Raise the achievement level of students in area equal to that of students in other metropolitan areas	Percent completing high school	50 percent		6. Ethnic cultural studies program	All schools
				7. Drop-out academy	One unit
5. Incorporate in-service education as basic part of program for teachers and administrative personnel in inner-city schools to develop sensitivity to needs of children in these schools	Hours, teachers, schools	1 hour daily per teacher at 9 schools	B. Development of teaching and administrative personnel	1. Teacher team leaders	20-25 percent staff increase
				2. In-service training (conducted by team leaders)	One hour daily per teacher at 9 schools
				3. Child-parent centers	9 schools
				4. School-opening in-service program	All schools
6. Reduce teacher-pupil ratio from 1:35 to 1:25 and adult-pupil ratio to 1:23 or less to meet special needs of area residents	Number of schools affected	9 schools			

Objective	Indicator	Target/Impact		Item	Target/Impact
7. Improve quality and quantity of facilities in area schools	Mobil classrooms added or new classrooms constructed	30 mobile classrooms	C. Improvement of facilities	1. Child-parent centers	9 schools
				2. Cultural-educational cluster construction (long-range)	1 facility
				3. Magnet school construction (long-range)	1 facility
8. Broaden range of educational opportunities and programs to meet needs of residents in area	Schools kept open after hours	9 schools	D. Coordination of educational resources	1. Cultural programs and field trips	Increased activities
9. Increase level of educational service available to Model Area adults	Percent in formal elementary education	6 percent	E. Improvement of informal and adult education	1. Adult education program	Added in 5 schools (total 9)
	Percent in informal education	6 percent		2. CO-PLUS schools (after-hour use)	3 giving high-school diploma; 9 schools, open an additional 6 hours per day and weekends
	Percent working toward high school diploma	6 percent		3. Neighborhood library center	1 facility
				4. Volunteer tutors program	Expand from 540 to 930 tutors
			F. Development of supportive educational programs and services	1. Various ESEA programs and supporting staff	Total of 450 paraprofessionals for 9 schools
				2. Free breakfast program	All Model Area children
			G. Development of community participation	1. Community use of schools (after-hour use)	Increased at 9 schools
				2. CO-PLUS schools (staff-community planning)	9 schools

Note: Achievement Targets and Five-Year Impacts are for the West Model Neighborhood, one of four in Chicago.
Source: City of Chicago, Model Cities Program, Part II: Five-Year Forecast (1969).

The structure of Tables 3.1 and 3.2 also illustrates one of the more important and complicating features of multiple programs-objectives comparisons. Because sets of objectives and programs are interrelated, they can virtually never be analyzed in isolation. A single objective may be (and usually is) affected by more than one alternative program or project, while a single program may (and usually does) affect more than one objective. Moreover, objectives are often closely interrelated, so that the achievement of one will carry with it the achievement of others.

Similarly, alternative programs may also be closely related, such that the inauguration of one is required for the successful implementation of another, with possible time-phased sequencing or scheduling interplays. Often an individual program proposal assumes that a host of other programs are maintained somewhere near their existing levels Tables 3.1 and 3.2 thus show how it may often be necessary to group like objectives and like programs together, with the understanding that it may often be difficult or impossible to separate or distinguish the individual impacts of one program, or the achievement of one objective, from others.

Continuing Planning and Evaluation

Individual Model Cities participants have, in general, only begun to come to grips with some of the hard problems to be faced in the third and fourth steps of the systems approach. These steps are to be undertaken during the continuing planning and evaluation phase of the program. Though individual participants as yet have little experience to report, preliminary thinking indicates that successful evaluation of Model Cities Programs will constitute a major and difficult undertaking. [3] A number of consultant research studies have been authorized by HUD that would provide assistance to localities for conducting evaluation. *

---

*These research studies include the development of a prototype CDA information system intended to provide each local agency with a set of procedures for collecting and processing data relevant to program evaluation and performance review; a comparative study of the planning processes followed by 11 first-round and ten second-round cities in preparing their comprehensive programs; a research design and strategy for HUD-conducted model neighborhood resident surveys intended to examine selected aspects of program impact in a sample of cities; specialized studies of program impact in seven cities, utilizing the perceptions, contacts, and evaluations of neighborhood resident observers; a projected study of the institutional changes induced by the

Generally, the continuing planning phase of the First-Year Program is intended to revise, update, and refine the comprehensive program document and to develop a Second-Year Action Program. Key inputs into this continuing planning process will be the analyses and evaluations of the impacts of First-Year projects (as well as existing and modified programs) on model neighborhood residents. Should these projects and programs (singly or in combination) be continued, replaced, reorganized, increased, or decreased during the second year?

The principal criteria for evaluating projects and programs in this way will, of course, center upon their relative impact or effectiveness in achieving previously stated objectives. In one way or another, it must be possible to ascertain how each program will affect (or has affected) the quantitative measures associated with each objective. In fact, perhaps because the Model Cities Program is primarily intended as a program of action, relatively little time has been allowed for the development of predictive mathematical models, models that might quantitatively relate selected alternative programs to selected objectives.

Instead, the prediction of effectiveness of Model Cities (systems step 3) is treated primarily as a problem of measuring the actual impact of alternative programs during the First Year. The implied "prediction" is that a program will in general continue to accomplish whatever it was able to accomplish during this testing and monitoring phase. The urgency of public action within model neighborhoods generally dictates that promising programs be implemented at once and that formal predictions of effectiveness be supplanted by ongoing measurements of effectiveness.

It might eventually be possible in some instances to develop statistical or simulation models for predicting the effectiveness of programs proposed for implementation in the Second-Year Program or beyond. These could conceivably utilize data collected in the monitoring of current and First-Year programs, particularly data pertaining to the characteristics and attitudes of model neighborhood residents. The value of prediction is, of course, that it enables the sifting out of less desirable programs without actually trying them out first.

As presently foreseen, however, the bulk of Model Cities prediction—as well as evaluation (as systems step 4)—will be based on the ongoing monitoring of actual projects and programs. The crucial role of improved information resources is then more or less trans-

---

program in a sample of cities; the preparation of "experience reports" on significant Model Cities projects and activities in selected cities; and the provision of direct technical assistance to some 25 CDAs in the conduct of their continuing planning and evaluation programs.

ferred from the "normal prediction phase to an expanded evaluation
phase," as these two steps in the systems approach are essentially com
bined. The Model Cities Program consequently well illustrates the
problems and needs involved in generating and collecting data that
measure objectives (outputs), programs (inputs), and the intervening
variables, factors, and conditions that help programs contribute to
achieving objectives.

Two basic kinds of data will be needed in Model Cities evaluation:
data on neighborhood residents and data on project-program operations.[4] Data on neighborhood residents will in general relate to and
document previously established objectives. Initial conditions or need
must be measured, and subsequent changes in those conditions (as they
pertain to objectives) must be observed. In some way it must be possible to determine whether these changes took place as a result of
Model Cities Programs, or were due to outside influences.

Two major sources of data on neighborhood residents can be used
agency administrative records and specially conducted surveys. Agen
records (including, but not limited to, the files of those agencies that
may actually be participating in the Program) can in some cases be
used to monitor changes in the model-neighborhood population, if
available on a monthly or quarterly basis. Improvements in record-
keeping procedures may be necessary to provide access to such data.
Records used might include the administrative files of public aid departments, state employment services, community action agencies,
local school boards, or public health departments.

A second source of data on neighborhood residents may come from
surveys measuring neighborhood attitudes or opinions. These attitudes
should relate to stated community objectives and to the assessment of
progress being made in achieving them. Interview surveys provide a
major tool of this sort—usually an expensive one, but often the only
effective one in getting at current conditions, needs, and program-
project effectiveness in meeting needs. Many of the questions asked
on such surveys will provide data not available from agency records
or elsewhere, especially where the attitudes and satisfactions of
neighborhood residents are the chief items of concern in meeting objectives. Residents themselves can provide valuable help in designing
and conducting such surveys. Special follow-up surveys aimed specifically at those who participated in particular programs may also be
desirable.

Periodic interview or questionnaire surveys might be supplemente
by other more indirect and less formal methods for feeling a neighborhood's pulse: the reports of staff members and caseworkers on their
field contacts with residents, meetings with neighborhood organization
participation of residents in advising and guiding the development of

programs themselves, examination of service requests or waiting lists for particular programs, and so on.

While these kinds of information are essential in gauging progress toward meeting objectives, parallel data must be collected on the various projects and programs contributing to that progress. Particularly important here is the need to collect cost data for given levels of program impact so that comparative statements of relative costs and effectiveness for alternative programs aimed at the same objective may be developed. These cost-effectiveness comparisons constitute a primary technique for evaluating the merits of different programs.

Data on the internal operation and administration of projects-programs will also be needed, partly to support program-cost calculations but mainly to determine whether the program is doing what it was intended to do. Records should be kept on the numbers of persons served by a project, their needs and characteristics, the types of assistance given to them, their length of contact with the project, the way the program was organized, the gaps and overlaps in service, coordination with other agencies, the need for follow-up surveys, and other operating features. Alternatives should be evaluated not only in terms of effectiveness (achieving objectives) but also in terms of efficiency (smooth operations). The best alternative might be simply the reorganization of an existing program.

OTHER PLANNING PROCESSES

Although the Model Cities Program currently represents the most serious and ambitious attempt to structure an ongoing urban planning process more systematically, as well as the most extensive attempt in terms of the number of cities involved, it is by no means the first such attempt. A number of individual cities have in recent years developed innovative approaches to other planning processes that in one way or another also represent basic systems approaches. Although these efforts generally are not as ambitious or all-encompassing as those being undertaken by Model Cities participants, they nevertheless deal with planning processes equally in need of more systematic treatment. There is no reason to suspect that further systems work applied to these processes would not be equally productive.

In the following sections, examples of systems analysis applied to three other planning processes are discussed: the Wichita Capital Improvement Program (CIP), the Philadelphia Community Renewal Program (CRP), and the Southeastern Wisconsin Regional Land-Use and Transportation Plan. Possible applications to comprehensive city

planning are also examined. Each example represents, of course, onl
one among many possible ways to approach that particular planning
process more objectively. Other cities and metropolitan areas might
be expected to develop their own unique variation of a basic systems
approach, just as different Model Cities Programs each have their ow
particular organizational or structural emphases. These examples ar
intended only to illustrate how one particular planning agency did in
fact approach or analyze a basic local planning function.

Table 3. 3 summarizes the differences and similarities of the thre
examples. Together they illustrate a variety of methods or techniques
for handling each step of the four-step systems approach. In Wichita,
for example, as shown in Table 3. 3, the identification of objectives
was conducted only indirectly, the identification of proposed capital
improvement projects was direct and fairly rigorous, the prediction
of effectiveness was carried out subjectively, and emphasis was given
to the quantitative evaluation of alternatives. In contrast, again as
shown in Table 3. 3, the Philadelphia CRP stressed the identification o
a hierarchy of goals, objectives, and programs, with the identificatior
of alternative programs only preliminary and the remaining two steps
not completed. In Southeastern Wisconsin, steps 1 and 3 (identifying
objectives and predicting effectiveness) stressed quantitative methods
of analysis, while the identification of programs was generalized and
the evaluation of alternatives subjective.

Capital Improvement Programming

Wichita's systematic approach to the CIP was developed through
participation in the Metropolitan Data Center Project. [5] This approach
involved primarily the development of computer programs for the proc
essing of a series of numerical estimates of project need or importanc
for individual capital improvements. These relatively simple progran
assigned weights, calculated ratios, and performed other algebraic
operations that permitted the attachment of a single priority score to
each capital project. In general, the list of proposed projects within
each functional sector (water, parks, public buildings, sewers, thor-
oughfares, bridges, drainage, urban renewal) could then be compared
with an available sector budget, and those with the highest scores suc-
cessively recommended until the budget ran out. Individual budgets
were assigned to each functional sector, and priority rankings determined only within that sector. Comparison of projects between sector
was not permitted, since their priority scores were in general based
on different grounds.

TABLE 3.3

Systematic Analysis of Planning Processes

Basic Steps in the Systems Approach	Planning Agency Example		
	Wichita CIP	Philadelphia CRP	S.E. Wisc. Land-Use Transp. Plan
1. Identifying Objectives	Indirect. "Priority determinants," identified in terms of project, neighborhood, and community factors, are associated with each alternative project. Many of these imply local goals and objectives.	Hierarchical. A detailed four-level hierarchy of objectives, subobjectives, and supporting programs is defined for a single goal area—housing and the physical environment.	Quantitative. Specific objectives for land-use and transportation development are advanced and related to supporting planning principles and quantitative achievement standards.
2. Identifying Programs	Rigorous. Each suggested capital improvement is charted for rating against all relevant priority determinants. Other basic project data are also collected.	Preliminary. Individual program plan statements and analyses are proposed that would relate each proposed program to specific objectives and to quantified targets for goal achievement.	Generalized. Four broad alternative plans were designed (controlled existing trends, corridor plan, satellite cities plan, unplanned development) and described in terms of planning standards and other features.
3. Predicting Effectiveness	Subjective. All proposed projects receive a series of judgmental scores (on a 1-10 scale) that indicate their expected impact upon or importance to each relevant priority determinant.	Incomplete. The impact of alternative programs upon objectives would be measured and analyzed.	Quantitative. Transportation planning models and quantitative comparisons of forecasted land-use demands with availabilities were primarily used to estimate impact upon appropriate planning standards.
4. Evaluating Alternatives	Quantitative. Subjective weights are assigned to different priority determinants, and relative numerical scores are summed by computer. Priorities are assigned by highest total score.	Incomplete. Alternative program costs would be compared with relative levels of goal achievement.	Subjective. Comparisons of alternative plans according to their relative achievement of standards revealed little difference among them. A subjective rating technique was then utilized.

The identification and subsequent utilization of priority determinants, or those factors that in some way indicate a project's relative need or importance, are crucial to this analysis procedure. Three types of priority determinants were identified:

1. Project factors, referring to such characteristics as extent of the city to be served, population to be served, master plan status, esthetic value, citizen response, increase in tax base, crime prevention, estimated useful life, and many others—from 17 to 40 per project, depending on the functional sector
2. Neighborhood factors, which vary by the location of each project, with neighborhoods themselves rated according to some 25 characteristics, including extent and kind of desired future development, desired future intensity, minimum levels of development desired, and structural maintenance levels desired
3. Community factors, including extent and kind of desired community wide development, use of state and federal funds, basic financing and taxing policies, and some 17 other factors.

Selecting these priority determinants or factors essentially represents an indirect statement of neighborhood and community goals and objectives. The task at hand here basically involves the identification of objectives, the first step in a fundamental systems approach. However, by choosing to deal with a very diverse and mixed group of factors, it is possible that some of the elements included may not be particularly relevant as part of an explicit set of objectives, or it may be difficult consistently to interpret them as objectives. For example it may be difficult to redefine an objective that states how much population should be served by a proposed project or what its desirable useful life should be. In general, however, most of the factors identified do appear to imply objectives of one kind or another. Many could readily be associated with an accompanying specific objective; others actually represent objectives themselves. However, the use of factors rather than explicit objectives tends to result in a less rigorous and clear-cut systems approach—many implied objectives are often fuzzy or ambiguous.

The second basic step in systems analysis, identifying programs, is quite straightforward and direct in this example. A list of all possible capital improvements for the next 20 to 50 years is compiled in each of the functional sectors. Each is identified according to administrative and expected cost characteristics, and then entered on project rating sheets. Subsequent determination of project ratings in step 3 will then in effect amount to program or project identification specifically in terms of objectives.

Step 3, predicting effectiveness, is carried out at a simplified, entirely subjective level. Each priority determinant or factor is rated on a one-to-ten scale by those knowledgeable and experienced in capital-improvement programming. The impact of each project upon each determinant is, as a result, forecasted subjectively. While many factors are in fact quite difficult to measure objectively, it might be expected that others could eventually receive more rigorous or objective treatment. This prototype or illustrative example does serve to demonstrate forcefully that most of the factors that presently influence the preparation of urban capital-improvement programs are already receiving direct or indirect subjective consideration.

The evaluation of alternative projects (step 4) is accomplished with the help of the computer processing routines. A key facet of this evaluation phase involves the assignment of two sets of weights to priority determinants. It is first suggested that in summing the ratings received for individual determinants, the following weights be assigned: project factors, 60; neighborhood factors, 15; and community factors, 25. These reflect the assumed relative importance of each type of factor. Second, among the project factors, three are selected for special emphasis: citizen expression for or against the project (weight of 4.0), protection of life and property (2.0), and value as a community promotional device (2.0). These three factors (and their implied objectives) thus emerge as the most important of all those identified. It is stressed that the overall priority scores are intended only as a guide to the subsequent final evaluation of projects by government decision makers.

The Community Renewal Program

One of the earliest attempts at making urban planning more goal oriented and systematic began with the Philadelphia Community Renewal Program in 1962.[6] These early ideas were in fact patterned after some of the program budgeting concepts being used by the U.S. Department of Defense. The CRP was seen as only one among many local governmental programs that could benefit from a clearer definition of goals and objectives and from the identification of interrelationships among different agency programs as they contribute to common goals.

It was proposed that the CRP be developed within a larger framework, within the context of a comprehensive, citywide program and budget analysis—the annual Development Program. While some of these initial proposals and programming concepts were not carried to

full development in the final version of the CRP, they represent a basic
example of systems thinking. [7] In fact, the city's department of finance
is now responsible for exploring the coordinated development of a
multiagency, citywide Development Program, and many of the city's
municipal agencies have already begun preliminary program budgeting
studies of their own operations. [8] The Philadelphia CRP systems approach has had considerable local influence.

It was felt from the beginning that the sound evaluation or charting
of year-to-year progress of the CRP (as well as other governmental
programs) demanded a set of objectives for different levels of program
activity. Objectives at each level should bear a clear relationship to
one another, and should each be expressed so as to suggest one or more
performance measures of program accomplishment. Furthermore, the
CRP should work toward defining methods for measuring the impact of
alternative renewal programs upon CRP-related objectives and for relating these impacts to relative program costs. It must be possible to
test the feasibility as well as the relative desirability of both goals and
the programs that might achieve them. Attention should be devoted to
the development of program plans or statements that depict a mobiliza-
tion of resources toward definable objectives. These alternative uses
of resources would be posed in relation to one another under a basic
program comparison approach that would clarify the possible choices
for achieving goals. Ideally, such a budget analysis of programs would
permit cost comparisons of alternative means for achieving the same
objective.

As a first step in illustrating how such a program-budgeting approach might be applied to the Philadelphia CRP, a system of citywide
goals and supporting objectives was suggested. Goals in six major
functional categories were identified: people, property, housing and
the physical environment, transportation, economic growth, and general support. The housing and physical environment category was felt
to be most closely related to the urban renewal and renewal-related
programs of the CRP, and a detailed four-level hierarchy of supporting
objectives and programs was drafted.

The basic goal for the housing and physical environment category
is "to assure that every family and individual who desires to live in
Philadelphia has an opportunity to satisfy reasonable housing wants in
a good physical environment." Four first-level program categories,
each with an associated objective, were distinguished: new construction
and conversion, acquisition of dwelling accommodations, maintenance
and improvement, and controls and regulations. One of the objectives
here, for example, is "to assure that owners and occupants of existing
dwellings have an opportunity to satisfy reasonable housing wants in
terms of maintenance and improvements in their dwellings and immediate surroundings."

The second level of the hierarchy also identified program categories with associated objectives. The objective just mentioned had four such subobjectives in relation to maintenance level, property rehabilitation, area improvements, and area reconstruction. The last two levels of the hierarchy involve even more specific program designations and breakdowns, until actual programs themselves are being identified (such as area code inspections, dilapidated-building demolition, residential parking programs).

This integrated system of goals, objectives, subobjectives, and supporting programs represents a fundamental "means-ends chain" of continuous interrelationships, each level supporting (or being supported by) the next. Given such a hierarchical goal statement, which provides the basic framework for step 1 of the systems approach, it is proposed that an analysis of existing conditions be undertaken to give dimension to or quantify the actual needs that must be met so that objectives can be converted into work or program targets for the short-range time period (one to six years) of the Development Program.

The second and perhaps most crucial phase suggested for the CRP involves the inventory of existing programs. In order for the system of objectives and quantified needs to be meaningful, uniform reporting of all programs that may contribute to the achievement of objectives is required. A program plan such as that shown in Table 3.4 is proposed for each existing agency program. Especially important here is the identification of agency goals and objectives for each program and the comparison and reconciliation of these with their relevant counterparts within the hierarchical goal system.

The approximate level of impact of each program must be identified. The program-reporting categories "Program Objectives" and "Specific Targets for Accomplishment" must be sufficiently clear and quantifiable. The performance potential of each program for achieving objectives must be discernible. While such a program analysis was attempted only in an abbreviated form for a subarea prototype study, it does cover the essential elements involved under step 2 of the systems approach.[9] Such an analysis should also be applied to new or modified programs once the need for such programs can be ascertained by an overall comparison of existing programs with quantified objectives or program targets.

Steps 3 and 4 of the systems approach were not, at this early stage, considered in detail. It is implied that they will essentially build upon the Program Plan analyses described above. Prediction of effectiveness and evaluation of alternatives must be carried out more or less on a program-by-program basis. For many programs associated with the CRP, particularly those whose impact is measured in terms of the number of housing units constructed, demolished, converted, rehabilitated, or maintained, the prediction of impact is relatively straightfor-

TABLE 3.4

Suggested Program Plan Format:
Philadelphia Community Renewal Program

Program No.		Date:	Agency:
Public ( )		Permanent ( )	
Private ( )		Temporary ( )	
		Research ( )	
Existing Program ( )		Pilot ( )	
New Program ( )		Demonstration ( )	
Modified Program ( )			
Program Title:			
Program Objectives:	Indicate the primary and secondary goals to which this program applies. Identify more specific objectives and subobjectives. Identify specific agency objectives for this program.		
Program Description:	Itemize program components, subprograms, or major activities. Describe agency criteria for applying the program. Describe phasing of activities as necessary.		
Basis for Involvement:	State specific statutory or other authority for conducting the program.		
Preconditions for Effectiveness:	Describe the particular needs, problems, conditions, or services this program is designed to meet, remedy, or provide.		
Program Relationships:	Describe the administrative organization for this program, including its tie-in with other agencies, public and private.		
Specific Targets for Accomplishment:	For each objective stated earlier, define a target for accomplishment expressed (a) in numerical units, (b) over a period of years reasonable for this program, and (c) in cumulative as well as annual terms.		
Program Evaluation Methods:	Identify methods for charting, reporting, controlling, or appraising progress toward each target expressed above.		
Resources Required:	Show in tabular form the dollars spent on this program by source, capital or operating fund, annual and five-year past experience, annual and five-year projection, and expenditure category.		
Alternative Programs Considered:	Describe possible alternatives for meeting the same general objectives and why these alternatives were rejected.		
Problems or Difficulties:	Describe problems foreseen and possible remedies for the successful operation of the program.		

ward (how many units <u>would</u> be affected?), and the real problem for
analysis lies in determining the unit costs of alternative public actions.
Many of the subsequent difficulties in evaluating alternatives do not
appear to have been fully anticipated. However, the critical need to
uncover workable measures of program accomplishment or impact,
the need to relate these measures to quantified program targets or objectives, and the need to relate these targets and objectives to one
another in some organized way are all emphasized.

Land-Use/Transportation Planning

The transportation/land-use plan for the Southeastern Wisconsin
region has been developed through a basic seven-step planning process. [10] As shown in Figure 3.2, this process represents an expansion
and adaptation of the fundamental four-step systems approach, adding
three steps—initial study design, inventory of existing conditions, and
final selection and adoption of a recommended plan—and treating each
of the other four steps somewhat differently. For example, the identification of objectives appears as the closely knit formulation of interrelated objectives, principles, and standards. The design of
alternative plans is in this instance preceded by an analysis and
forecast of basic population and economic growth factors affecting all
alternatives equally.

Parts of the prediction of effectiveness (systems step 3) are involved in this preceding step, in that alternative plans are consciously
preadjusted to estimated growth levels, while other aspects of effectiveness prediction are actually combined with the evaluation of alternatives in step 3, the plan test and evaluation phase. The final
selection (but not necessarily the adoption) of a preferred plan, mentioned above, might have been incorporated directly as a part of this
evaluation phase. While such a seven-step process is generally typical
of other transportation/land-use plans, it may or may not be appropriate in other planning contexts. [11] Reinterpretation of this process in
terms of the four steps of the systems approach is shown in Table 3.3.

Overall, this example represents one of the most detailed and
fully developed applications of systems analysis yet attempted in urban
planning. Three kinds of regional development objectives were identified and adopted by SEWRPC: general objectives, land-use development
objectives, and transportation-system development objectives. The
extreme difficulty of formulating goals and objectives for a broad region encompassing multiple and often conflicting interests is acknowledged, and the participation of elected officials and citizen leaders in
the goal-formulation task is stressed.

FIGURE 3.2

The Land-Use/Transportation Planning Process; Southeastern Wisconsin Regional Planning Commission

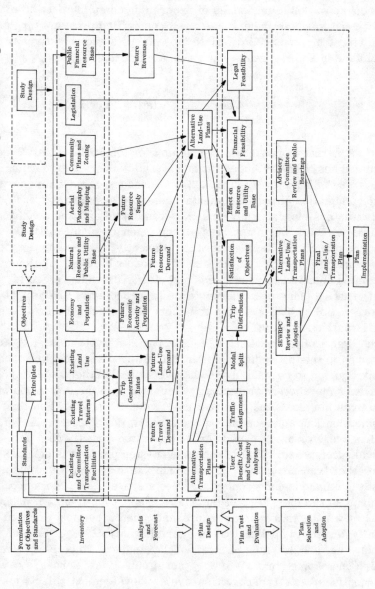

General objectives were essentially qualitative or difficult to relate
directly to alternative development plans. Nine such objectives were
identified (e.g., "A wide range of employment opportunities through
a broad, diversified economic base"; "Protection, wise use, and sound
development of the natural resource base"). More specific and related
objectives for land-use (eight objectives) and for transportation (seven
objectives) could be related measurably to physical development plans.
Quantifiable standards were consequently advanced for assessing how
well each proposed plan may meet each objective, and underlying planning principles for each objective were given. In all, some 20 planning
and over 70 development standards were identified. Examples are
given in Table 3.5.

The synthesis or design of alternative development plans (systems
step 2) is based upon the inputs provided by the three preceding planning operations—formulation of objectives and standards, inventory
and data collection, and analysis and forecasts. Alternatives are necessarily generalized from among innumerable possible variations to focus
on four broad structural extremes: controlled existing trends, corridor
plan, satellite cities plan, and unplanned development. Generation of
some of the more detailed features and interrelationships of these alternatives is exceedingly complex, and was essentially carried out on
an intuitive, "cut-and-try," mapping-oriented basis.

Many planning standards were actually used as criteria in the design of plans themselves, so that plan design, testing, and evaluation
(systems steps 2, 3, and 4) essentially formed a continuous, overlapping process. The use of some standards as common design criteria
(such as those involving land-use proportions and densities) permitted
the subsequent prediction of their impact upon other standards (primarily those involving natural resources and transportation). Each
alternative plan was in fact eventually identified and described in terms
of all regional development objectives and standards.

Prediction of the effectiveness or impact (systems step 3) of each
broad alternative plan, in terms of those selected objectives and standards not used as design criteria, was accomplished through the use of
several techniques. First, the traditional series of transportation-
planning computer models for forecasting trip generation, modal split,
and trip distribution, and for traffic assignment to existing and proposed transportation networks, were utilized. These models were
actually used both in the design of feasible and efficient transportation
systems and in predicting resulting transportation requirements in
terms of regional objectives. Second, conventional techniques for
comparing forecasted land-use demands with subarea land-use availa-
bilities and design allocations were used, showing their expected relationship to appropriate development objectives and standards. Third,

TABLE 3.5

Land-Use-Planning Objectives, Principles, and Standards:
Southeastern Wisconsin Regional Planning Commission

Objective no. 5

The development and conservation of residential areas within a physical environment that is healthy, safe, convenient, and attractive.

Principle

Residential areas developed in designed planning units can assist in stabilizing community property values, preserving residential amenities, and promoting efficiency in the provision of public and community service facilities, can best provide a desirable environment for family life, and can provide the population with improved levels of safety and convenience.

Standards

1. Residential planning units should be physically self-contained within clearly defined and relatively permanent isolating boundaries, such as arterial streets and highways, major park and open-space reservations, or significant natural features, such as rivers, streams, or hills.
2. Residential planning units should contain enough area to provide housing for the population served by one elementary school and one neighborhood park; an internal street system that discourages penetration of the unit by through traffic; and all of the community and commercial facilities necessary to meet the day-to-day living requirements of the family within the immediate vicinity of its dwelling unit. To meet these requirements at varied residential densities, the following specific standards should be met:

Land Use	Low-Density Development (2 miles square) Percent of Area	Medium-Density Development (1 mile square) Percent of Area	High-Density Development (1/2 mile square) Percent of Area
Residential	80.0	71.0	66.0
Streets and utilities	16.5	23.0	25.0
Parks and playgrounds	1.5	2.5	3.5
Public elementary school	0.5	1.5	2.5
Other governmental and institutional	1.0	1.0	1.5
Commercial	0.5	1.0	1.5
Total	100.0	100.0	100.0

3. Each residential planning unit should be designed to include a wide range of housing types, designs, and costs.

Objective no. 7

The preservation and provision of open space to enhance the total quality of the regional environment, maximize essential natural resource availability, give form and structure to urban development, and facilitate the ultimate attainment of a balanced year-round outdoor recreational program providing a full range of facilities for all age groups.

Principle

Open space is the fundamental element required for the preservation, wise use, and development of such natural resources as soil, water, woodlands, wetlands, and wildlife; it provides the opportunity to add to the physical, intellectual, and spiritual growth of the population; it enhances the economic and esthetic value of certain types of development and is essential to outdoor recreational pursuits.

Standards

1. Local park and recreation open spaces should be provided within a maximum service radius of one-half mile of every dwelling unit in an urban area, and each site should be of sufficient size to accommodate the maximum tributary service area population at a use intensity of 675 persons per acre.

2. Regional park and recreation open spaces should be provided within an approximately one-hour travel time of every dwelling unit in the Region and should have a minimum site area of 250 acres.

3. Areas having unique scientific, cultural, scenic, or educational value should not be allocated to any urban or agricultural land uses, and adjacent surrounding areas should be retained in open-space use, such as agriculture or limited recreation.

the feasibility or realism of alternative land-use plans was experimentally tested through the use of preliminary land-use simulation and plan design models. [12] Each of these techniques and mathematical models was primarily intended to predict or estimate the impact that each plan will have on relevant regional objectives and standards by the design year 1990.

Evaluation of alternative development plans (systems step 4) was accomplished through the comparison of their relative impact upon all quantified regional objectives and standards. Some standards, as noted above, were used as criteria for the actual design of alternatives, so that these standards were uniformly met by each plan alternative (not including unplanned development). Examples include the amount of land (per thousand persons of population increase) allocated to low-density residential development or the location of all new industrial development within properly planned industrial districts. Other standards were only partially met or otherwise varied slightly in their level of achievement. Examples include the percentage of medium/ and high-density residential development to be served by public sewer and water utilities and the total vehicle miles of travel per day.

Importantly, however, the great majority of both land-use and transportation standards are either adequately met or subject to being met by local community or private action. In terms of the predicted achievement of stated objectives, there is consequently very little difference among the three alternative development plans. A technique known as the "rank-based expected value method" for subjectively choosing among alternatives was consequently devised. This technique is based on a complicated series of numerical (1, 2, or 3) rankings of standards, objectives, and plans themselves, combined with subjective estimates of the probability of implementing each plan. [13]

It was separately concluded, however, that because there was little variation among alternatives, that alternative that represents the least radical departure from recent historic development trends and commitments should be recommended. The Controlled Existing Trends Plan was selected in both instances.

Comprehensive City Planning

The comprehensive plan or general plan typically conducted by city or county planning departments represents a fourth broad arena for applying the systems approach in urban planning. The comprehensive planning process has many parallels with the Model Cities Program and the Community Renewal Program and, in fact, most of the approaches to systems analysis that might be attempted under these

programs would have equal validity here. The comprehensive plan
provides a broader context for these two more specialized planning
activities. It also generally provides a context for citywide or metropolitan capital-improvements programming. The comprehensive plan
of most smaller cities and metropolitan areas often includes a
transportation/land-use plan. Consequently, many of the systems
approaches that might be associated with these two remaining planning
processes could also be transferred to comprehensive planning.

Perhaps because the comprehensive planning process is generally
broader in scope and purpose, and particularly because it is intention-
ally less specific in identifying alternative plans and programs, relatively little has been accomplished in making the process more
systematic. There does, however, appear to be a growing interest in
at least the first step of the systems approach, the identification of
objectives. Many local planning agencies are now exploring the role
of "policies planning" as a part of the comprehensive planning process. [14] Policies planning is in general a particular way of treating the
identification of goals and objectives so that a series of normative
statements or policies for evaluating specific plans and proposals may
be generated.

Policies thereby lie somewhere between broad objectives and more
specific programs and serve as a means for relating or interpreting
one in terms of the other. They are something akin to the planning
principles used in the SEWRPC study. Importantly, policies afford a
large measure of flexibility in terms of commitment to specific types
of plans or programs. Instead of actually identifying and evaluating
multiple alternative programs as a part of the comprehensive plan,
policies planning offers a short-cut method for developing generalized
evaluation criteria, without necessarily undertaking the evaluation itself. The development of quantitative criteria or standards may or
may not be attempted. It is often assumed under policies planning that
specific projects and programs will be evaluated as they arise.

An essential feature of policies planning also lies in its broad
guidelines for the direction and character of future growth and development. These guidelines describe in general terms the changes in
existing conditions that are desired and in effect provide a framework
or basis for generating development proposals as well as for evaluating
them. For example, the Comprehensive Plan of Chicago is divided into
two basic parts—the Policies Plan and the generalized Improvement
Plan. [15] The second is more or less based upon the first and sketches
broad program or action areas, with generalized targets for each given
in relation to each of seven policy areas (residential areas, recreation
and park land, education, public safety and health, business, industry,
and transportation). The general pattern of the Chicago Policies Plan
has been to specifically identify a total of some 76 objectives for the

seven policy areas, each supported by a narrative discussion of related policies, needs, issues, or planning proposals. Measures or quantitative indexes for gauging the achievement of most of these objectives are not, however, suggested.

While policies planning has much to offer in the way of strengthening and sharpening the process of comprehensive urban planning, even further gains appear to be possible. These could be achieved through extending and expanding policies planning to encompass at least the first two steps of the systems approach—identifying objectives and identifying programs. The full identification of objectives would involve a more rigorous treatment than current policies plans seem inclined to give. Wherever possible, quantitative measures of goal achievement should be attached to each objective or policy, some attempt should be made to compare existing conditions with desired conditions, and appropriate goal-achievement targets or standards should be advanced. Policies plans themselves can be made more explicit. In addition, it may be desirable to identify broad program or action areas more explicitly in terms of their potential impacts upon specific objectives. Finally, for selected comprehensive-plan components, it may also be desirable to identify alternative programs, develop methods for predicting effectiveness, and explore techniques for evaluating these alternatives.

ANALYZING URBAN SYSTEMS

The systematic study of individual components of the comprehensive plan represents a second major opportunity or level for applying the systems approach in urban planning. Typically, the objectives for the plan components or systems, such as residential land use, business, industry, transportation, recreation, education, public safety, or public health, may have already been explored as part of the comprehensive planning process (or as part of any of the four basic planning processes outlined in the preceding section). While more rigorous or systematic approaches to urban planning processes, and particularly to the policies planning phase of comprehensive planning, should continue to be explored, the sheer complexity of urban functions and interrelationships generally limits progress at these broad levels. The systems approach at these overall process levels seems primarily concerned with the careful indentification and delineation of objectives and with the initial identification of selected (often generalized) program alternatives.

Further progress in developing our capabilities for urban-oriented systems analysis, especially in terms of the second, third, and fourth steps of the basic systems approach, may perhaps best be accomplished through the study of individual systems, problems, and governmental operations. A shift in the scale of analysis or investigation seems necessary, so that alternative programs can be expressed with more detail and realism, so that the difficult problems of predicting effectiveness (primarily those involving data collection, model building, and the analysis of program-objective interrelationships) may be more manageably handled, and so that the evaluation of alternatives may be conducted in more concrete and specific terms. Experience has shown, however, that the third and fourth steps of the systems approach are exceedingly difficult to complete successfully, even where the scope of analysis has been restricted to individual urban systems, problems, or governmental operations.

In this section three examples of the analysis of urban systems will be briefly reviewed—the San Francisco housing market simulation model, the Los Angeles approach to parks and recreation planning, and New York studies of health facilities and services. Again, it should be stressed that these are examples only of approaches taken by specific cities to the analysis of particular systems, approaches that may or may not be appropriate or applicable in other cities.

Table 3.6 presents a summary evaluation of each example, spelled out in terms of the four steps of the systems approach. It is comparable to Table 3.3, presented earlier. It should also be noted that these are only three of the many urban systems that might merit more systematic study. While the eight possible systems mentioned above represent basic functional categories, many different subsystems could be identified or outlined within each category. For example, housing and residential areas could be broken down into subsystems distinguished by life cycle (inner-city slums versus fringe subdivisions), by location (individual communities or subareas), by type (public housing versus high-rise luxury apartments), or in other ways. With these many possibilities for study, the analysis of urban systems is just beginning.

Housing Market Simulation Model

The San Francisco Simulation Model, originally developed in support of the Community Renewal Program, essentially represents an attempt to develop a computer model of the economic interrelationships of housing supply and demand. [16] Because so much time and effort were devoted to the development of the model itself, to serve as a third-step systems device for predicting the effectiveness of alternative governmental programs, steps 1, 2, and 4 in the systems approach appear to have been somewhat slighted (see Figure 3.3 and Table 3.6).

TABLE 3.6

Systematic Analysis of Urban Systems

Basic Steps in the Systems Approach	Project		
	S. F. Housing Market Simulation Model	L.A. Neighborhood Recreation Priorities	N.Y.C. Health Facilities and Services
1. Identifying Objectives	Implicit. The single goal of a well-balanced housing supply is advanced, and more specific objectives are implied by the types of data to be utilized.	Indirect. Four socioeconomic characteristics (youth population, population density, family income, juvenile delinquency) are identified as indicators of recreation needs. Objectives are indirectly related to them.	Generalized. Major problems are reviewed, four broad goals are advanced, and nine major guidelines or objectives for policy making are suggested.
2. Identifying Programs	Indirect. Alternative programs and policies are identified in terms of basic housing data on type, condition, quantity, and cost but are not related to objectives.	Generalized. Three basic types of programs (professional staff, park acreage, recreation centers) are identified as recreation resources but are related only indirectly to objectives.	Indirect. Seven major program approaches are recommended, but more specific alternatives are not advanced, and there is no direct alignment against objectives.
3. Predicting Effectiveness	Quantitative. Major emphasis was placed on the development of an elaborate computer simulation model of housing market supply and demand within the central city.	Implicit. It is assumed that need characteristics will persist into the future, and that recreation resources can help meet them. No specific prediction techniques are used.	Preliminary. A major study of the health-care system in terms of interrelated elements (needs, facilities, practices, organizations) is proposed.
4. Evaluating Alternatives	Incomplete. Forecasted housing changes will be matched against subsequently determined objectives.	Quantitative. Standardized relative scores for each of the seven variables are computed for each community. Individual cumulative need indexes are subtracted from resource indexes to derive relative priority indices.	Incomplete. Subsequent research findings would be used to evaluate objectives as well as programs.

FIGURE 3.3

Role of the Housing Market Simulation Model: San Francisco Department of City Planning

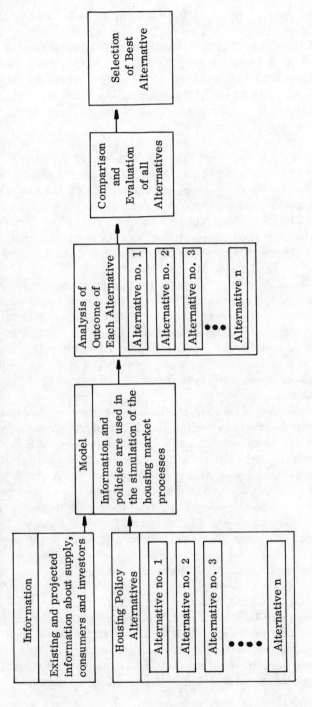

For instance, beyond the broad goal of an adequate and suitable supply of housing, objectives for San Francisco's housing system are not explicitly identified and explored. It is assumed that enough information about the housing supply, in terms of type, condition, quantity, and cost, is included in the model so that any reasonable or logical objective can be tested for achievement. The actual formulation of objectives is more or less left as part of the fourth systems step, evaluation of alternatives.

Alternative programs and policies affecting the housing system are consequently not identified directly in terms of objectives, but rather in terms of those basic characteristics of housing supply that objectives will eventually address—type, condition, quantity, and cost. Nine basic types of housing are distinguished, and each type is further described in terms of four building condition categories. Eight subareas of the city (or locational categories) are also distinguished, and these vary both by the predominant types of housing found there and by the cost or rental range of the housing.

The housing stock of the city is thereby represented by up to 288 separate types, the products of these three partitions. Alternative governmental actions may be aimed at these different housing characteristics, particularly those involving location or subarea. The following kinds of governmental action are provided for within the model: zoning change, code enforcement, removal of units for a public purpose, redevelopment of areas for new housing, and the provision of public housing.

Innumerable combinations and permutations of specific policies and proposed actions in each of these five areas could be tested through the operation of the model, each new combination calling for a new run of the model. This kind of flexibility in handling multiple alternatives is one of the model's most important attributes. A single run of the model is quite complex, and may be briefly summarized as follows. The time period for a complete run is presently 18 years, divided into nine two-year segments. During each of the two-year periods, four basic kinds of operations or calculations must be performed:

1. Project housing demand: Forecast the number of households expected within each of 84 different household categories, varying by size, family cycle, income, and race.
2. Match demand against supply: Using estimates of rent-paying ability and housing preferences, determine which household demands will be unsatisfied, and which housing types underutilized.
3. Execute governmental actions: Alter the housing supply according to a predetermined series of proposed public actions.

4. Modify housing supply: Predict the response of the private housing
   market in adjusting rental levels so that underutilized housing may
   meet unsatisfied household demands.

   The evaluation phase of this systems approach example was left
relatively unstructured and depends primarily upon those goals and
objectives for housing that local decision makers and planners may
wish to advance. In general, the results of a nine-period run (or the
results after any period among the nine) will be expressed in terms of
an updated housing supply, adjusted primarily by the private market to
meet changing demand conditions. Alternative sets of governmental
policies and actions will affect the status of this housing supply, and
their relative effectiveness in terms of meeting objectives (quantitative
or qualitative) can presumably be compared and evaluated.
   Quantitative objectives must necessarily be expressed in terms of
the types of housing expected to be available, the physical conditions
of that housing, associated rental levels, and the quantities expected
to be available under each type, condition, and rental. Perhaps other
objectives, in terms of locational factors or minority-group household
demands, could also be set. Consideration should also be given to the
effects of alternative population (housing demand) forecasts upon relative program impacts, recognizing the element of uncertainty present
in such forecasts.

Neighborhood Recreation Priorities

   Recent studies in Los Angeles have worked toward developing
techniques for estimating priorities among the city's neighborhoods
for the provision of additional recreation facilities and services.[17]
Only neighborhood-type facilities operated by the City Department of
Recreation and Parks (playgrounds, tot lots, recreation centers, field
houses) were considered. Other important elements or subsystems
within an overall urban recreation system were left out, including
larger regional parks (under city, county, or state jurisdiction),
school-operated recreation facilities, or voluntary agency facilities.
It is noted that eventual consideration must be given to the role played
by these other resources when proposals for change in the city's facilities and services are made.
   The technique actually developed for evaluating neighborhood recreation needs and priorities, thereby giving an indication of the relative
importance of any specific proposal for improvement, is comparatively
simple and straightforward. It is based upon a modified systems approach. Table 3.6 indicates that emphasis has been given to the fourth

step of the approach, and that the other three steps have been treated
less thoroughly.

The indentification of objectives for this recreation subsystem is
indirect, with primary attention devoted to the identification of socio-
economic and demographic characteristics that reflect recreation
needs. After a review of more than 25 such characteristics, four
were settled upon as basic factors related to "social needs" as well
as recreation needs. These four factors in turn suggest somewhat indirectly the objectives toward which the city's recreation programs
should aim. The four factors are

1. Youth population (5-19 years). Recreation agencies typically place
   heavier emphasis upon youth-oriented programs and services. A
   higher youth population indicates a need for increased recreation
   and leisure-time services.
2. Population density. Greater population density normally indicates
   a need for increased recreation services to help counter the lack
   of residential play space.
3. Median family income. Lower-income families are generally more
   dependent upon community-supported recreation facilities and services, having less ability to provide their own leisure-time activities.
4. Juvenile delinquency rate. This index is assumed to provide a
   measure of the need for expanded recreation services, in order to
   help reduce social tensions and disorganization through the provision
   of socially approved recreation outlets and activities.

These four characteristics or variables were then quantitatively
aggregated to develop a single need index for each neighborhood. Similarly, after analyzing various alternatives, an index of recreation resources was developed, utilizing three basic measures of neighborhood
recreation services. The use of these three variables essentially
amounts to the identification of alternative programs, though at a
somewhat generalized level. Because objectives are not explicitly outlined, there is no opportunity to relate programs to objectives quantitatively. However, an indirect relationship does exist, primarily
involving the population-related need variables above. The three
measures of recreation resources or programs are

1. Number of full-time and part-time professional recreation staff
   hours per 1,000 population per year in a neighborhood
2. Acreage of neighborhood recreation facilities and centers per 1,000
   population
3. Number of recreation facilities and centers per 1,000 population.

Other possible variables are suggested ("developed indoor space, developed outdoor space"), and it is also observed that the resources of other institutions and agencies could conceivably be included in these computations.

The third stage of the systems approach, predicting effectiveness, is only implicitly considered. Because programs are generalized and only indirectly related to objectives (which are themselves only indirectly represented), no specific predictions of effectiveness are attempted. It is simply assumed that neighborhood needs-objectives will continue into the future, and that these three recreation programs-resources indexes will be successful, in part at least, in reducing needs.

The most important phase of this example centers on the evaluation of alternatives—in this case, the determination of relative recreation priorities among 61 Los Angeles communities. Note that here "alternative programs" are really being treated in terms of where they might be applied. The undertaking of overall recreation improvements in any specific community is the actual alternative being evaluated and program to which priority scores are assigned. The calculation of individual priority scores for each community is not complicated, as shown in Figure 3.4. The raw score or value for each of seven variables is standardized along a zero-to-100 scale, so that need indexes and resource indexes may be summed. The resulting priority index is simply the subtraction of individual cumulative need indexes from resource indexes for each community.

FIGURE 3.4

Neighborhood Recreation Priorities Formula:
Los Angeles Recreation and Youth Services Planning Council

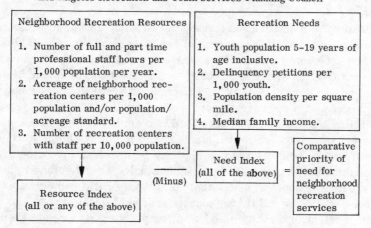

Health Facilities and Services

An early study of New York City's health care system provides
another interesting example of applying the systems approach in the
analysis of a specific urban system. [18] This example is only preliminary in nature, however, and a more thorough and in-depth investigation of health facilities and services is expected from current studies
by the Rand Corporation's New York City Project. [19] In Table 3.6 it is
indicated that in this example none of the four steps of the systems
approach is investigated in any depth.

This initial study is divided into two primary parts: (a) a brief
analysis of problems with the present health-care system, leading to
the identification of preliminary improvement objectives or guidelines
and to the recommendation of generalized program approaches for
future action and decision making, and (b) a brief proposal for the
further structural analysis of health facilities and services as an actual
operating system, composed of functional elements or interrelated
components. Continuing studies would provide the basis for predicting
effectiveness and evaluating alternative improvement programs. The
identification of additional objectives and more specific programs would
also be included.

Though essentially still only a proposal for more detailed study,
the report provides another example of the many possible variations or
adaptations that may be made when applying the systems approach to
the analysis of a specific planning process, system, problem, or governmental operation. As shown in Table 3.6, the initial identification
of objectives is generalized, and the identification of programs is indirect in terms of those objectives. Though these will eventually require more rigorous delineation, they provide an appropriate starting
point.

After the identification and review of some 23 major problems and
deficiencies in existing patterns of health services (e.g., "There are
serious deficiencies in facilities and services for the care of long-
term patients"; "There is probably a sufficient total number of general
care beds in New York City, but these beds are poorly distributed"),
four broad goals regarding coordination, availability, quality, and
flexibility are advanced. These lead to a series of nine major guidelines or objectives for future planning and policy decisions. These
objectives are generalized (e.g., "City policy should be aimed at
strengthening the partnership between municipal and voluntary hospitals
and medical schools in order to achieve systematic and coordinated resources and to spread throughout the entire hospital system the best
medical talent in the city") and no attempt is made to relate them to
quantitative standards of achievement.

On the basis of these problems, goals, and objectives, a group of seven major recommendations or program approaches for future action, supported by 16 more specific program and policy recommendations, are suggested. These are also somewhat generalized, and in some cases alternative courses of action in implementing a broad recommendation are discussed. Because these are only preliminary in nature, and because there is no real specificity in identifying clear-cut alternative policies, programs, and projects, no direct or rigorous matching of recommended action with objectives is attempted. Examples of some of these policy-program proposals include the following:

• Facilities that must be replaced by the City and additional facilities that are required should, whenever feasible, be constructed adjacent to voluntary general teaching hospitals or medical schools.
• Any long-term care facility that the City constructs should be an integral part of a general hospital complex.
• The City should give high priority to the replacement, if required, of its hospitals that are below this desired size (350-bed capacity).

Given this initial statement on objectives and program approaches, the next phase of the study involves an analysis of the inner workings of the health-care system. A procedure for undertaking such an analysis is sketched, with the understanding that its results and findings are primarily intended for use in evaluating objectives as well as alternative programs—and in generating new objectives and programs. The health care system is defined in terms of four kinds of elements: (a) urban residents and their health characteristics and needs, (b) physical facilities and the health services provided therein, (c) operating practices, laws, regulations, procedures, and economic constraints affecting the delivery of services, and (d) the organizations and institutions, and their interrelationships, that administer health services.

Effective study of such a system will require the identification of interrelationships between elements, basically in terms of inputs (health needs), processes (delivery of services), and outputs (community objectives). In addition, the health-care system is cross-classified in terms of six planning or programming categories: overall system management, community medical-service centers, hospital coordination, chronic-care facilities, unified information system, and leadership coordination. A research effort of considerable magnitude is implied in bringing all of these system considerations under study.

ANALYZING URBAN PROBLEMS

The systematic analysis of urban problems is even less advanced than that of urban systems. Little has been accomplished in the way of specific examples of systems studies in this third broad level of potential application. In general, the task of analyzing a particular urban social or economic problem may sometimes represent a major component within the larger analysis of an urban system. There are no clear distinctions between "system" and "problem," however, and the orientation chosen may often reflect the origins, sponsorship, or purposes of a specific study. Systems tend to imply or involve the spatial distribution of physical facilities, while problems tend to imply the social and economic characteristics of different neighborhoods, activities, or institutions. While the study of social and economic problems has usually not received as much attention from urban planners as the study of physical patterns of urban development, there is growing evidence that such problems will in the future demand more careful consideration.

The Model Cities Program is itself a major indication of the increasing importance of socioeconomic as well as physical factors in the comprehensive planning of major urban subareas—in this case, the poverty neighborhoods of our central cities. The Model Cities Program is concerned with a wide range of social and economic problems: substandard housing, restricted housing opportunities, substandard family income levels, unemployment and underemployment, dependence upon welfare payments, inadequate educational facilities and programs, disease and ill health, crime and delinquency, restricted recreational and cultural opportunities, poor accessibility to job opportunities, blighted neighborhood environments, and inadequate citizen participation in neighborhood improvement programs. In the process of systematically developing and evaluating governmental programs aimed at alleviating such problems, individual Model Cities agencies are also committed to the development of more rigorous analytic frameworks and techniques. They will thereby provide a major proving ground for the systematic analysis of urban problems. *

---

*Urban social and economic problems are not, of course, restricted to central city poverty neighborhoods. Similar, but less severe problems occur in other urban and suburban neighborhoods. In addition, other types of urban socioeconomic problems might involve air and water pollution, refuse disposal, and open space preservation.

As an example, a preliminary paper describing subemployment conditions in the Dayton Model City Area represents an initial step in the local analysis of this problem area. [20] The first step in this pre-liminary discussion involved simply the definition of the problem and its magnitude. Subemployment includes both unemployed persons and those who may be working part time or intermittently. Statistical com-parisons are made with the rest of the metropolitan area. Second, an initial examination of the probable causes of subemployment was under-taken. "Personal factors," such as lack of necessary education, train-ing, experience, age, or poor health, and "job market factors," including shortage of unskilled jobs, low-paying jobs, or inaccessibility to available jobs, were both identified. Third, community objectives and related evaluation criteria were suggested for this problem area. This first attempt at identifying objectives is sketched in Table 3.7.

The remainder of the Dayton paper briefly describes the public and private employment-related programs that currently may have some effect upon achieving objectives and resolving subemployment problems, suggests a series of additional alternative programs, and proposes a procedure for the analysis and evaluation of these alterna-tives. Among the alternatives identified are the existing Youth Oppor-tunity Program and Model City Manpower Program, coordination of existing scattered agency services (public and private), educational and/or on-the-job training programs, educational programs to reduce racial discrimination barriers, encouragement of new industrial loca-tion in the model neighborhood, and provision of direct financial support to existing employment service agencies.

Anticipated tasks and problems for further analysis include the collection of data regarding the activities and services of these indepen-dent agencies, the collection of data that profile the current status and characteristics of the model neighborhood labor force, a description of employment opportunities on the current job market (identified by specific skill categories), analysis of relative cost-effectiveness trade-offs among alternative programs, evaluation of those alternatives in terms of achieving objectives, and the design of an ongoing data collec-tion system for future analyses and reviews of program alternatives. Though a great deal of further work along these overall lines will be necessary, the beginnings of a basic systems approach analysis of the general problem of subemployment are here.

A second broad indication of the growing importance of social and economic considerations in urban planning lies in the recent emergence of "social planning" as a valid component of comprehensive planning. [21] Because much of such social planning is problem oriented, the need for systematic and continuing analyses of basic urban social and economic problems is substantial. While the Model Cities Program is currently

TABLE 3.7

Community Objectives and Evaluation Criteria:
Dayton Subemployment Issue Paper

Problem:	Excessive subemployment in the Dayton Model City Area.
Goal:	To reduce subemployment in the Dayton Model City Area.
Objective A:	To provide employment opportunities to those seeking employment. Evaluation criteria: 1. Number of unemployed people (unemployment rate in the traditional sense) 2. Ratio of unemployed to the labor force 3. Number of employed who previously were unemployed
Objective B:	To provide an employment environment in which those individuals who are no longer seeking work (nonpartici-pants) are motivated to seek and find jobs. Evaluation criteria: Same as above except that the term "unemployed" is expanded to include the "nonparticipants" as well.
Objective C:	To provide jobs of a "self-satisfying" nature. Evaluation criteria: 1. Results of sample attitude survey of job satisfaction 2. Results of sample survey of job-advancement history
Objective D:	To provide employment opportunities that permit financial self-sufficiency and a reasonable standard of living. Evaluation criteria: 1. Number of families/individuals with incomes below the "poverty" level income 2. Changes in family/individual incomes 3. Number of families/individuals brought above the "poverty" level income 4. Number of families/individuals no longer needing welfare assistance 5. Changes in total welfare payments per family/individual
Objective E:	To reduce the incidence and intensity of crime, delinquency, and civil disturbance. Evaluation criterion: Number and/or rates of "incidents" by geographic area.

the focus of comprehensive social and physical planning for high-problem urban subareas, it should be placed within this larger perspective. Both within and outside of the Model Cities Program, the need for a clearer understanding of urban problems and their potential solutions should be expected to grow.

More than one local planning or administrative agency might take the lead in analyzing different types of urban problems, if only because of the fragmented administration of the many public programs aimed at promoting economic and social welfare—human resources departments, health departments, youth and senior-citizen commissions, welfare agencies, manpower training, environmental health, and educational agencies. The coordination of these investigations, as well as the conduct of some of them, especially those closely allied with the physical environment, offers a major new role for the local comprehensive planning agency.

IMPROVING GOVERNMENTAL OPERATIONS

A final broad area for applying the systems approach in urban planning centers upon the needs and possibilities for improving the operations of specific governmental agencies. * While in some respects this appears to be the most finely grained or detailed level of systems analysis, opportunities for meaningful study are still abundant. Many of these opportunities lie within the province of administrative agencies themselves, as they attempt to reorganize their budgeting procedures and organizational structure along more systematic, objectives-oriented lines. Much of the PPBS literature, including those reports and articles dealing specifically with municipal program budgeting, indicates that this more rigorous approach to governmental programming and decision making must of necessity be undertaken by administrators themselves, if it is to be at all effective. [22]

While different municipal and other local governmental agencies must take the lead in this broad area of systems analysis, local planning departments can also be of considerable assistance. It might be expected, for example, that planning agency studies of various

---

*While not mentioned in this report, the systems analysis of urban planning itself is also a valid application of the systems approach. Here the concern lies with evaluating whether urban planning activities have been effective, with whether planners and planning agencies have been able usefully to influence the course of urban growth and change.

planning processes could be of major value to particular operating agencies, especially in terms of substance (objectives and programs), and possibly in terms of methodology (prediction and evaluation). The same would apply in the study of individual urban systems. As part of planning's basic advisory role, the guidance and direction for more detailed agency operational analyses should be broadly provided by these larger studies.

In addition, the above discussion suggests that urban-problems analysis might be undertaken by individual operating agencies, by planning departments, or by both in cooperation. The coordination of multiple-agency studies of this type may also be assigned to the planning staff. It is at this same cooperative, coordinative level that planning agencies may directly assist in systems analyses aimed at improving particular governmental operations. Local planners are probably most able to provide assistance in investigating those agency services and operations that have an important spatial, physical, or social problem dimension.

An example of a cooperative systems study of the spatial distribution of a certain class of public facilities is found in an East Lansing, Michigan, analysis of alternative fire station locations.[23] This study is one of several that have attempted to extend the use of already developed transportation planning models (mainly as a part of the prediction phase) to the study of other governmental services.[24]

Four local public agencies participated as part of the East Lansing Project Team: the city manager's office, city planning department, fire department, and building department. The services of an outside consultant (in this case, the Institute of Applied Technology of the National Bureau of Standards) were also utilized.

A single major objective was identified in the East Lansing study— to provide the best possible level of fire protection service. The dimensions of the definition of "best possible service" imply a series of more specific subobjectives. Because the computer model used to predict effectiveness calls for the identification of links and nodes, with each node representing a single city block (and with each link representing the streets that connect those blocks), the rest of the analysis was forced to adopt this link-node orientation.

The fire-proneness or degree of fire hazard associated with each block or node then became one of the critical measures of the level of fire protection service. Six variables relating to the structural characteristics of buildings within each block were distinguished, and a weighted combination of these variables was used to derive relative measures of fire protection need for each block. These variables are population, building height, construction type, age, area in square feet, and occupancy type. Since each variable has a range of "demand" for fire protection services, the implied subobjectives are that the greatest needs along each dimension are to be adequately met. The weighting formula for combining these six variables into a single fire-hazard rating (first for individual structures, which are then summed for each block) was derived on a trial-and-error basis, and was found to correlate with the frequency of past fires across the city.

The identification of alternatives was in this example quite straight-forward. Twelve alternative feasible fire station locations were selected for testing. These could each be tested singly or in combinations of two or three. (One, two, or three new stations were being contemplated to replace or supplement the existing central fire station.) In addition, several different configurations of future land development were also identified. First, based upon the city's 1980 development plan, two basic alternatives for the distribution of future growth were distinguished. Second, it was decided to analyze each of these two alternatives in three ways: on a citywide basis, north half only (six potential fire station locations, with the Michigan State University campus excluded), and south half only (with the other six potential locations).

The prediction of effectiveness phase of the East Lansing study used an already developed transportation-planning model, one that assigns vehicular traffic to a street and freeway network made up of links (street segments) and nodes (street intersections). One of the key features of this network assignment model is its use of minimum travel-time paths. Traffic going from any one point (node) to any other is routed over that series of links that results in the shortest total travel time. In applying this to fire station location analysis, the model finds the shortest total travel time between that node (or nodes) designated as a fire station location to all other nodes (in this case city blocks, which each have a predetermined fire hazard rating).

These two basic characteristics of fire-protection service—travel time and fire-hazard rating—form the heart of the analysis. For each city block, the fire-hazard rating is multiplied by the total travel time required to reach that block, and then, for each alternative fire station location or set of locations, the products for individual blocks are summed. The alternative with the smallest sum is to be preferred, since overall it tends to reach the most hazardous blocks in the shortest time. Hence, the evaluation phase of this analysis proceeds quite simply and directly from the prediction phase.

GUIDELINES FOR SYSTEMS ANALYSIS

Applying the systems approach in urban planning is not an easy
assignment. Though the potential gains in improved governmental
planning and decision making are large, the analytic effort and data
resources required are also likely to be large. Effective systems
analysis is also likely to be expensive. Whether these increased
efforts and expenditures will, in fact, be worthwhile remains at present
an open question. Systems analysis in urban planning is in its infancy.
Only further experimentation and testing of the systems approach will
be able to establish its areas of useful application as well as its limitations. As the examples reviewed above illustrate, many different
planning processes, urban systems, urban problems, and governmenta
operations appear open to more systematic analysis, using many different strategies and techniques.

The fact that effective systems analysis involves a long-term
research and planning commitment is evidenced by the slow progress
and incomplete accomplishments of those planning agencies that have
explored the approach. A number of the agency efforts reviewed in this
report have not advanced far beyond the goal-identification stage, with
perhaps an initial investigation of the program-identification stage.
Whatever has been achieved during these first two steps has been far
from exhaustive—for all of the examples discussed. Those agencies
that have explored the prediction and evaluation stages have faced
serious problems in model building and/or the treatment of multiple
objectives. Their solutions to these problems have been highly individualized and subject to considerable further thought and analysis.

Though systems analysis is not easy, the weight of current
opinion among experienced PPB analysts and other systems experts
seems to indicate that its potential benefits outweigh the difficulty of
its execution. Even if incompletely or inconclusively carried out,
systems analysis is valuable simply in forcing the identification and
acknowledgment of relevant objectives and plan-program-project
alternatives. Whatever final recommendations or decisions are made,
they will be made with the benefit of having faced directly, in part at
least, the assumptions, implied objectives, and indirect value judgments involved. There is likely to remain, however, a certain reluctance or resistance among many public officials and politicians to "too
much" PPBS. Flexibility for political maneuvering and bargaining,
as well as a desire to perpetuate existing, familiar bureaucratic
arrangements, are to some extent threatened by a more rational,
objective examination of governmental activities.

This chapter has suggested that within urban planning agencies
and activities, as distinguished from specific local governments and
governmental departments, the systems approach may be applied at
any one of four different levels. In general, it appears preferable for
analyses of broader planning processes (the first level) to focus upon
the first two steps of the systems approach—identifying objectives and
programs. Steps 3 and 4—predicting effectiveness and evaluating
alternatives—appear best left to more specific and manageable analyses
of particular urban systems, problems, or governmental operations.

Experience seems to indicate that the breadth of planning processes
is such that overall prediction and evaluation become extremely complicated, overwhelming tasks. These tasks should generally be related to
individual components or subject areas (systems, problems, governmental operations) of concern within a planning process. Within these
more specific analysis contexts, a more detailed examination of objectives and alternative programs will probably also be required. All four
steps of the systems approach should consequently be investigated.

Individual planning agencies interested in the application of systems
analysis to their planning activities need not and probably should not
attempt a full-scale initial effort. Instead, they should first grapple
with the identification of objectives (systems step 1). Staff members
might be assigned to explore how local objectives have been expressed,
by whom, and how they might be measured. Often the agency's
planning activities should be broken down by subject area, and local
objectives within each area examined. Next would come the identification of plans, programs, or projects that relate to objectives within
each subject area (systems step 2). Perhaps a current planning
proposal is the subject of much local debate or controversy. A systematic identification of its objectives (and its alternatives) might be both
timely and useful.

Following this initial, preliminary identification of programs and
objectives (perhaps using a simple programs-objectives matrix or
goals-achievement comparison matrix to match programs against
their relevant objectives), the agency might wish to conduct a more
detailed analysis of some specific system, subsystem, or problem.
Some subject areas (systems, problems) might be given priority in
terms of the agency's activities or the city's interests. Further analysis of these priority areas should begin by investigating the prediction-
evaluation needs and problems a systems approach would involve
(systems steps 3 and 4). Data needs and availability should be explored
at an early date. The role of mathematical modeling should be carefully considered. In general, initial modeling and prediction efforts
should be kept modest in scope and at a manageable level. It is
important that a planning agency begin all of its systems analysis work

at a modest scale, expanding as capabilities develop and resources become available. A long-term work program for the agency's systems analysis efforts might be sketched, discussed, and organized. The thought of using "systems analysis" need not be an overwhelming idea.

In this section, some 20 guidelines for applying the systems approach in urban planning are presented. They are intended as a checklist for the design of systems analysis work programs, as well as for the initial explorations preceding and following such programs. These guidelines have been suggested by a review of the various examples already discussed, and are by no means intended as a complete list. Since urban-oriented systems analysis is only in its beginning stages, the guidelines are essentially preliminary in nature. They are also primarily oriented toward some of the major problems of systems analysis. As summarized in Table 3.8, these guidelines are organized according to the four basic steps of the systems approach. They are briefly described and explained in the following paragraphs.

Identifying Objectives

1. Objectives should be expressed quantitatively wherever possible. Measurement is, of course, the cornerstone of the systems approach. It permits relative levels of goal achievement to be compared. Unless the achievement of an objective can in some way be measured quantitatively, that objective is in danger of being insufficiently considered or of being left out altogether. Not all objectives will be amenable to measurement, however, and those that are not will have to be considered subjectively or qualitatively later in the analysis. Other objectives are likely to be open only to partial measurement, expecially those involving citizen attitudes and satisfactions. For example, the "job satisfaction" objective shown in Table 3.7 (Objective C) is likely to be at best only partially measurable.

2. Sets of objectives should be defined in consistent, comparable terms. Goals and objectives can be identified at varying levels of abstraction, from the very vague (such as increased personal freedom) to the very specific (reduce the drop-out rate at Wilson High School). Where multiple objectives for a certain process, system, or problem are being advanced, they should be expressed at comparable levels of detail, using the same kinds of general language. This permits alternative programs to be evaluated according to consistent ground rules. It tends to avoid the use of objectives biased toward or implying particular program alternatives. The Model Cities objectives shown in Tables 3.1 and 3.2 display, in part, this kind of consistency.

3. Different sets of objectives can be defined within the same subject area. An important aspect of the systems approach is its

TABLE 3.8

Guidelines for Systems Analysis in Urban Planning

Identifying objectives
1. Objectives should be expressed quantitatively wherever possible.
2. Sets of objectives should be defined in consistent, comparable terms.
3. Different sets of objectives can be defined within the same subject area.
4. Different quantitative measures for the same objective should be explored.
5. The more specifically an objective is stated, the more it resembles an actual program.

Identifying programs
6. Programs should be expressed in terms of the objectives to which they apply.
7. Programs will usually apply to more than one objective.
8. Sets of programs should be defined in consistent, comparable terms.
9. A common unit of input measurement among programs (such as dollars) may be desirable.
10. The identification or design of alternative programs is especially difficult and important.

Predicting effectiveness
11. Objectives are likely to be interdependent.
12. Programs are likely to be interdependent.
13. The collection of appropriate and relevant data on program-objective characteristics and interrelationships is essential.
14. Mathematical modeling and statistical analysis should be kept at a manageable level.
15. Prediction can sometimes be assumed or approximated, without the use of detailed mathematical modeling.

Evaluating alternatives
16. The comparison of program costs with relative levels of effectiveness may be desirable.
17. The assignment of subjective weights among objectives may be important.
18. The development of a single score to evaluate alternative programs may be desirable.
19. Nonquantitative objectives should receive due consideration.
20. Systems analysis and evaluation are only an aid to governmental decision making.

emphasis upon analytic process, upon the continual revision, modification, and improvement of all the elements used within that process—objectives, programs, analytic methods. Objectives in particular should be open to change. Many goals and objectives are in fact quite difficult to identify, and agreement upon them may not be easy. Goals may be advanced by many different community groups, private organizations, politicians, citizens, consultants, administrators, or planners. Conditions may change, and goals may change with them. As a result, the objectives used within any specific systems analysis should not be regarded as permanent ones.

4. Different quantitative measures for the same objectives should be explored. A single quantitative measure for the achievement of a particular objective is likely to reflect only one aspect of that objective. Other measures will reflect other aspects, and, in many cases, more than one measure is desirable to capture the sometimes hidden implications of specific objectives. One of the difficulties of quantitative measurement is its tendency to restrict or limit one's view of the objective at hand, to give only a partial insight into that objective. Consequently, the indexes used to gauge the achievement of objectives should also be open to continual revision and augmentation. As an example, a number of the Southeastern Wisconsin objectives shown in Table 3.4 have been related to multiple indexes. In addition, the development of new output-oriented quantitative measures may be called for in cases where input-oriented measures of goal achievement have initially been used (as with the Model Cities education objectives shown in Table 3.2).

5. The more specifically an objective is stated, the more it resembles an actual program. The means-ends continuum, where the grouping and regrouping of specific programs tends to suggest objectives for those programs, and the grouping of objectives tends in turn to suggest broader goals, is another important aspect of the systems approach. The hierarchy of objectives explored by the Philadelphia CRP illustrates this relationship. The mixing or confusing of programs with objectives can lead to difficulties in systems analysis, since for analysis and evaluation purposes the two must be kept separate. In general, objectives should be stated at a more general level than program alternatives.

Identifying Programs

6. Programs should be expressed in terms of the objectives to which they apply. One of the critical problems of the systems approach lies in the proper identification and measurement of program alternatives. Normally, the budgets and records of various governmental

agencies are organized by object-of-expenditure categories that usually
have little to do with the agency's stated or implied objectives. For
example, expenditures made under one object classification (such as
personal services or machinery and equipment) may pertain to several
different objectives, and this must be ascertained. A reorganization
of record keeping will often be required. It is important to identify
program costs separately in relation to objectives pursued. Further
problems in program measurement are commonly associated with
program overlap, both within and between different agencies. Some
agencies may fund several unrelated (and often uncoordinated) programs, all aimed at the same objective or objectives. Other agencies
may duplicate in part the services and programs provided by "competing" agencies. In general, it is desirable to identify all (or nearly all)
of the programs that apply to particular objectives.

7. Programs will usually apply to more than one objective. If a
particular subject area is examined thoroughly enough, it will usually
be found that program alternatives are intended to achieve multiple
objectives (stated, implied, quantitative, qualitative). In turn, more
than one program alternative will usually apply to a single objective.
Though this makes the analysis process much more complicated, it is
important to identify and explore these multiple program-objective
interrelationships. The Southeastern Wisconsin example illustrates
how broad metropolitan development alternatives apply to a host of
different objectives, while the San Francisco example shows how a
single stated objective for housing programs actually implies a series
of more specific objectives.

8. Sets of programs should be defined in consistent, comparable
terms. Where a series of program alternatives has been identified for
systematic evaluation, it is important that they be stated in comparable
terms. They should be related to objectives in a similar way, so that
it will be possible to compare their relative levels of goal achievement.
They must represent realistic, feasible alternatives, consistently
measurable in the same way as other alternatives. Some, but not all,
of the Model Cities Program shown in Tables 3.1 and 3.2 exhibit this
kind of comparability. For example, the various housing-impacts upon
the total number of housing units.

9. A common unit of input measurement (such as dollars) may be
desirable. Very often it will be desirable to make trade-off comparisons between different programs. That is, during later prediction and
evaluation phases, it may be instructive to raise or lower the level of
investment in one program (given a fixed level of desired goal achievement), to see how other program investments must subsequently be
lowered or raised. It might be informative to raise or lower a desired
level of goal achievement, in order to see which program investments

would be most affected. To make incremental comparisons of this type, a common unit of program input measurement is required. This almost always turns out to be dollars, though other units (such as man-hours) would also work, if uniformly available and applicable.

10. The identification or design of alternative programs is especially difficult and important. Just as objectives are open to continuing revision and refinement, alternative programs aimed at achieving objectives should also be subject to improvement and innovation. Initially, a set of alternatives might be built around existing governmental (or private) plans, programs, or policies, supplemented by a few key suggestions for improvement. The design of entirely new alternatives, as well as the modification of existing ones, should be seen as a continuing process, built in part upon the criticisms and problems identified by those participating in the goal-formulation process, as well as upon the creative insights of program administrators and planners. Additional alternatives should also be expected to result from continuing improvements in data collection and the analysis of programs-objectives interrelationships.

Predicting Effectiveness

11. Objectives are likely to be interdependent. One of the many perplexing aspects of the prediction and analysis phase of the systems approach lies in the frequent interdependencies among and between both objectives and programs. Tables 3.1 and 3.2 serve to suggest interdependencies of both types in relation to the Model Cities Program. The Philadelphia CRP's hierarchy of objectives also demonstrated directly how objectives are interrelated. In some cases, objectives may be in conflict, calling for some sort of compromise among performance standards or achievement targets. Often the interdependency of objectives will be such that the achievement of one will depend upon (or lead to) the achievement of others.

12. Programs are likely to be interdependent. Interdependencies among programs are more serious because it is alternative programs that are to be evaluated. If one program depends upon the presence of others in order to be successful, then this relationship must be acknowledged. If its relative level of success depends upon the relative levels of investment in other programs, the situation becomes more complicated. In particular, it is often difficult to distinguish separately the impacts of a single program when a number of different programs (or environmental conditions) serve simultaneously to affect the achievement of relevant objectives. This is especially true in the case of social-service programs (such as those being incorporated within Model Cities Programs). The San Francisco example shows that it

is also true in relation to housing programs. Other problems may lie with time-phased or sequential program interdependencies, and in dealing with the relative time spans of program impact in general.

13. The collection of appropriate and relevant data on program-objective characteristics and interrelationships is essential. This may be the single most important dimension of the systems-analysis process. Without real-world data to show how objectives are affected by alternative programs, social and economic conditions, system and problem characteristics, and critical environmental factors and, in general, how objectives themselves affect each other and how they may be defined and measured in different ways, other phases within the systems approach become empty exercises. Considerable understanding of the particular subject area under study, and especially of the kinds of data available (or potentially available) to describe that subject area, is therefore necessary. The East Lansing project showed that a systems approach to the study of fire-station locations did much to reveal the weaknesses and strengths of the existing record-keeping system. The San Francisco and Southeastern Wisconsin programs both required large amounts of data, and the collection and processing of that data constituted major technical assignments.

14. Mathematical modeling and statistical analysis should be kept at a manageable level. Two of the examples reviewed placed extensive reliance upon mathematical computer models, and in retrospect the planners involved felt that too much emphasis had generally been given to this aspect of the systems-analysis process. In East Lansing, the use of a predetermined transportation-planning model was criticized as being insensitive to the special features of the governmental operation under study. Fire department operations were fitted to the model, rather than vice versa. There was also a certain lack of coordination between model experts and those familiar with local fire protection needs and experience.

In San Francisco, the housing market simulation model was eventually found to be too cumbersome for effective use, its results too difficult to analyze and interpret, and its function and operation poorly understood by local planners. In this example, the model-building phase of the systems analysis absorbed a large and disproportionate share of the total effort. The model itself became unduly complex and more important than the purposes it was intended to serve. The important lesson to be learned here is that the model-building activities of the prediction phase of the systems approach should not be permitted to get out of hand. Outside of established transportation planning models, urban model-building is presently quite experimental in nature, a research frontier calling for long-term research commitments. Such commitments should be made wisely, with a full understanding of and appreciation for the time and expense involved.

15. Prediction can sometimes be assumed or approximated, without the use of detailed mathematical modeling. It should be stressed that complicated model building is not an absolutely essential component of the systems-analysis process. Other less precise but more realistic approaches to prediction have also been advanced. While model building may be conceptually preferable, its informational demands may become enormous, its analytic development time-consuming and expensive, and its reliability and eventual utility uncertain. The Model Cities strategy for "prediction," with its emphasis on ongoing data collection, program monitoring and review, neighborhood resident surveys, and the current short-term evaluation of programs in terms of observed impacts, represents an alternative to formal mathematical modeling. Here, prediction is implied as a part of actual evaluation. The Los Angeles example also gives prediction an implicit role within its overall systems approach.

Evaluating Alternatives

16. The comparison of program costs with relative levels of effectiveness may be desirable. One of the major strong points of PPBS is its emphasis upon cost-effectiveness comparisons for different program or project alternatives. Both the Model Cities Program and the Philadelphia CRP stressed this orientation. In general, given a maximum level of permitted expenditures, the aim is to find that alternative that will be most effective. Conversely, given a desired minimum level of effectiveness, the aim is to find the least costly alternative that will meet that minimum. The first of these situations is commonly referred to as achieving "economy," the second as achieving "efficiency." If levels of effectiveness can be cast in dollar terms (though this is not essential), the analysis is sometimes referred to as cost-benefit analysis. If all the necessary costs and effectiveness estimates can be made, this form of evaluation will often be desirable.

17. The assignment of subjective weights to objectives may be important. In some cases, it may not be felt that all objectives are of equal importance. In both the Wichita CIP and the Southeastern Wisconsin Transportation/Land-Use Plan, subjective weights were assigned to objectives to account for the relative differences among them. The determination of these weights is one of the most difficult tasks of systems analysis (regardless of the analytic context), though it is not necessarily a required one. The difficulty lies in deciding who should assign the weights, and how they should go about doing it. In these two examples, preliminary weights were assigned by planners themselves.

18. The development of a single score to evaluate alternative programs may be desirable. In both the Wichita and Southeastern Wisconsin examples, the weighting of objectives was used to develop a single

score for evaluating each alternative program (capital improvement project or transportation/land-use plan). In addition, the Los Angeles program was designed to generate a single recreation-need index or score for each local community. This technique has the obvious advantage of permitting the entire evaluation to be summarized with a simple series of rank or priority numbers, one for each alternative under consideration. It implies, however, that all important objectives have been considered (and are represented), and that any weighting of objectives has been satisfactorily conducted.

19. Nonquantitative objectives should receive due consideration. Because it is unlikely that all relevant objectives will actually be measurable (as well as analyzable in relation to programs), steps should be taken to explicitly include qualitative objectives and other important decision factors somewhere within the evaluation stage. It may be possible to isolate certain qualitative or intangible objectives and show how much they might be "worth" in terms of a trade-off with quantified objectives. In any event, in communicating the results of any systems analysis to political and administrative decision makers, care should be taken to display those objectives that could not be quantified, as well as those that were.

20. Systems analysis and evaluation are only an aid to governmental decision making. Finally, it should be stressed that, regardless of the results of any particular systems analysis, the final decision regarding choice among program alternatives rests with governmental officials. Effective systems analysis is not interchangeable with decision making but is only conducted in support of decision making. In the final analysis, intangible or political factors are likely to play an important role and perhaps influence actual decision making in ways that were not anticipated at the time systematic analysis was conducted. The systems approach is essentially only a more rigorous version of the basic advisory role of urban planning.

NOTES

1. U.S. Department of Housing and Urban Development, Improving the Quality of Urban Life: A Program Guide to Model Neighborhoods in Demonstration Cities (Washington, D.C.: Government Printing Office, 1966); Model Cities Administration, "Model Cities Planning Requirements," CDA Letter No. 1 (Washington, D.C.: HUD, 1967); Model Cities Administration, "Comprehensive Program Submission Requirements," CDA Letter No. 4 (Washington, D.C.: HUD, 1968).

2. Model Cities Administration, "Measures of Living Quality in Model Neighborhoods," Technical Assistance Bulletin No. 2 (Washington, D.C.: HUD, 1968).

3. A required component of every First-Year Action Program is a preliminary statement on continuing planning and evaluation activities, which in varying degrees among the first-round participants showed an awareness of the magnitude of the evaluation assignment. Assistance was provided by HUD in the form of a draft document that describes in some detail the many important considerations involved in developing evaluation strategies. See Model Cities Administration, "Evaluation of Model Cities Programs," Technical Assistance Bulletin, draft (Washington, D.C.: HUD, 1969).

4. See ibid., Ch. 7.

5. Manly Johnson and E. P. Alworth, eds., Metropolitan Data Center Project, Demonstration Project No. Oklahoma D-1 (Washington, D.C.: Urban Renewal Administration, Housing and Home Finance Agency, 1966).

6. Philadelphia Community Renewal Program, Community Renewal Programming, Technical Report No. 4 (December 1962).

7. Philadelphia Community Renewal Program, Major Policies and Proposals (February 1967).

8. Selma J. Mushkin, "PPB in Cities," Public Administration Review 29 (March-April 1969); Graeme M. Taylor, "PPB in the City of Philadelphia," ICH 13C21 (Cambridge, Mass.: Intercollegiate Case Clearinghouse, Harvard University Business School, 1968). See Taylor, "PPB in New York City," ICH 13C22 (Cambridge, Mass.: Intercollegiate Case Clearinghouse, Harvard University Business School, 1968), for a description of similar program-budgeting innovations in New York City.

9. Philadelphia Community Renewal Program, Development Programming as Applied to West Philadelphia, Technical Report No. 8 (February 1964).

10. Southeastern Wisconsin Regional Planning Commission, (SEWRPC) Land Use-Transportation Study: Forecasts and Alternative Plans, 1990, Planning Report No. 7, 2 (1966).

11. For a review and analysis of this plan-making process in 12 other major metropolitan areas, with particular emphasis upon the evaluation of alternative plans, see David E. Boyce and Norman D. Day, Metropolitan Plan Evaluation Methodology (Philadelphia: Institute for Environmental Studies, University of Pennsylvania, 1969).

12. See Kenneth J. Schlager, "A Recursive Programming Theory of the Residential Land Development Process," Highway Research Record, no. 126 (Washington, D.C.: Highway Research Board, 1966); Kenneth J. Schlager, "A Land-Use Plan Design Model," Journal of the American Institute of Planners 31 (May 1965); SEWRPC, A Mathematical Approach to Urban Design, Technical Report No. 3 (1966); SEWRPC Land Use-Transportation Study: Recommended Regional Land Use and

Transportation Plans, 1990, Planning Report No. 7, 3 (1966), for descriptions of these experimental models. In general, other urban development models, such as those discussed in the May 1965 issue of
the AIP Journal and elsewhere, are also intended for application during
this prediction of effectiveness phase of land-use/transportation planning, with some possible overlap into the preceding design of alternative phase.

13. SEWRPC, Land Use-Transportation Study, vol. 2. See also
Kenneth J. Schlager, "The Rank-Base Expected Value Method of Plan
Evaluation," Highway Research Record, no. 238 (Washington, D.C.:
Highway Research Board, 1968).

14. Franklyn H. Beal, "Defining Development Objectives," in
Principles and Practice of Urban Planning, William I. Goodman and
Eric C. Freund, eds. (Washington, D.C.: International Managers'
Association, 1968).

15. Chicago Department of Development and Planning, The Comprehensive Plan of Chicago (1966). See also Chicago Department of
City Planning, Basic Policies for the Comprehensive Plan of Chicago
(1964).

16. San Francisco Department of City Planning, Status of the San
Francisco Simulation Model (1968). See also Harry B. Wolfe and
Martin L. Ernst, "Simulation Models and Urban Planning," in Opera-
tions Research for Public Systems, Philip M. Morse and Laura W.
Bacon, eds. (Cambridge, Mass.: MIT Press, 1967); Arthur D. Little,
Inc., Model of the San Francisco Housing Market, Technical Paper
No. 8 (San Francisco: San Francisco Community Renewal Program,
1966); Ira M. Robinson, Harry B. Wolfe, and Robert L. Barringer,
"A Simulation Model for Renewal Programming," AIP Journal 31 (May
1965).

17. Edwin J. Staley, "Determining Neighborhood Recreation Pri-
orities: An Instrument," Journal of Leisure Research 1 (Winter 1969);
Recreation and Youth Services Planning Council, Study of Recreation
Needs and Services: South Central Los Angeles (Los Angeles: The
Council, 1966).

18. System Development Corporation, System Analysis and Planning for Public Health Care in the City of New York: An Initial Study
(New York: The Health Research Council of the City of New York,
1966).

19. The Rand Corporation undertook a series of long-term systems
research projects for the City of New York, beginning in 1967. Included
among these projects are a Health Services Administration Study, Fire
Department Study, Police Department Study, Research on Housing
Problems, and a Study of Public Safety in High-Rise Public Housing.
Some of the early reports available from this series are Clarence Teng,

The New York City Health Budget in Program Terms, Memorandum
RM-5774-NYC (Santa Monica, Calif.: The Rand Corporation, 1969);
A. J. Tenzer, J. B. Benton, and C. Teng, Applying the Concepts of
Program Budgeting to the New York City Police Department, Memo-
randum RM-5846-NYC (Santa Monica, Calif.: The Rand Corporation,
1969); David Dreyfuss and Joan Hendrickson, A Guide to Government
Activities in New York City's Housing Markets, Memorandum RM-
5673-NYC (Santa Monica, Calif.: The Rand Corporation, 1968).

    20. State-Local Finances Project, A First Step to Analysis: The
Issue Paper, PPB Note 11 (Washington, D.C.: George Washington
University, 1968). For specific analyses of other socioeconomic problem areas, see Robert G. Spiegelman, "A Benefit/Cost Model to Evaluate Educational Programs," Socioeconomic Planning Sciences (August
1968); Clark C. Abt, "Design for an Education System Cost-Effectiveness Model," Socio-Economic Planning Sciences (April 1969); Gilbert
Kruschwitz, Alan Colker, and Donald Lamb, "A Community Action
Program Impact Model," Socio-Economic Planning Sciences (June
1969). In addition, for more general discussions of the application of
systems analysis in the study of urban problems, see Helen O. Nicol,
"Guaranteed Income Maintenance: A Public Welfare Systems Model,"
in Planning Programming Budgeting: A Systems Approach to Management, Fremont J. Lyden and Ernest G. Miller, eds. (Chicago: Markham, 1967); Robert Elkin, "Framework for Decision-Making: Applying
PPBS to Public Welfare Program Structure," Public Welfare (April
1969); Arthur Spindler, "Systems Analysis in Public Welfare," Public
Welfare (July 1968).

    21. See Martin Rein, "Social Planning: The Search for Legitimacy,"
AIP Journal 35 (July 1969); Michael P. Brooks and Michael A. Stegman,
"Urban Social Policy, Race, and the Education of Planners," AIP
Journal 34 (September 1968); Norton E. Long, "Planning for Social
Change," ASPO Newsletter (1968); Bernard J. Frieden, "The Changing
Prospects for Social Planning," AIP Journal 33 (September 1967); John
W. Dyckman, "Social Planning, Social Planners, and Planned Soci-
eties," AIP Journal 32 (March 1966); Harvey S. Perloff, "New Direc-
tions in Social Planning," AIP Journal 31 (November 1965); Harvey S.
Perloff, "Common Goals and the Linking of Physical and Social Plan-
ning," ASPO Newsletter (1965); Melvin M. Webber, "Comprehensive
Planning and Social Responsibility," AIP Journal 29 (November 1963).
See also Bernard J. Frieden and Robert Morris, eds., Urban Planning
and Social Policy (New York: Basic Books, 1968).

    22. The State-Local Finances Project of George Washington Univer-
sity offers some preliminary examples of the systems approach applied
to general municipal and county governmental operations. See State-
Local Finances Project, PPB Pilot Project Reports from the Partici-

pating 5 States, 5 Counties, and 5 Cities (Washington, D.C.: George
Washington University, 1969); State-Local Finances Project, Implementing PPB in State, City, County (Washington, D.C.: George Washington University, 1969); State-Local Finances Project, Teaching Cases
in Program Planning for State, City, County Objectives (Washington,
D.C.: George Washington University, 1969).

23. East Lansing Project Team, "East Lansing: A Facilities Location Analysis," mimeographed (Washington, D.C.: International City
Managers' Association, 1968). A contrasting analysis of fire station
location in New York City is presented in E. H. Blum and J. M. Chai-
ken, "Application of Incidence Analysis to Deployment of Fire Compa-
nies" (paper presented at the 4th Annual Symposium on the Application
of Computers to the Problems of Urban Society, Association for Computing Machinery, October 1969). This paper is based upon work by
the Rand Corporation, cited in note 19 above.

24. Systems studies of governmental distribution or collection services, or of the central location of neighborhood and community service
facilities, are growing in number. For example, analyses of school
location and districting are presented in T. Ploughman, W. Darnton,
and W. Heuser, "An Assignment Program to Establish School Attendance Boundaries and Forecast Construction Needs," Socio-Economic
Planning Sciences (July 1968); Richard J. O'Brien, "Model for Planning
the Location and Size of Urban Schools," Socio-Economic Planning
Sciences (April 1969); Gordon A. Marker, "Some Aspects of Educational
Park Planning," Socio-Economic Planning Sciences (April 1969). School
redistricting models are described in S. Clarke and J. Surkis, "An
Operations Research Approach to Racial Desegregation of School Sys-
tems," Socio-Economic Planning Sciences (July 1968); Leila B. Hick-
man and Howard M. Taylor, "School Rezoning to Achieve Racial
Balance: A Linear Programming Approach," Socio-Economic Planning
Sciences (August 1969). In addition, systems studies of broader edu-
cational operations and planning activities are presented in M. Szekely,
M. Stankard, and R. Sisson, "Design of a Planning Model for an Urban
School District," Socio-Economic Planning Sciences (July 1968), as
well as in a number of papers presented at the Symposium on Opera-
tions Analysis of Education, whose proceedings are published in Socio-
Economic Planning Sciences (April 1969).

For an analysis of hospital-location patterns in Chicago, see
Richard Morrill and Robert Earickson, "Locational Efficiency of Chicago Area Hospitals: An Experimental Model," Health Services Research 4 (Summer 1969); Robert Earickson, "A Behavioural Approach
to Simulation Models of Patient Use of Physicians and Hospitals,"
Working Papers 3.11-3.13 (Chicago: Chicago Regional Hospital Study,
1969). For an analysis of public ambulance service in New York City,

see E. S. Savas, Simulation and Cost-Effectiveness Analysis of New York's Emergency Ambulance Service (New York: Office of the Mayor, 1968); Richard J. Gill, "Emergency Ambulance Service," ICH 13C25 and ICH 13C26 (Cambridge, Mass.: Intercollegiate Case Clearinghouse, Harvard University Business School, 1968.

Analyses of police station location and patrol unit operations are presented in J. Surkis, G. R. Gordon, and N. Hauser, "A Simulation Model of New York City Police Department's Response System" (paper presented at the 2d Conference on Applications of Simulation, Association for Computing Machinery, December 1968); David L. Bussard, "Los Angeles Police Department Operations Simulation," Papers, 4th Annual Symposium on the Application of Computers to the Problems of Urban Society (New York: Association for Computing Machinery, October 1969).

Many of these examples have not, however, been carried through as fully developed systems analyses but have concentrated mainly on the model-building, prediction of effectiveness phase. Some are oriented mainly toward an analysis of the services of a specific agency (ambulance services, police patrol operations), while others are oriented more toward the analysis of a system of multiple-agency facilities. Some of the latter could, with further development, become important components of larger studies of urban systems, such as those involving hospitals (health-care systems) or schools (educational system). Others are already well on their way toward an objectives-oriented, systematic form of overall study design.

4

EVALUATING REGIONAL
PLANS AND
COMMUNITY IMPACT

The roots of comprehensive regional planning lie less in the communities that might benefit from integrated structuring of land uses and services and more in the federal legislation that underlies the Highway Trust Fund and other urban investment programs. As a result, the institutions that perform comprehensive regional planning, and the activities they pursue, are often politically and functionally isolated from the communities in which the ultimate consequences of regional planning, good or bad, must be felt. While institutional and political issues fostering this absence of vertical integration of comprehensive planning are critical, the planner must give special recognition to the influence of planning techniques themselves on this problem.

This chapter defines this problem in specific terms and reviews the state of the art of comprehensive plan evaluation in this context. An approach for better linking regional plan evaluation with community impacts is suggested, including potential strategies for building local participation into regional plan evaluation.

CONTEXT OF THE PROBLEM

Regional, comprehensive planning is common to every major metropolitan area in the United States. The functions these planning

---

Coauthored with Joseph L. Schofer. Reprinted with permission from Journal of the Urban Planning and Development Division, Proceedings of the American Society of Civil Engineers, vol. 100, no. UP1 (March 1974).

activities perform are needed and desired at the community level. A variety of community-serving functional systems act at the regional scale, and so their development and maintenance must be planned at that scale. Furthermore, some systems with localized functional characteristics create spillover effects that go beyond the jurisdictions within which those systems operate. Consequently, there is a need for coordinated efforts, at larger than community scale, in the planning of those systems.

Thus, while it is the nature of regional planning to play a large-scale, integrative role, there are significant benefits to be derived from it by individual citizens of the communities that make up the region.

Yet the primary impetus for comprehensive regional planning stems from the legislative framework of federally-sponsored programs, which require some form of regional coordinative role as a requisite for local funding under those programs. The Federal Highway Act of 1962 represents perhaps the clearest statement of this requirement, but a variety of other federal programs have called for similar integration of planning at the local level. Currently, the Department of Housing and Urban Development supports this type of planning, and the Office of Management and Budget Circular A-95 requires that a variety of requests for federal funding be cleared first through a regional review agency.

Meeting federal requirements for regional planning does not necessarily insure that effective regional planning will be performed. This is due, in part, to the tendency to plan only in a perfunctory manner. More typically, however, effectiveness of regional planning is limited because accomplishing the task well presents challenging technical and political problems.

A major factor that limits the effectiveness of regional planning is the isolation of planning agencies from a regional power base. With their constituencies divided among numerous political jurisdictions, few of which are anxious to share policy-making power, regional planning agencies are frequently too weak to implement their products. The combination of a poorly defined constituency and the opposition of local governments to intervention by external bodies, along with the nature of federal requirements for regional planning, makes it feasible for regional planning agencies to concentrate their resources on macroscopic, long-range planning. It is the exception, rather than the rule, to find the areawide planning organization (APO) engaging in detailed planning or the assessment of localized needs and impacts.

This broad-scale focus has an influence on the effectiveness of the regional planning process. Failure to examine detailed planning issues reduces the probability of plan implementation by increasing the likeli-

hood that regional plans will be locally infeasible. The unresponsive-
ness of large-scale plans to community needs makes it easier for local
governments to reject the recommendations of the regional agency,
further weakening its effectiveness. Finally, the absence of concern
for detail at the regional level virtually guarantees the absence of a
community constituency for the APO. Thus, regional planning often
functions in a vacuum, and the evident needs for integrated planning
are not met in fact even if they are met in spirit.

While the planner must recognize the influence of these environmental factors on his own efforts, in the short run there is little he can
do to respond in a political sense. It is imperative, however, that the
planner recognize the influence these factors have had on the evolution
of his tools. For the planner's major opportunities to respond to the
need for regional planning lie in the development of more responsive
methods for planning.

Indeed, an examination of typical regional planning methods illustrates their insensitivity to matters of detail, particularly with respect
to localized needs and impacts of alternative plans. The evaluation
component of the regional planning process provides an important
example of this problem.

Often plan evaluation at the regional level is superficial, involving
the presentation of summaries of plan characteristics, not impacts, to
a regionally-constituted commission that then makes a decision regarding acceptance or rejection of plan alternatives. The perfunctory nature
of evaluation may extend to the A-95 review activity, which is often
conducted in the absence of a systematic evaluative framework. In
either instance, when impact measures are introduced, they are typically prepared for the regional level only, and tend to be limited to the
easiest-to-measure concepts, such as trip lengths, acres of open space,
or the costs of services.

Yet no one lives at the regional level. Daily activities are limited
to one, or a few, neighborhoods within the region, along with travel
between these neighborhoods or communities. Citizens become concerned about the impacts of proposed projects when they can identify
the effects of plans upon the quality of life in their neighborhoods. In
fact, the principal consequences of regional plans may be measurable
only at the local level. We are interested in regionally integrated
transportation and waste-water treatment facilities because we wish
to insure the quality of these services in the communities and corridors
in which we function. Spillovers are important because the quality of
life in our residential or working communities may be affected by what
happens in an adjacent community.

Evaluation of regional plans without consideration of local needs
and impacts then fails to consider the most fundamental characteristics

of those plans. To improve the effectiveness of the regional planning
process, by improving the quality, and feasibility of implementation,
of its products, it is imperative that methods be developed to insure
comprehensive evaluation of alternative plans. The mandate to do this
exists in federal legislation, including recent requirements for assessment of social and environmental impacts specified in the 1969 Environmental Policy Act. What is needed is a set of tools that makes it
possible to evaluate such plans from both the regional and localized
perspective.

The remainder of this chapter focuses on assessment of regional
plan evaluation methods that promise to respond more effectively to
the need for this integrated perspective. An alternative approach is
then outlined.

COMPREHENSIVE REGIONAL PLAN EVALUATION METHODS

This section outlines some key issues in regional plan evaluation
methodology. These are organized around five elements: (a) the evaluation process, (b) criteria and measures, (c) goals and objectives,
(d) comparison formats, and (e) citizen participation.

For each of the five elements the need is stressed for better
identifying and linking macro- and microlevel impacts. Attention is
focused on the degree to which detailed, community-level impacts are
specifically considered at a broader regional level. The existence of a
a well-defined set of areawide goals and objectives is assumed,
together with the existence of appropriate regional forecasting and
simulation models.

PLANNING/EVALUATION PROCESS

Goals-Objectives Hierarchy

Essential to assessment of goal-achievement characteristics of
alternative plans is specification of objectives, the attainment of each
of which can be measured by one or more criteria. [1] This need for
specificity in objectives is evident in several metropolitan planning
efforts that attempted to be more systematic. [2] In Milwaukee, e.g.,
great care was taken to define a hierarchy of goals, objectives, subobjectives, and measurable criteria. [3] In Louisville loosely stated goals
created difficulties in defining suitable measures of effectiveness. [4]

A recent study of evaluation methods also concluded that a hierarchical structuring of goals and objectives was useful in identifying meaningful criteria.[5] In this structuring process, broad goals would be established first, and then the implications of each of these for more specific ends (system objectives) would be listed, leading in turn to still more specific performance objectives under each of the system objectives, and so on, until specific measures were identified at the end of each "branch" on the hierarchy.

This hierarchical value system lends itself naturally to treating the relationship between regional and community-scale plan impacts. The appropriate hierarchical structuring of regional goals and objectives, linking regional goals to more detailed community objectives, represents a promising means for coordinated assessment of both macro and microaspects of regional plans. Continuity between goals at different levels, explicit recognition of cross-linkages, and acknowledgment of changing focus and scale should all be important aspects of this activity, providing a systematic, comprehensive framework for plan evaluation.[6]

Experience of this type at the regional planning level appears skimpy, often stopping at the upper ends of a goals hierarchy. The establishment of a meaningful goal set is often viewed as a nonessential process performed only for public-relations purposes. This may be due to the absence of an identifiable constituency for regional planning. It may also be attributed to a failure of the planner to understand the utility of such a value system in design and evaluation. Finally, ineffective treatment of planning goals may also be attributed to the absence of methods for goal formulation.[7]

Regional-Subregional Differences

The Southeastern Wisconsin Regional Planning Commission (SEWRPC) planning process found an important dimension of goals-objectives hierarchies to be the different geographic levels at which various objectives applied.[8] The three general spatial contexts of region, community, and neighborhood were found to be both relevant and meaningful. At each of these levels a certain class of objectives applied. A regional goal would imply a group of detailed community-level objectives, while community objectives would imply a related set of more detailed subobjectives for neighborhoods at the next level of the hierarchy.

Attaching this spatial characteristic to levels in a goals hierarchy recognizes the relationship between the specificity of goals and the characteristics of the plan components that respond to them. Goals

and objectives at the regional level, e.g., are appropriate for evaluatin
components that are regional in their implications, such as transportation technologies, network structures, and patterns of urban form.
More detailed plan elements that have subarea implications and dif-
erences, including the location and design of facilities, can no longer
be evaluated by regional goals alone but require more detailed objectives responsive to conditions at the subarea level.

Different levels of geographic scale for the impact of public investments respond to clearly different clients and needs to be fulfilled. The
Boston Transportation Planning Review, a regional study conducted in
response to subregional issues, produced its reports in a series of
subregional packages representing an example of how a shift downward
in scale brings local needs and issues to the forefront.[9]

Effective regional plan evaluation calls for goal/alternative comparisons at all levels of a goals hierarchy, including the macroscopic
and the microscopic scale. To date, regional and subarea or project-
oriented planning/evaluation activities have been conducted separately,
typically by different agencies at different points in time. Too often,
particularly in transportation planning, regional network plans were
assessed at a much too general, regional level only. Individual
projects or routes have sometimes been rejected by citizens' groups
and policy makers, in part because critical, local impacts were not
adequately considered when the route was included in the recommended
system plan.[10]

More typically, local negative impacts have been judged unimpor-
tant by planners and decision makers in the context of larger-scale,
regional benefits. These microimpacts, which represent a large portion of the negative impacts of a total system plan, were never considered adequately in regional-scale planning.[11] The inability of
planning to deal with these levels of analysis has led to much citizen
opposition and notably poor transportation and other facilities. The
need to introduce sufficient sensitivity to local differences in evaluating
alternative regional plans has become critical not only to insure the
quality and feasibility of plans but also to maintain the credibility of
the regional planning agency.

Iterative Process

Accompanying the need for a more detailed evaluation of alternatives is a parallel need for the development and assessment of
alternatives to be seen as a cyclic process. One-shot planning efforts
facilitate the omission of microscale impacts, and serve to isolate

the planning agency from affected citizens. Freezing the once-made regional plan makes it difficult to make adjustments to meet local needs and fails to recognize that the plan comprises a collection of smaller components. To avoid independent, one-shot, areawide, all-inclusive alternatives, both the preparation and the evaluation of alternatives should occur in stages, as an iterative and continuing process.[12]

There should be two general phases. First, starting at an area-wide level, and working individually within functional components (transportation, open space, housing, etc.), a generalized set of alter-natives within each component could be developed. A preliminary evaluation of these could be conducted, matching them to construct plans across functional sectors. Second, the component-based process could be repeated at increasing levels of detail, beginning with the re-sults of the evaluation of alternatives of the previous cycle. More de-tailed plan elements within each functional sector would be further integrated, and again, alternatives within each functional area would be selectively combined into overall areawide alternatives.

It has also been suggested that alternatives first be formulated, analyzed, and screened preliminarily and evaluated at the sector or submetropolitan level.[13] This might lead to more responsive alterna-tives, especially from the perspective of the level at which their im-plementation would be undertaken. As a second step, subarea alternatives would be integrated between functional sectors to yield comprehensive development and public facility alternatives at two levels: (a) sets of alternatives within each geographic sector and (b) selected sets of areawide metropolitan alternatives involving a further reconciliation and matching of possible conflicts between sectors.

If the arguments in favor of regional planning are correct, of course, it will be important that such a strategy insure the strength of the regional integration component of areawide planning. Iterative feedback between levels will be critical, regardless of which is started first. To accomplish this cycling between both functional components and levels of geographic detail, it may be necessary to create new in-stitutional strategies for regional planning that would insure that the mandate to pursue this form of analysis existed in the planning agency.

No regional planning agency has yet inaugurated a fully coordinated, cycling process of this type, though several are now engaged in the up-dating and revision of a regional comprehensive plan adopted previously. However, there are signs that the level of thoroughness and detail, in some form of iterative or internal cycling pattern, will increase for these second-generation regional plans. In some cases a major thrust toward integrating regional and local-level planning may lie in extensive subarea or corridor planning on an interagency task force basis.[14] Still, to accomplish this, care must be taken to include significant sensitivity to the needs of the local client, i.e., the affected citizen.

CRITERIA AND MEASURES

Types of Measurement

Three types of measures of effectiveness may be used in plan
evaluation: costable or dollar-valued criteria, other quantitative criteria, and criteria measured by subjective methods. Some of the important measurement issues affecting evaluation are included in the
following.

Collection of objective, quantifiable (including monetary) data to
document existing conditions and to forecast future conditions is a difficult and expensive proposition, particularly for several levels of
analysis. Difficult, and consistent, decisions must be made regarding
the unit of identification, time horizon for collection and forecasting,
the level of aggregation, and the fact that individual measures only
represent a partial aspect of the phenomenon being measured. These
problems served to limit the range and scale of consequences examined
in previous regional plan evaluations.

Subjective measurement (e.g., ordinal ranking of alternatives)
proceeds in part from the premise that it is easier to rank intangible
benefits and costs in terms of perceived quality than to assign a more
objective benefit or cost value. Furthermore, the use of subjective
estimation and evaluation procedures may be especially appropriate
for cases where the fundamental issues relate to significant differences
in perception of impacts on the part of different communities. It is essential for the evaluation procedure to capture these differences in an
organized manner, which requires an effective citizen participation
mechanism at the community level.

Selecting candidate measures or criteria will require ingenuity,
creativity, as well as informed judgment. An initial simplifying step
can often lie in compiling a "master list" of measures from past planning studies and analyses. [15] However, special emphasis must be placed
on identification of the unique needs and impacts in the planning context
at hand.

Forecasting Criteria

Regional plans are evaluated over some future time period. Some
of the measures of future impacts may be provided by regional forecasting and simulation models. Others will have to be derived through
additional, special studies.

Model-Based Criteria

Some of the criteria measuring the objective attainment of plans
will be produced by standard forecasting models. Indeed, effective
forecasting models should be structured to meet the information needs
of evaluation. For example, transportation-modeling outputs relate to
aggregate regional travel (vehicle-miles, average speed, etc.) but represent only a start of alternative transportation plans. In a few regions,
efforts have also been made to enrich the output of land-use forecasting
models to provide data more relevant to plan evaluation. [16]

Forecasting Other Quantitative Criteria

The attainment of many objectives can be quantitatively measured,
but forecasts of their future values in relation to alternative plans will
not be an output of the existing models. Some means for forecasting
them must be developed; that these measures are not now generated by
regional-level models is a major factor in their exclusion from plan
evaluation.

Noise impacts of transportation alternatives are a good example.
Regional simulation models do not function at a level of detail that
allows estimation of neighborhood noise levels. Furthermore, it is
difficult to aggregate noise impacts to produce a regional total. Thus,
noise tends to be ignored, for at the detailed, local planning level, the
regional plan has been fixed, and the existing tools for adequately predicting noise impacts are typically unavailable. [17]

Forecasting Qualitative/Subjective Criteria

The use of subjective criteria should also be considered. Deter-
minations should be made regarding who (e.g., experts in various
functional areas) should make such forecasts and how they should be
made. Recent experience suggests the usefulness of panels of experts
for forecasting the impacts of large-scale public systems. For
example, a subjective matrix-evaluation technique for social and environmental impact assessment of wastewater treatment alternatives
has been developed and applied in the Chicago region under the sponsorship of the U.S. Army Corps of Engineers. [18] In the case of some
neighborhood impacts, neighborhood residents themselves may be the
appropriate experts to consult. There is a considerable need for effective techniques for gathering information on expected impacts from
such groups. [19]

GOALS AND GOAL WEIGHTING

The systematic use of goals and objectives in regional planning
calls for the development of trade-off techniques for comparing the
differential attainment of various goals among alternative plans. The
relative importance of different goals to different community interests
must be explored in some way to achieve meaningful evaluation results.
Experience in goal weighting at the regional planning level is scanty,
but both experimental and practical applications in small interest-group
contexts have burgeoned in recent years.[20] At the regional level, perhaps the most critical problem is the identification of the appropriate
client groups for participation in the weighting process.

Weighting Techniques

Several methods for developing priority weights have been suggested.[21] These include ordinal ranking, rating along a common scale,
and ranking via a paired-comparisons method. Potentially relevant
alternative techniques, and various modifications of these three, appear
in the survey research literature.[22] These methods should be assessed
conceptually and experimentally to determine their utility in goal weighting. Such assessment may well reveal that other, more interactive,
techniques may be necessary to specify goal-attainment trade-off preferences adequately.

For example, one study suggests that direct interviews, conducted
on both individual and group bases, may be necessary to communicate
the implications of certain objectives properly and to stimulate the
necessary thought on the part of each participant.[23] It may be desirable
to make objectives more "real" by confronting participants with well-
specified plan alternatives, together with information on the consequences of these alternatives, and with a tentative set of objectives that
the participant may revise. This might be accomplished through the
construction of comprehensive scenarios as the basis for judgment of
priorities.

Differences in Values

Value conflicts and differences among individuals and groups participating in goal weighting should be expected. In a recent study, because a consensus on a common weighting scheme could not be reached

a goal-weighting procedure and related attempts to develop an overall weighted summary index were abandoned. [24] Disagreements were then dealt with subjectively. This illustrates the need to develop techniques for better identifying and dealing with goal conflicts in the evaluation process.

Because of potential conflicts among community groups regarding the relative importance of goals, it may be desirable to obtain the separate assessments or ratings of each group and then compare their utilities by assigning relative weights to the groups themselves. This weighting of interest groups falls short of any attempt to transform varying utility rankings onto a single absolute scale. Great difficulty has been found in attempting to derive a single utility scale. [25] Still, the knowledge of the distinct weighting sets would be of use in evaluating the components of alternative regional plans.

Because of uncertainty regarding changes in values through time, as well as in relation to a particular evaluation context (e.g., regional versus local), methods for assessing the sensitivity of evaluation results to the goal weights assigned take on special importance. In fact, as suggested in a Pennsylvania example, it may be desirable to take several alternative weighting schemes and carry them through the evaluation process completely, and then examine the results. [26] This is the thrust of the rank sensitivity-comparison technique utilized in the Twin Cities example, [27] and of conceptual developments in the use of goal-weight distributions instead of point estimates. [28]

COMPARISON FORMATS

Multidimensionality

Because a large body of information on alternative plans is likely to be generated, consideration should be given to means for organizing communicating, and illustrating the results of plan evaluation, both to policy makers and to the public.

The difficulty decision makers have had in processing multidimensional information is the reason that goal-weighting schemes have been of major interest in evaluation. [29] The emerging nature of these methods and the unlikelihood of their being totally successful in collapsing dimensionality suggest the continued need to pursue methods of presenting complex information sets to decision makers. The methods to be used should include not only summary indexes, such as benefit/cost and cost-effectiveness ratios based on goal attainment weights but also devices for displaying multidimensional characteristics, such as comparison profiles, maps, charts, graphs, verbal descriptions, and other means. There should be a strong link between these communications media and mechanisms for community participation and interaction in plan evaluation.

Serious reservations have been expressed regarding the use of summary indexes alone, stressing that what is needed is more, rather than less, information, and improved means for displaying that information. [30]

Greater emphasis should be placed upon the presentation and communication aspects of evaluation. Rather than oversimplifying a complex situation, obscuring too much valuable information, devices should be sought that clarify and illustrate the differences between alternatives. [31] Community factor profiles represent a communicative device of this type. This is not to rule out, however, the development of a group of summarizing index scores for sets of impacts or objectives, where loss of detail is not significant. [32]

Time Streams of Effects

The timing of different impacts should also be communicated clearly. The fact that different costs and benefits will be incurred at different dates suggests the need for discount rates, whereby longer-range costs and benefits receive less emphasis. [33] Discounting future impacts back to a so-called present value simply means that the further in the future an impact may lie, the less its value is at the present.

Certainly it is desirable to reconcile costs and benefits in terms of a single comparison year. Yet compressing time streams through the use of interest rates, in fact, may cover up significant differences between alternatives. In such cases, and where the timing of impacts is otherwise of special importance, direct consideration of time streams of effects may be necessary. This presents a special challenge for the presentation of evaluation results, as well as for the process of impact forecasting.

The definition of the time period of analysis often can be crucial in influencing the results of evaluation, particularly in comparing short-range and long-range impacts. [34] Specification of the time frame must also account for the likelihood that local impacts may occur at different time periods than regional impacts. This is particularly obvious for those impacts related to the construction period.

PARTICIPATION

Much of the interest in citizen participation in recent years, particularly in transportation planning, has been generated at the project level.[35] Community opposition to freeway projects in a number of cities, e.g., has expanded consideration of community and environmental values in highway-corridor planning. Citizen participation has been viewed as a mechanism for capturing these values, and emphasis has been placed on improving techniques for achieving effective community interaction at the project level of planning, i.e., oriented toward the implementation of a particular highway segment contained within the broader regional plan. Community values become most intensely felt and expressed at this level, when the microscale impacts of a specific facility upon adjacent neighborhoods can be seen much more clearly.[36]

However, at a broader regional or metropolitan planning level it has not seemed possible to delineate alternative plans in sufficient detail to permit citizen participation. It might also seem somewhat premature to begin identifying and evaluating subarea, project-type alternatives, when the staging of such alternatives is actually anticipated to extend far into the future.

On the other hand, caution is required to avoid yielding to such difficulties at the risk of great costs in the future. A major problem in regional planning, particularly transportation planning, seems to be the tendency for early commitment to an overall plan, the real implications of which have not been considered effectively. Citizen participation as a mechanism for introducing the evaluation of local impacts of regional plans may indeed serve an important function in the regional planning process. To accomplish this, however, requires an effective participation method for this planning level. Some means of compromise between the microlevel of participation associated with project level or neighborhood/subarea plan evaluation, and broader, regional-level plan evaluation should be sought.

AN ALTERNATE APPROACH

In this section an alternative approach to regional plan evaluation is outlined. A version of this approach is being implemented by the San Diego Region Comprehensive Planning Organization (CPO). It attempts to overcome some of the problems considered earlier, particularly in relation to the assessment of community impacts in the regional planning context. The San Diego CPO is devoting more resources and has allowed a significantly longer time frame for the conduct of evaluation activities, in comparison with other regional planning programs. [37]

Figure 4.1 describes the structure of this strategy. Interrelationship between the three phases of the planning/evaluation process—goal formulation, plan development, and plan evaluation—emphasize that this approach is designed to be an integral part of the regional planning process and not simply a component to be added to the end of plan making. Close linkages between all elements are clearly required, including recycling between evaluation, goal formulation, and plan development to foster an understanding of local/regional impacts and trade-offs. Opportunities for expanded community participation through iterative evaluation are included in this process. The need to give balanced consideration to both macrolevel and microlevel plan consequences is emphasized.

Details of the Proposed Strategy

The essential features of the recommended approach are the development of plan-impact forecasts for both the regional and the community levels; the presentation of effective but simple impact

FIGURE 4.1

Plan Evaluation in the Regional Planning Process

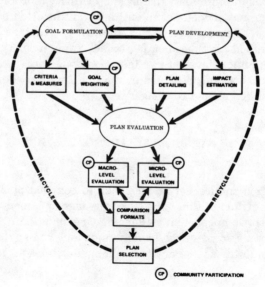

summaries to decision makers and citizen participants; the systematic, subjective assessment of plan impacts by such lay groups; and the iterative cycling of these subjective assessments among evaluators, and between evaluators and plan designers. While it is expected that the use of this general evaluation strategy, irrespective of specific techniques involved in its implementation, will improve regional plan evaluation, some more specific components are recommended for illustrative purposes.

To provide an informative bridge between forecasts of the impacts of regional development alternatives and subjective evaluation, an expanded cost-effectiveness framework is suggested. Cost-effectiveness analysis is an extension of the traditional cost-benefit approach to include nonmonetary impacts and to relate impacts to the attainment of goals and objectives, i.e. effectiveness. It focuses on a comprehensive assessment of goal-achievement, rather than simply capturing only the easily-measured benefits and costs. [38]

Cost-effectiveness analysis provides a quantitative framework describing the goal achievement properties of alternative plans at various levels of analysis. It organizes the numerical descriptors of plan effectiveness derived from forecasting models and other sources so that more subjective, and participative, techniques can be used to reduce the dimensionality of the information set for use in the decision process.

Figure 4.2 shows a cost-effectiveness summary sheet, prepared by planners to describe the effectiveness of each plan in meeting various goals. These summary data serve as inputs to subjective evaluation and decision making by representatives of affected communities and by regional policy makers.

To use this approach, individual goals, specific objectives, and associated criteria must be carefully defined through broadly based participative processes for preparing initial goal definitions, or at least for ratification of planner-developed definitions.

While the development of comprehensive goals and objectives may be the most difficult step in the evaluation process, it may also be the most important. Without such a value framework, there is no rational basis for evaluation by any method.

The summary sheet provides easily compared descriptors of goal-related plan impacts that should be prepared both for the affected communities and for the region as a whole. To the extent desired, effectiveness indicators can be aggregated using priority weights for each objective, and ratios of effectiveness to applicable costs can be computed. Data for use in this summary sheet should be available from planning models, special studies, and subjective assessments.

FIGURE 4.2

Cost-Effectiveness Summary Sheet

GOAL AREA: _____

ALTERNATIVE PLAN: _____ _____

Objectives	Criteria	Forecasted Impact	Normalized Impact	Relative Weight	Weighted Score
1.	a.				
	b.				
	c.				
2.	a.				
	b.				
3.	a.				
4.	a.				
5.	a.				
	b.				
	c.				
	d.				
6.	a.				

Summary Score	XXX
Applicable Costs	$$$
Cost-Effectiveness Ratio	XX/$$

To permit trade-offs and comparisons between objectives, it may be useful to convert measures of effectiveness to a common scale through "normalization," where each impact value would be converted to a percentage of the maximum or minimum value that might have bee achieved. For consistency in evaluation, only one average or "best" measure (among several possible measures) should be associated with each objective in the weighted scoring and comparative analyses.

The relative weights assigned to each objective could be derived from Delphi surveys (or similar techniques) in which various community groups and policy makers participate. [39] It would be useful to introduce different sets of community-developed weights at this point so that weighted plan scores might be generated to reflect the views of various interest groups. These weighted effectiveness scores woul be computed in each goal area and for each plan alternative. The final entry in the cost-effectiveness summary sheet would then consist of the calculation of a simple cost-effectiveness ratio, introducing applicable capital and operating costs for each alternative.

Facilitating Plan Comparisons

To develop a combined assessment for each plan over all goal areas, data from the summary sheets should be presented to citizens' groups and decision makers for subjective assessment. A format for accomplishing this is shown in Figure 4.3. Here, the evaluator is presented with current and predicted regional level values of each criterion for all alternative plans. Comparison of plans is accomplished by scanning across the table for each evaluative dimension, on a simple preference scale, perhaps ranging from zero to five.

Another device, such as that shown in Figure 4.4, is needed to explore differences in terms of microlevel or community impacts. Different comparison sheets, again one for each goal area, could be prepared to highlight the critical impacts of each of the important communities within the region. On each sheet, forecasted values and current values would again be shown for each community-level criterion. To promote consistency with the regional analysis, values of criteria for the regional level would also be included.

The preparation of Figure 4.4 would require the forecasting of impacts at the community level. While this represents a significant additional effort in regional planning, it is essential if the problems associated with the local impacts of regional plans are to be avoided.

Based on the information from formal forecasting procedures, community participants could use Figure 4.4 to make subjective assessments, again along a simple preference scale, of the alternative plans. But because impact forecasts alone are not likely to provide a sufficiently meaningful description of localized, community impacts, supplementary information may be desirable.

These might include architectural perspective drawings, as well as plan-view maps. Physical models may also be appropriate, and in some cases the preparation of narrative scenarios might clarify future conditions under each alternative plan. To allay fears regarding certain impacts, special presentations such as audio tapes simulating expected noise levels and special studies of air and water pollution might be developed at the community level. These efforts should provide participants with a comprehensive understanding of the expected quality of life under each alternative. Special studies need be carried only far enough to highlight the major community differences in impacts among alternative plans.

The participative effort should probably be carried out in group meetings, where all participants are offered the same information sets and have a chance to analyze, clarify, and comment on plan impacts. A format based on the charrette process is likely to be successful in this context.[40]

FIGURE 4.3

Regional Level Plan Comparison Sheet

GOAL AREA _____

OBJECTIVES	CRITERIA	PLAN EFFECTIVENESS CHARACTERISTICS			
		Alternative A	Alternative B	Alternative C	Alternative D
1.	a.				
	b.				
	c.				
2.	a.				
	b.				
3.	a.				
4.	a.				
5.	a.				
	b.				
	c.				
	d.				
6.	a.				
SUMMARY SCORE					
APPLICABLE COSTS					
COST-EFFECTIVENESS RATIO					

EXISTING CRITERION VALUE

FORECAST CRITERION VALUE

SUBJECTIVE RATING

FIGURE 4.4

Community Level Plan Comparison Sheet

GOAL AREA _____ COMMUNITY _____

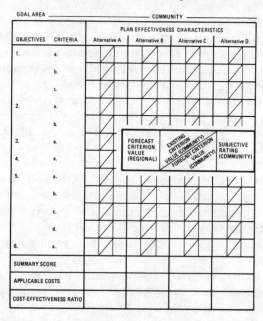

OBJECTIVES	CRITERIA	PLAN EFFECTIVENESS CHARACTERISTICS			
		Alternative A	Alternative B	Alternative C	Alternative D
1.	a.				
	b.				
	c.				
2.	a.				
	b.				
3.	a.				
4.	a.				
5.	a.				
	b.				
	c.				
	d.				
6.	a.				
SUMMARY SCORE					
APPLICABLE COSTS					
COST-EFFECTIVENESS RATIO					

FORECAST CRITERION VALUE (REGIONAL)

EXISTING CRITERION VALUE (COMMUNITY)

FORECAST CRITERION VALUE (COMMUNITY)

SUBJECTIVE RATING (COMMUNITY)

It should be relatively easy to summarize the results of both community and regional level subjective assessments. This can be accomplished by computing the mean subjective scores of plans on objectives, as well as the range of the distributions. Given previously or newly established goal weights, mean values for the aggregate scores of each plan on all goals can also be developed, along with ranges for the aggregate scores. Subjective assessments at each level would thus be conducted in two phases: (a) Each alternative would be rated on each objective (with mean scores computed), and (b) the objectives themselves would be weighted (with weighted mean scores computed).

Results of subjective assessment efforts at both levels of analysis should be returned to the original participants to give them an opportunity to revise their evaluations based on the views of all evaluators. The use of this Delphi-like iterative process could be a move toward establishing a consensus of evaluators at both regional and community levels.

It has also been shown that such iterative decision-making methods can lead to areas of persistent disagreement.[41] Such information, serving to highlight conflicts between regional and local-level impacts and between different communities at the local level, can be the most useful output of the evaluation process. Precise definitions of the areas and nature of disagreements can focus continuing attempts at conflict resolution, through clarification of impact forecasts, and open examinations of expected plan characteristics.

Perhaps of more importance to the planning process, such information can be used to modify alternative plans, using the iterative strategy shown in Figure 4.1.[42] In this way, plan design and participative evaluation through the community level can be linked, with the objective being the development and implementation of better plans, rather than simply the application of a new evaluation methodology.

CONCLUSIONS

Regional planning, and regional plan evaluation, must be more responsive to the community-scale impacts of proposed plans if the planning process is to produce viable, i.e., implementable, products. To accomplish this, ways must be found to sensitize planners to these critical impacts in plan evaluation. The proposed strategy would accomplish this by including the evaluation of localized effects on goal attainment and the quality of community life in the regional plan evaluation process. The focus would be on the development of information on expected regional and community impacts, in formats suitable for use in community interaction processes.

These processes would then provide an opportunity for subjective assessment of plan impacts by regional and community participants. Through organized interactive efforts, participants would be given the opportunity to make positive contributions to plan evaluation and plan design. Using an iterative design-evaluation process, participative evaluation from both local and regional levels can be used to effect the products of the planning process. This should serve not only to increa the interest of the public in citizen participation, but also to increase the responsiveness of regional plans to the needs of people.

While some detailed characteristics of this approach have been suggested herein, it is felt that the most important contributions will come from the use of this overall strategy, with whatever specific tec niques seem feasible.

NOTES

1. M. Wachs and J. L. Schofer, "Abstract Values and Concrete Highways," Traffic Quarterly (January 1969).

2. See Barton-Aschman Associates, Inc., "Guidelines for Long-Range Transportation Planning in the Twin Cities Region" (Minneapoli St. Paul, Minn.: Twin Cities Metropolitan Council, December 1971); W. Jessiman, D. Brand, A. Tumminia, and C. R. Brussee, "A Rational Decision-making Technique for Transportation Planning," Highway Research Record, no. 180 (Washington, D.C.: Highway Research Board, 1967); C. G. Schimpeler and W. L. Grecco, "Systems Evaluation: An Approach Based on Community Structure and Values," Highw Research Record, no. 238 (Washington, D.C.: Highway Research Board, 1968); K. Schlager, "The Rank-Based Expected Value Method of Plan Evaluation," Highway Research Record, no. 238 (Washington, D.C.: Highway Research Board, 1968).

3. Southeastern Wisconsin Regional Planning Commission, "Land Use/Transportation Study: Recommended Regional Land-Use and Transportation Plans," Planning Report No. 7, 3 (Waukesha, Wisc.: SEWRPC, November 1966); Schlager, op. cit.

4. Schimpeler and Grecco, op. cit.

5. F. S. Pardee, C. T. Phillips, and K. V. Smith, "Measureme and Evaluation of Alternative Regional Transportation Mixes: Volume 2, Methodology," RM-63-24-DOT (Santa Monica, Calif.: Rand Corporation, August 1970).

6. Wachs and Schofer, op. cit.

7. M. Skutsch and J. L. Schofer, "Goals Delphis for Urban Planning: Concepts in Their Design," Socio-Economic Planning Sciences 7 (1973).

8. J. E. Seley, "Development of a Sophisticated Opposition: The Lower Manhattan Expressway Issue" (Philadelphia: The Wharton School of Finance and Commerce, University of Pennsylvania, 1970).

9. A. M. Voorhees and Associates et al., "North Shore Draft Environmental Impact Statement, Preliminary Location Report, Program Package Evaluation Report" (Boston: The Commonwealth of Massachusetts, 1972).

10. A. Lupo, F. Colcord, and E. P. Fowler, Rites of Way; The Politics of Transportation in Boston and the U.S. City (Boston: Little, Brown, 1971); Seley, op. cit.

11. M. Wachs, B. M. Hudson, and J. L. Schofer, "Integrating Localized and Systemwide Objectives in Transportation Planning," Research Report (Los Angeles: School of Architecture and Urban Planning, UCLA, 1973).

12. D. E. Boyce, N. D. Day, and C. McDonald, "Metropolitan Plan Making" (Philadelphia: Regional Science Research Institute, 1970).

13. M. F. Hufschmidt, The Metropolitan Planning Process: An Exploratory Study (Chapel Hill, N.C.: University of North Carolina, August 1970).

14. Barton-Aschman Associates, Inc., and Creighton, Hamburg, Inc., "Development of Transportation Planning Work Program for the Delaware Valley Regional Planning Commission: Summary Report; Work Paper No. 3, Interagency Relationships; Work Paper No. 5, Implementation Strategies" (Philadelphia: Pennsylvania Department of Transportation, June 1973).

15. Pardee et al., op. cit.

16. Oak Ridge National Laboratory, "The Environment and Technology Assessment," Progress Report, June-December 1970 (Oak Ridge, Tenn.: The Laboratory, 1971); San Diego Region Comprehensive Planning Organization, "The Regional Model System" (San Diego, Calif.: The Organization, April 1972).

17. G. C. Gordon et al., "Highway Noise: A Design Guide for Highway Engineers," National Cooperative Highway Research Program Report 117 (Washington, D.C.: Highway Research Board, 1971).

18. Department of the Army, Chicago District Corps of Engineers, "Wastewater Management Study for Chicago—South End of Lake Michigan" (Chicago: The Department, July 1973), App. E.

19. G. Fellman, "Sociological Field Work Is Essential in Studying Community Values," Highway Research Record, no. 305 (Washington, D.C.: Highway Research Board, 1970).

20. G. S. Rutherford et al., "Goal Formulation for Socio-Technical Systems," Journal of the Urban Planning and Development Division 99, no. UP2, Proc. Paper 9987 (September 1973).

21. M. Scheibe, M. Skutsch, and J. L. Schofer, "Experiments in Delphi Methodology," in Delphi and Its Applications, H. Linstone and M. Turroff, eds. (1973); Skutsch and Schofer, op. cit.

22. W. S. Torgerson, Theory and Methods of Scaling (New York: Wiley, 1958.

23. Pardee et al., op. cit.

24. S. J. Bellomo and S. C. Provost, "Toward an Evaluation of Subarea Transportation Systems," Highway Research Record, no. 293 (Washington, D.C.: Highway Research Board, 1969).

25. C. H. Oglesby, B. Bishop, and G. E. Willeke, "A Method for Recisions Among Freeway Location Alternatives Based on User and Community Consequences," Highway Research Record, no. 305 (Washington, D.C.: Highway Research Board, 1970).

26. J. N. Bloom et al., "A Resource Allocation Model for Transportation Planning," Highway Research Record, no. 285 (Washington, D.C.: Highway Research Board, 1969).

27. Barton-Aschman Associates, Inc., "Guidelines . . . ," op. cit.

28. K. M. Goodman, "A Computerized Investigation and Sensitivi Analysis of a Linear Weighting Scheme for the Evaluation of Alternatives for Complex Urban Systems," thesis, Northwestern University, Evanston, Ill., 1971.

29. Jessiman et al., op. cit.

30. Oglesby et al., op. cit.

31. E. N. Thomas and J. L. Schofer, "Strategies for the Evaluation of Alternative Transportation Plans," National Cooperative Highway Research Program Report 96 (Washington, D.C.: Highway Research Board, 1970).

32. W. A. Steger and T. R. Lakshmanan, "Plan Evaluation Methodologies: Some Aspects of Decision Requirements and Analytical Response," Urban Development Models, Special Report 97, G. C. Hemmens, ed. (Washington, D.C.: Highway Research Board, 1968).

33. M. Hill, "A Goals-Achievement Matrix for Evaluating Alternative Plans," Journal of the American Institute of Planners 34 (January 1968).

34. Oglesby et al., op. cit.

35. H. Bleiker, J. H. Suhrbier, and M. L. Manheim, "Community Interaction as an Integral Part of the Highway Decision-making Process," Highway Research Record, no. 356 (Washington, D.C.: Highway Research Board, 1971); E. L. Falk, "Measurement of Community Values: The Spokane Experiment," Highway Research Record, no. 229 (Washington, D.C.: Highway Research Board, 1968); M. L. Manheim and J. H. Suhrbeir, "Community Values in Transportation

Project Planning," Transportation Research Forum, Proceeding, 12th Annual Meeting, Oxford, Ind. (1971).

36. Wachs et al., op. cit.

37. Barton-Aschman Associates, Inc., "Plan Evaluation and Selection Process: Final Report" (San Diego, Calif.: San Diego Region CPO, June 1972). Summary report also available.

38. N. Lichfield, "Cost-Benefit Analysis in City Planning," Journal of the American Institute of Planners 24 (November 1960); Thomas and Schofer, op. cit.

39. Scheibe et al., op. cit.

40. W. L. Riddick, Charrette Processes (York, Pa.: Shumway, 1971).

41. Scheibe et al., op. cit.

42. D. G. Stuart, "Staging the Evaluation of Alternative Regional Plans," presented at American Institute of Planners Confer-In 1972, Boston, October 1972.

5

URBAN INDICATORS:
THEIR ROLE
IN PLANNING

How can urban officials tell how well their city is doing? Is it a "good" place to live? Is it getting better or worse?

How can urban planners, in turn, tell how well they are doing? Do their plans and programs deal with the most serious needs and problems of the city? Are they aimed in the right direction? Most important, are these plans and programs contributing to a better environment? Do they make any difference, and, if so, how much difference?

These questions call for a particular kind of urban information—not just ordinary data or statistics, but "indicators" that measure quantitatively how well-off the city is. Urban indicators can be defined quite simply as measures of well-being or the quality of life within urban areas, along social, economic, cultural, environmental, and other related dimensions.

Urban indicators have a significant potential for improving the planning process. However, agency experience with them is presently quite limited. In this chapter, a preliminary framework for using indicators in urban planning is suggested. Using various examples, three different possible categories of urban indicator are identified. Various data resources are discussed, and several different roles within the planning process are outlined. Planning agency responsibility in further developing urban indicators is stressed and recommended.

Such urban indicators are usually used on a comparative basis. That is, they "indicate" the relative well-being of the city in comparis

---

Reprinted with permission from American Society of Planning Officials, <u>Planning Advisory Service Report No. 281</u> (June 1972).

with the same numbers collected for last year (or other previous years), in comparison with other cities, by comparing different subareas within the same city, and in comparison with the desired levels and directions of change that have been stated in the goals and objectives of the urban area.

The link between goals and indicators is an especially significant one. Indicators can show how much or how well a particular goal or objective has been achieved. If a specific standard of achievement has been set, they can indicate whether that standard has in fact been met.

There is consequently an important tie between the growing interest in urban indicators and the emergence of planning-programming-budgeting systems (PPBS) in urban public administration. The systems approach of PPBS calls for more clarity and precision in the planning and evaluation of public programs, in relation to the varying problems, needs, and goals of the city, and of its different subareas and communities. Greatly improved information resources are required for effective PPBS approaches, and urban indicators are useful improvements.

It should be stressed at the beginning, however, that urban indicators are in an early stage of development, and that much room remains for improvement. Very few cities, and very few urban or regional planning agencies, have to date attempted to use them. Because of this lack of experience, this chapter suggests a possible framework for using urban indicators, but this framework remains to be tested in practice.

The framework is organized around a classification of indicators by the types of information they provide. This classification scheme is in turn related to potential uses for indicators in urban planning. Each type suggests a certain level of planning and/or evaluation activities. There is consequently a strong interface with other innovative concepts in planning, such as state of the region reports, goals-oriented planning, and cost-effectiveness evaluation strategies. All of these related concepts, it should be emphasized, must also be further refined in the course of practical application.

What kinds of urban indicators should be sought? In general, one class of useful indicators deals with the city as a whole, or with its major subdistricts. These so-called social indicators provide a broad indication of overall condition. However, other types of more specific, plan- and program-related measures will probably also be required. Some of these more detailed urban indicators might deal with the impacts upon different population groups and geographic areas of particular plans and programs. Others might deal with the efficiency with which particular programs have been administered and with their ability to meet previously established targets and budgets.

Figure 5.1 suggests a preliminary sketch-concept of how urban indicators might be used in urban planning. In their broadest sense,

FIGURE 5.1

Urban Indicators in Urban Planning

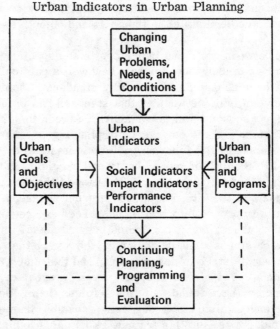

urban indicators of all types should probably be collected in a regular sequence, in response to changing urban problems, needs, and conditions, in order to document the direction and degree of change. These changing urban conditions in turn are often reflected in a broad range of urban goals and objectives that themselves can also be strongly reflected in most types of urban indicators. Because urban indicators should probably also be sensitive to the variety of alternative urban plans and programs that will be proposed and implemented in pursuit of desired goals, it becomes helpful to distinguish the three levels of urban indicators illustrated—social, impact, and performance.

Figure 5.1 also suggests that an important thrust for urban indicators can lie in facilitating the matching of urban plans and programs with the goals and objectives they are designed to achieve. Some indicators might tend simply to show how certain urban problems have become more or less serious and how certain goals and objectives assumed greater or lesser priority. Other indicators, however, can show how particular plans and programs have been (or could be) able to ameliorate problems, by showing progress in relation to past conditions and by showing progress in relation to stated goals and objectives.

New or innovative plans and programs could also be assessed on the basis of their potential for achieving greater gains—as measured by anticipated impacts upon key indicators. The overall result of these applications of urban indicators is, as illustrated in Figure 5.1, a continuing planning, programming, and evaluation activity that recycles through both the refinement of urban goals and objectives and the improvement of urban plans and programs.

The potentials for urban indicators shown in Figure 5.1 cannot be achieved, however, without solving several serious, but seemingly surmountable, problems. Among these problems are the practical difficulties involved in the proper identification of urban goals. Adequate participation, achieving consensus, and sufficient specificity are important considerations here. Similarly, proper definition of alternative plans and programs in terms related to applicable indicators can present practical problems in specificity. The need to identify goals and plans/programs carefully is discussed a number of times in the following pages.

Other important problems involve the data sources from which indicators may be derived. Often, needed data are not currently available, or available in an unsuitable form. It may be costly and time-consuming to correct these deficiencies. The forecasting of some indicators may also be costly. If mathematical models are already incorporated within an agency's planning program, some of these forecasting costs may already be absorbed, however. Various data sources and problems are discussed further in a subsequent section.

The remainder of the chapter is organized as follows. The first of the three following sections provides a more careful definition of the three different types of urban indicators (social, impact, performance). The second section then examines briefly the three basic information resources from which indicators may be derived—public agency records, community surveys, and the 1970 Census.

The third section describes and illustrates how urban indicators could be better employed in urban planning—in the development of state of the city or region reports, in facilitating more systematic planning and programming activities, and in permitting more meaningful evaluation of plans and programs already in some state of implementation. The final section of the chapter then discusses some of the factors involved in assigning responsibilities for the development of urban indicators to urban planning agencies. An appendix lists some basic questions that could be used in compiling potential agency data indicators.

URBAN INDICATORS DEFINED

This section describes how three different types of urban indicators may be distinguished and illustrates, by example, how specific indicators in each category have been utilized.

Social indicators, that have received a good deal of attention at the national level, deal with general community change.[1] They are usually areawide in context, and provide a general index of how well-off the urban area is. Impact indicators are detailed in nature, and can be utilized to assess the effectiveness of public agency plans and programs They are especially useful in cost-effectiveness strategies for planning and evaluation. Performance indicators, the most detailed of the three deal more with managerial and financial aspects of public agency plans and programs, and are therefore most useful in assessing the efficienc of program administration. They can also be used to generate cost-efficiency analyses.

The most general types of urban indicators, social indicators, can be broadly defined as measures of the aggregate well-being among the persons and families within a society, a city, or a neighborhood.[2]

These indicators, such as crime rates, disease rates, substandar housing rates, or unemployment rates, help gauge the quality of life within the geographic area to which they are referenced. However, the are general indicators of well-being, affected by many different public programs, plans, and policies. It is usually quite difficult to determin the degree of influence that any particular program may have on the ob served level of a given social indicator.

A recent report exploring the role of social indicators at the national level also illustrates in a general way their relevance at the urb level.[3] Table 5.1 outlines a series of major goals and related indicators described in that report, as they relate to five general program or functional areas. As the table suggests, a series of multiple indicators is needed under each program area, even though these have bee stated in the broadest of terms. Thus, at least 14 different measures can be associated with the broad objective of "reducing crime." Similarly, at least 22 different indicators can be mentioned as potential measures of "increased learning," each of which assesses a slightly different dimension of educational attainment. Each of the indicators listed might also be associated with more specific objectives—such as increasing the proportion of high school graduates.

Another approach to the identification and use of urban social indi cators lies in a recent comparative study of Washington, D.C., and 1 other large metropolitan areas.[4] As indicated in Table 5.2, Washington and the other areas were analyzed along 14 different dimensions, each representing some aspect of the quality of urban life. Only a single indicator was matched against each of these different dimensior Note that specific goals and objectives are not stated, though it is evident that the implication for improvement along each of these dimensions is a matter of concern. Relative rankings among the 18 cities also represent some measure of the seriousness of the associated conditions, and also thereby imply the urgency with which goals might be stated. All of the 14 indicators were determined for two points in time (such as 1964 and 1968), in order to gain some measure of progress or retrogression, both within each urban area and in comparison with the others.

Neither of the indicators and associated or implied objectives listed in Tables 5.1 and 5.2 should be regarded as preferred or all-inclusive. They are clearly exploratory in nature. Additional goals and indicators could easily be added, and many of these would be likely to present slightly different pictures. In the Washington study, for example, while the number of infant deaths per 1,000 live births was used as a measure of health, as many as 60 indicators in the health field could have been chosen. In other fields, however, the choice of pertinent data was quite limited. For many quality-of-life dimensions, it may well be desirable to derive a combined index that represents a number of different indicators pertaining to that dimension.

While social indicators can be extremely valuable in indicating the current and changing status of key urban problems, it is difficult, as noted above, to relate them to particular public programs and plans. In order to better assess these plans and programs themselves, indicators that are more closely related to the characteristics of local public services, rather than to the general characteristics of the society at large, are likely to be needed. For example, student achievement rates on a grade-level basis, for particular schools or for participants in particular educational programs, are more revealing than simply the overall percentage of high school graduates within the city or neighborhood.

In general, this increased specificity can enable indicators to be more closely associated with individual programs and program-related objectives, in order to facilitate local planning and evaluation efforts. Like social indicators, impact indicators are also in an early stage of development. In many cases, data relating to the actual or anticipated impact of different public projects is difficult to assemble.

This difficulty was demonstrated in a recent evaluation of selected Model Cities Projects conducted for the city of Chicago.[5] An attempt was made in part to outline how achievement and attitudinal indicators of student, teacher, parent, and community impacts of educational programs and projects could be utilized. Full use of these indicators was not made in the actual evaluation project conducted, largely because of the relatively short duration of the evaluation assignment. This education project, known as Cooperative Planned Urban Schools (CO-PLUS), consisted of a series of eight coordinated project components aimed at providing a saturation of personnel, materials, and services in seven elementary schools.

TABLE 5.1

Major Goals and Indicators: Toward a Social Report

Area	Goal	Indicator
Health	Improve Health	Life expectancy by age, sex, and race Disease incidence rates by race and income Age-specific death rates by sex Life expectancy free of bed-disability and institutional confinement by age, sex, and race Infant mortality rates by race Mental hospitalization rates Maternal mortality rates by race Frequency of physician and dentist visits by race and income
Education	Increase Learning	Percentage of high school graduates, by age, race, income Percentage of college graduates, by age, race, income School achievement testing, grades 1-3-6-9-12, by race and family income Armed Forces Qualification Test, by race and family income College entrance scholastic aptitude test, by race and family income College enrollment rate, by tested ability and socioeconomic status

Area	Goal	Indicator
Public Safety	Reduce Crime	Crimes per 100,000 persons (homicide, rape, aggravated assault, robbery, burglary, larceny, auto theft) Value of property involved in theft, per $1,000 of appropriable property Victimization rates by age and sex Victimization rates by race and income Percent of persons expressing fear of neighborhood crime (via survey) Criminal arrests by age bracket per 100,000 persons
Income	Increase Family Economic Security	Median family income, by race Median personal income, by race and sex
	Reduce the Number of Povery Income Families	Number of families with incomes below poverty levels, by age, family status, and sex of head
Environment	Reduce Pollution of the Natural Environment	Air pollution levels Dissolved oxygen rates Coliform bacteria counts
	Improve Quality of the Man-Made Environment	Substandard housing rates Overcrowded housing rates Indexes of residential segregation Proportion of non-poverty families living in poverty areas, by race Rents paid for comparable housing, by race

TABLE 5.2

Comparative Social Indicators: Washington, D.C.

Quality of Life	Indicator	Washington's Rank*	Quality of Life	Indicator	Washington's Rank*
Poverty	% Low Income Households	2nd	Traffic Safety	Traffic Death Rate	7th
Unemployment	% Unemployed	4th	Air Pollution	Air Pollution Index	8th
Racial Equality	Non-White/White Unemployment Rates	4th	Income Level	Per Capita Income	10th
Mental Health	Suicide Rate	5th	Housing	Cost of Housing	10th
Health	Infant Mortality Rate	7th	Social Disintegration	Narcotics Addiction Rate	13th
			Community Concern	Per Capita United Fund Contributions	14th
			Public Order	Reported Robbery Rate	16th
			Education	Draft Rejection Rate	18th
			Citizen Participation	Presidential Voting Rate	18th

* Among the nation's 18 largest metropolitan areas.

NOTE: Lower numerical rankings represent more favorable conditions as of most recent available data. In 3 cases, not all 18 areas are represented.

Table 5.3 lists the wide range of impact indicators that were
utilized and recommended by the evaluation consultant. Many of these
had previously been used in the Coleman Report,[6] a federally sponsored
study that attempted to define the outcomes of educational services in
terms of impact upon pupil achievement and motivation.

As Table 5.3 illustrates, the majority of the impact indicators
used in the CO-PLUS evaluation are project-specific in nature. Many
of them, particularly, deal with the perceptions of instructional team
leaders, teachers, and parents regarding improvements in the school
environment; while others deal with "harder" data—test scores,
attendance rates, teacher-turnover rates, etc. Four general sources
of data were utilized: test results and records of the board of education,
the results of a resident-attitude survey conducted by the Model Cities
agency (City Demonstration Agency: CDA) the CDA project-monitoring
information system, and specialized surveys conducted by the evaluation consultant.

In the Chicago project it was stressed that indicators of the type
shown in Table 5.3 should continue to be used in project assessments,
especially as an historical pattern of comparative data is accumulated.
However, it also became evident that additional indicators should
probably also be added. Table 5.4 identifies an illustrative list of
possible additional educational indicators. In many cases it will be
necessary to devise specialized measurement or survey techniques
in order to operationalize these indexes.

In general, it was recommended that all of these indicators
(Tables 5.3 and 5.4) be subject to further review and refinement,
since new and more meaningful indexes may emerge through further
analysis of educational services and problems, as other specialized
educational projects are devised that aim at particular problems, as
more carefully controlled project experimentation techniques are
used, and as information availability and measurement improvements
are made.

Of special importance in improving our ability to effectively
utilize impact-oriented urban indicators will be our ability to identify
meaningful and measurable objectives to which these indicators
relate. The close relationship between the indicators shown in Tables
5.3 and 5.4 and neighborhood objectives for educational well-being
and improvement should be stressed. As with more general social
indicators, the basic purpose of impact indicators will still be to
permit meaningful assessment of the attainment of community objectives.

To illustrate this key relationship between indicators and objectives, Table 5.5 shows how a variety of possible educational objectives,
expressed in fairly specific terms, might be associated with the five

TABLE 5.3

Education Indicators: Chicago Model Cities Program

Type	Indicator	Source
Student achievement and behavior	Student achievement tests, grades 1, 2, 3, 4, 5	Board of Education test results
	School attendance rates	Board of Education records
	Teacher opinions on: improved pupil attitudes increased energy levels pupil reaction to nutrition program	Consultant Survey
	Improved health, as implied by: no. of pupils receiving medical treatment no. of pupils receiving dental treatment	CDA Information System
Student attitudes and motivation	Interest in learning (11 questions) Self-concept (17 questions) Socialization (17 questions)	Consultant Survey
Teacher attitudes and sensitivity	Teacher turnover rates Identification of new teacher team effectiveness Identification of new curriculum needs Feeling of improved community relations	Board of Education Records Consultant Survey

Type	Indicator	Source
Teacher attitudes and sensitivity	Greater availability of teaching time	Board of Education Records
	Feeling of improved parent understanding	Consultant Survey
	Feeling of valuable participation by parents	
	Greater feeling of sensitivity to pupil needs	
Parent attitudes and perceptions	Estimates of parent-team effectiveness	Consultant Survey
	Feeling of CO-PLUS School Improvement	
	Desire to participate on planning teams again	CDA Information System
	Participation rates for parent-team planning committees	
Community attitudes and perceptions	Awareness of the CO-PLUS Program	CDA Resident Attitude Survey
	Feeling that it is doing a good job of serving children	
	Feeling that it is doing a good job of serving adults	
	Awareness of CO-PLUS job opportunities	
	Awareness of community evening school	
	Participation rates for community evening school	CDA Information System

TABLE 5.4

Possible Additional Education Indicators: Chicago Model Cities Program

Type	Indicator	Source
Student achievement and behavior	Truancy rates Dropout rates (HS) Detention rates Delinquency rates Disciplinary referral rates Teacher assault rates (HS) School tardiness rates School vandalism rates	Board of Education Records
Student attitudes and motivation	Self-directed study index Classroom climate index	Consultant Survey
	Participation in school recreation programs	Board of Education Records
Teacher attitudes and sensitivity	Teacher absenteeism Teacher effectiveness ratings	Board of Education Records Consultant Survey

Type	Indicator	Source
Parent attitudes and perceptions	Feeling of better understanding of children's needs	Consultant Survey
	Feeling that parent participation is valuable	Consultant Survey
Community attitudes and perceptions	Satisfaction with community evening school	Consultant Survey
	Career upgrading as a result of evening school	
	Family income increases due to evening school	
	Feeling that CO-PLUS Program has made schools more relevant to community	CDA Resident Attitude Survey
	Feeling that CO-PLUS Program will enable children to get better jobs	

156

categories of education indicators. Many of these illustrative objectives are stated directly in terms of the indicators with which they are associated. For example, "to improve student reading ability" would be assessed using the results of reading comprehension tests as indicators of goal achievement.

Many impact indicators might also be matched against the costs of the plans or programs to which they are related. The cost-effectiveness strategy for plan and program evaluation is especially relevant here. This strategy calls for major direct and indirect costs (particularly, of course, the costs of implementation for the sponsoring public agency) of each alternative to be associated with its varying levels of impact or effectiveness. A subset of cost-effectiveness indicators or ratios might then be defined, matching costs against particular impact indicators (for example, training costs per successful job placement, for three alternative job training programs.)

While most planners and researchers concerned with urban problems are likely to turn to impact indicators when they think of assessing the effects that various public programs have upon those problems, this view is often the exception rather than the rule for the typical public administrator.

An examination of the data and records processed by most urban public agencies (such as school boards, welfare agencies, health departments, police departments, housing and building departments, etc.) reveals that much of these data deal with routine administrative and budgetary operations. They deal largely with the quantity of services delivered, rather than with the eventual effects of those services. They represent a natural extension of the administrator's concern for who is doing what in his agency, and at what cost. When such data are compared with the aggregate costs of different programs, they also provide some measure of how well or efficiently the agency is performing.

There is an all-too-frequent tendency to confuse these "performance indicators" with impact indicators, since they do represent one result of the expenditure of dollars in any public service program. However, they usually are still only measures of how the agency spent its particular budget, and not what was actually accomplished for those persons and families receiving services (i.e., changes in their socioeconomic status).

Examples of such measures abound. For example, they include the number of persons employed or trained, the number of staff hours expended in a particular activity, children examined, facilities established, breakfasts served, individuals taking courses, families receiving particular types of services, vacant lots cleaned, dwelling units cleared, dwelling units rehabilitated, etc. Such measures do

TABLE 5.5

Possible Education Objectives:
Chicago Model Cities Program

Indicator Type	Possible Related Neighborhood Objectives
Student Achievement and Behavior	To raise student achievement levels. To improve student reading ability. To improve student mathematics ability. To increase school attendance rates. To reduce school vandalism rates. To improve the physical health of students.
Student Attitude and Motivation	To increase student motivation for learning. To improve the self-concept of students. To improve the socialization of students. To increase students' sense of environmental control. To increase student motivation for further schooling. To increase the percentage of high school graduates.
Teacher Attitudes and Sensitivity	To reduce teacher turnover rates. To increase teacher effectiveness. To reduce teacher absenteeism. To increase the time available for teaching. To increase teacher sensitivity to pupil needs. To improve teacher/parent/community relations.
Parent Attitudes and Perceptions	To increase parent understanding of educational procedures. To increase parent participation in educational planning. To increase parent understanding of pupil needs. To improve school/parent relations.
Community Attitudes and Perceptions	To increase community awareness of special educational services. To improve community attitudes toward youth education. To improve community attitudes toward adult education. To increase community awareness of adult education opportunities. To increase participation in community evening schools. To improve school/community relations.

TABLE 5.6

Typical Performance Indicators

Type	Indicator
Direct	Family visits completed Complaints investigated Textbooks purchased Paraprofessionals employed Committee meetings held Parent-teacher groups organized Staff members trained Staff hours expended Mobile classrooms provided Swimming pools constructed Kitchen units installed Family referrals made Brochures distributed Service requests received Orientation sessions held Building inspections completed Audio-visual equipment purchased
Intermediate	Students enrolled Children examined Breakfasts served Vacant lots cleaned Sidewalks repaired Students counseled Adults enrolled in evening school Families served Citizens on committees Citizens attending meetings Dwelling units cleared

provide an indication of program achievement in terms of providing services, but not in terms of achieving objectives that pertain to improving the quality of life within urban areas. They are all essentially measures of inputs (services provided), rather than expected outputs (neighborhood or family change).

Table 5.6 illustrates several examples of potential performance indicators. Note that a distinction can generally be made between measures that relate directly to services provided—such as number of paraprofessionals employed, number of orientation sessions held, number of parent-teacher groups organized, etc.—and what may be termed as intermediate measures of impact—such as number of students enrolled, number of students counseled, number of breakfasts served, or number of persons enrolled in evening school. Direct performance measures usually relate specifically to what the agency itself may have provided, in terms of staff, materials, facilities, meetings held, groups organized, etc. Each of these items can be easily related to cost and budget categories.

Intermediate measures, on the other hand, usually relate to the recipients of services, but still represent only the crudest measure of impact—simply whether a service was received or not. They thereby are probably more a measure of agency performance than anything else, which is why they are classed here. In general, only when it can be determined what changes resulted in the daily lives of recipients can the resultant data be classed in the impact-effectiveness category.

Still, however, it may often be useful to examine performance indicators as a means for quickly telling how well a project has been administered. Certainly, governmental decision makers and administrators look upon such data as quite important in managing the progress of programs. The point is that they should not see these direct and intermediate indicators of services provided as representing the full measure of what the agency has accomplished. Rather, the need for both performance and impact indicators should be better understood, by administrators, planners, and others.

The utility of performance indicators can often be increased considerably when they are matched against associated costs. The resulting cost-efficiency ratios or indexes give a measure of how well a project has been run. For example, expenditures per student, cost per dwelling unit inspection, and similar indicators can give a rough indication of value received for each public dollar spent. A more meaningful measure of value received, of course, will typically lie with the comparable cost-effectiveness indicators mentioned above. Other dimensions of cost-efficiency can also be derived via comparisons with predetermined schedules, budgets, staffing loads, service targets, and similar management targets.

BASIC INFORMATION RESOURCES

Where can urban indicators be obtained? Which urban data appear to have value as potential indicators, and which do not? This section reviews three general information resources from which urban indicators may be derived. The first, public-agency records, clearly contains the greatest overall potential for generating urban indicators of all three types, but is hampered by the presence of much data that are irrelevant or of marginal value in its present form. The second, community surveys, though much more expensive to collect, offers an opportunity for generating important perceptual or attitudinal indicators relating to urban conditions and programs. The third, 1970 Census data, is of more limited value, but still represents an important data resource for urban planning.

A major source of data from which urban indicators of all three types may be derived consists of public-agency records. These records may or may not be computerized, a factor that is helpful but not essential in the development of urban indicators. Computerized files may exist within single agencies or within coordinated interagency urban information systems or data banks. [7]

Two broad types of agency data should probably be distinguished— resource-related data, reflecting primarily the quantity of services delivered and the number of dollars spent by various categories, and client-related data, relating primarily to the individuals and families who have received services, and/or the geographic zones or subareas by which services are administered. The great bulk of this data of both types is, of course, used primarily for agency administrative purposes. This often includes the monitoring of agency and individual program progress, from a management point of view.

In terms of their potential utilization as urban indicators, it may be helpful to further distinguish three general categories of public-agency data. Both resource and client-related data would fall in each category.

1. Program-Project Data. The first category involves agency project/ program data generated directly within individual projects or activities. Many of these data will be likely to involve potential use as performance or efficiency indicators, relating to the details of project administration, while others may begin to involve potential for longer-term measures of project impact upon clients. Many of these data are fairly routine, involving matters of fiscal and administrative management in the provision of services. They can permit us, however, to get an indication of whether a project has been kept on schedule and within budgets. There appears to be a general need to increase the quantity of impact-related data contained within these types of agency records.

2. Intraagency Data. Another impact-related type of agency data consists of agencywide records that may involve more than one particular project, perhaps covering all related agency services or operations. Such data may permit comparisons between innovative and conventional services and their associated impacts. Data of this type could also be quite useful in situations where specialized programs were administered in only a few agencies, facilities, or jurisdictions, on an experimental or test basis. Other facilities or jurisdictions displaying similar characteristics would then serve, in effect, as a kind of control group against which the experimental services could be compared. Consequently, equivalent data for these control groups would be necessary in order to permit

meaningful comparisons. Again, client-related data would be
especially needed to permit an assessment of program or project
impact.
3. Interagency Data. The third type of agency data of potential value
   in developing urban indicators would, for a specific agency, relate
   to the projects and programs conducted by other agencies. These
   would include person- and family-based records kept by other
   agencies (such as school boards, health departments, welfare
   agencies, employment training centers, etc.) that may provide
   basic demographic and historical data whose collection need not be
   duplicated unnecessarily.

Again, client- and subarea-related data would probably be of
primary concern here, and both impact and/or general social indicators
would be likely to be generated. In fact, more general data of this
type, difficult to relate to an individual program, but more often
describing the characteristics of a neighborhood or community as a
whole, probably represent the primary multiple-agency source for
most urban social indicators. In many cases, the need for interagency cooperation in the delivery of complementary services (such
as day care services, preschool education, employment training for
working mothers) is usually accompanied by a need for interagency
records coordination.

Public agency data that may be computerized and/or incorporated
within an urban information system merit special attention, since these
data have considerable potential for detailed analysis, particularly
where a large number of observations or records are involved. The
possibility of matching different records referenced to a common
identification system (such as street addresses) offers a potential for
performing comparative analyses via computer that would be pro-
hibitively expensive otherwise. However, it should be stressed that
the bulk of the data files commonly included within management-
oriented urban information systems deal primarily with fiscal-related
performance indicators. They may be of some value in the area of
performance/efficiency analysis.

The types of data that are commonly computerized by municipal
agencies, county agencies, school boards, and other local governmental jurisdictions include cost accounting and inventory control,
purchasing and cash-flow analysis, personnel payroll and accounting,
hospital and health statistics, meter reading and billing, student class
scheduling and attendance reporting, property assessments and tax
billing, building and housing codes violations, zoning classification
and changes, arrest and conviction records, and similar records.
Where potentially useful for planning purposes, some of these data

may require reprocessing or reorganization (for example, by particular geographic areas).

An example of the use of computerized data files on a coordinated interagency basis for the development of both social and impact indicators is provided by the Neighborhood Early Warning System (NEWS) proposed for Washington, D.C.[8] Under this system, a common geographic referencing system (block-face location) would be used to match the records of the assessor's office, zoning board, housing department, building department, health department, welfare department, and police department. By monitoring, on a monthly and annual basis, selected key indicators derived from these agency files, such as welfare payments, criminal offenses, and housing code violations, it is proposed that a summary index of neighborhood deterioration be derived. This index, for a variety of neighborhoods across the urban area, would be monitored and computed on a month-to-month basis in order to identify those neighborhoods where critical change may be occurring. Table 5.7 lists the data-bank indicators that would be utilized.

Many urban social-action and community-improvement programs have as one of their most fundamental, yet elusive, goals, an improvement in local perceptions of community well-being.

Thorough utilization of urban indicators consequently suggests that indexes be devised for identifying changes in these more subjective, judgmental types of impacts. The best way to address the opinions, values, and attitudes held by individuals is probably to survey them—particularly when changes in these attitudes or perceptions from year to year are of critical concern. These types of measures have been referred to as "subjective social indicators"—measures of the perceptions of a neighborhood or target population regarding the planning and/or evaluation of programs aimed at that neighborhood or group.

It should be recognized, however, that collecting opinions from a sample of residents as a measure of problems and needs is an expensive proposition, fraught with many technical and procedural difficulties. In many cases such surveys may be inappropriate. They should not be used as a substitute for more objective information. As noted above, social and impact indicators derived from public-agency records may often be able to document progress or retrogression in various problem or program areas satisfactorily. Subjective social indicators of this type are consequently supplementary, aimed more at obtaining community relevancy than precise measurement. The literature on concepts and methods for conducting community surveys is extensive, and a recent report has developed a prototype series of questions relevant to the identification of subjective social indicators.[9]

TABLE 5.7

Computerized Urban Indicators: Washington, D. C.

Source	Indicator
Assessor's Office	Assessed value of land Assessed value of improvements Assessed value per square foot Year of last reassessment Sales information Depreciation index
Zoning Board	Land use category Number of floors Class, relative to quality of original construction
Building Department	Type of licensed business activities Number and type of rental dwelling units
Housing Department	Address of housing code violation Type of violation
Health Department	Address of health violation Type of violation
Welfare Department	Address of welfare recipient Type of welfare received Number of persons receiving welfare
Police Department	Address of criminal offense Type of offense

This project discusses in detail the methodology and pretesting involved in survey design, and reviews some of the key conceptual problems involved in interpreting the results of any value-oriented survey. The sample questions were developed in a series of 15 different perceptual areas, all contributing to some degree to the development of an overall "social profile" of the neighborhood area or areas surveyed. Among these question areas are specific satisfactions and dissatisfactions with the community as a place to live (implicitly, resident-held perceptions of problems and goals), perceptions of the responsiveness and relevance of local government, experience with social-service agencies and programs, and attitudes toward community action aimed at solving specific problems.

The National Opinion Research Center (NORC) reports suggest four different methods for gathering survey data regarding community-perceived problems and conditions. It is suggested that the first set of questions on this topic be open-ended—simply asking what three or four things are liked best or least about living in the neighborhood. These could be followed by so-called omnibus questions, both positively and negatively oriented, listing some 10 to 15 different conditions (such as housing conditions, food prices, neighborhood appearance, public transportation, medical care, fire protection, police protection, unemployment, etc.), and asking for comparative ratings among them (excellent, good, fair, or poor, for example).

However, the answers gained here are likely to be somewhat superficial in nature. If particular problem areas are especially important to the survey, additional, more detailed questions regarding the different aspects of these problems should be asked as well. Finally, it is also suggested that a simple one-question measure of overall satisfaction or dissatisfaction with the neighborhood should probably also be added.

While questions dealing with general community conditions are likely to yield measures of the social-indicator type, more specific questions dealing with particular public agency services can also yield responses of the impact-indicator type. The NORC study suggests four broad categories of questions that might be utilized here. A first type of question, especially in relation to those problem areas seen as most serious by the respondent, would be to elicit his opinion regarding the ability of the community to deal effectively with that problem. His willingness to participate in local efforts to deal with the problem might also be probed.

Related to and extending this line of questioning could be a series of queries that address the respondent's perception of local government—his ease of access to government officials, the effect of city government in general upon his own life, its effect upon his neighborhood, and open-ended questions regarding the programs the respondent might like to see implemented. A third series of questions might then deal directly with the services provided by specific agencies. These could deal with knowledge of an agency and its purpose, respondent's contacts with the agency, if any, and his general evaluation of how well the agency is doing.

Demographic and housing data collected during the 1970 Census will be of somewhat limited value in supporting the development of urban indicators. Its main drawback is simply that it is collected too infrequently (every ten years), while most urban indicators should probably be collected on an annual basis. However, the 1970 Census could provide a base line against which to measure future change in some indicators, primarily related to broader measures of community change (social indicators).[10] Data for small geographic areas may, in some cases, also be associated with the impacts of a particular program.

In cases where the need for annually updated data is not serious, census figures might also be quite valuable in providing some of the secondary demographic data needed to analyze indicator/program relationships. These include such basic demographic data (summarized for a variety of geographic areas, such as enumeration districts, block groups, census tracts, community areas, traffic analysis, zones, etc.), as age, race, marital status, family income, education, household size, and unemployment. The relationship between these variables various urban problems, and associated public service programs may help to clarify the relevance of those programs. Such data may in part document neighborhood or other subarea well-being, though annual change in such indicators would still be of primary concern. Among these possible census-derived urban indicators are: substandard housing rates, vacancy rates, average monthly rentals, overcrowding rates, average dwelling-unit size, age-composition ratios, median family income, racial-composition characteristics, average family size, and family-size characteristics.

Data collection improvements adopted for the 1970 Census may well be of great value in improving other urban indicators. These innovations have largely to do with the expanded usage of geographic coding guides that permit a wide variety of spacial data to be identified with a unique street-address location. Any data item, including much of the data collected by local public agencies, could also be so referenced as a part of original data collection. All data reported by street address could then, using census-developed computer programs, be summed by block or census tract, or aggregated according to other user-defined geographic units (enumeration districts, traffic analysis zones, neighborhood areas, public aid service districts, Model Cities neighborhoods, etc.). These census improvements in geographic coding, and the accompanying ability to aggregate and disaggregate data much more freely, could do much to improve the coordination of a wide variety of urban indicators.

USING URBAN INDICATORS

Urban indicators can be of considerable value in assessing current and projected urban conditions, as well as the effectiveness and efficiency of public-agency plans and programs. Their potential role in the urban planning process should consequently be further detailed.

One major use for urban indicators lies in the possible development of a regularly published "state of the city" report, showing where and how an urban area may have progressed or declined. A second potential use lies in strengthening the planning process itself, along more systematic, objectives-oriented lines. A third area of possible application involves the more rigorous evaluation of plans and programs already implemented, again in terms of appropriate urban objectives. All three uses for urban indicators are discussed in this section.

State of the City Reports

Much of the recent literature and thinking in the area of urban
indicators has dealt primarily with only one type—social indicators.
Furthermore, considerable attention has been given to social indicators
in terms of a national frame of reference. The focus of much of this
interest has centered upon the development of an annual status report
on the social well-being of the nation, comparable to the economic
report generated yearly by the President's Council of Economic
Advisors. As noted earlier, HEW produced a pilot effort of this type
in 1969. That report stressed the fact that many desirable measures
for gauging progress toward the achievement of social goals are
presently not available, hindering any complete or adequate social
accounting. Even though much progress remains to be made in the
quality of the data utilized, the concept of a national social report
has a good deal of attractiveness.

Most of the indicators that have been suggested for use in national-
level social reports deal with conditions that are largely urban in
nature, involving social mobility, income and poverty, public order
and safety, health and illness, the physical environment, and most
other aspects of society that are strongly influenced by urban con-
centrations of population. In fact, most social, economic, and environmental statistics deal with urban phenomena, and have their original
point of collection in urban areas.

The concept of an annual state of the city (or county or region)
report consequently represents a natural and logical extension of the
national social report idea, with all of its attendant attributes. Such
state of the city reports could be of great value in assisting both local
decision makers in setting priorities and identifying key areas of
change and impending difficulty, as well as state and national decision
makers in assessing comparative conditions within different urban
areas, as a guide, in part, in setting priorities among a wide range
of financial assistance programs.

A recent Michigan study offers an example of how such social
reporting might be undertaken at both state and local levels. [11] This
study recommended, at the state level, that an executive agency
(such as the research section of the state's bureau of the budget,
already producing an annual economic report) begin the preparation
of an annual social goals and indicators report to the governor. The
primary purpose of such a report would be the provision of regular
and reliable public information on the quality of life in the state. It is
further proposed that supplemental in-depth annual reports be prepared
in selected program areas, with lawful behavior, environmental

quality, health, and education indicators suggested as initial intensive
study areas.

A companion program for improving the quality of data available
for use as indicators in Michigan is also recommended. (The bulk of
the report represented a detailed assessment of the types of data now
available in six program areas.) Similar recommendations are made
for "quality of life reporting" in the Detroit metropolitan area, under
the sponsorship of the Southeast Michigan Council of Governments
(SEMCOG). Considerably more detail with regard to geographic subareas and different socioeconomic groups would be required.

Such annual state of the city or region reports could effectively
be coordinated with the annual reports already prepared by many
municipalities and public agencies—including most planning agencies.
In fact, the orientation of planning-agency annual reports toward the
examination of key urban indicators, primarily social indicators, but
perhaps including selected impact indicators in relation to major
programs, could considerably strengthen the value of that document.
Some of the key functions of such a report, including the provision of
an accounting to the public, generating support for the planning
activity, and educating the reader concerning the purposes and procedures of planning, could be broadened to include not only the
efforts and activities of the planning agency, but the changing status
of the urban area itself.[12] The projects, plans, and programs pursued
by the planning agency could then be better related to the range of
urban problems and opportunities that they actually address. Such an
approach might also assist in agency self-examination—by comparing
what the planning agency is doing with the changing status of key urban
problems.

Systematic Planning and Programming

Closely allied with and extending the concept of state of the city
reports is their possible incorporation within an overall systematic
planning process. Under such a process, annual or biennial state of
the city reports would represent the "current status" portion of a
broader plan or program aimed at improving the achievement of those
community goals and objectives around which the status report has
been organized.

Figure 5.2 illustrates a simple definition of the four basic phases
in the "systems approach," as utilized in public administration, civil
engineering, operations research, military and defense analysis,
and, increasingly, in urban and regional planning. The thrust of this

FIGURE 5. 2

Basic Steps in the Systems Approach

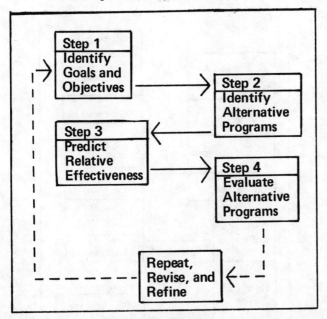

approach lies mainly in making planning more goals-oriented.
Greater emphasis on goals consequently calls for a more careful use
of urban data, particularly those data which can be classed as
"indicators" of goal-achievement. Regardless of the context of
application (planning or nonplanning), the underlying thrust of "system
analysis" is simply to be systematic, well-organized, and logical.
The four basic steps or phases include (a) identifying goals and objectives, (b) identifying alternative programs and policies, (c) predicting/
analyzing relative levels of effectiveness, (d) evaluating alternative
programs and policies.

Figure 5. 3 depicts a slightly expanded version of the systematic
planning process, permitting the potential utilization of urban indicators in support of that process to be more clearly identified.

Step 1 in the approach, identifying community objectives, would
deal with many of the goals and objectives around which state of the
city reports are organized. This step would involve the continuing
identification and clarification of local problems, needs, issues, and
conditions around which statements of desired improvement have been
made.

As noted in Figure 5. 3, these statements may originate with
political decision makers, public-agency administrators, or citizens

FIGURE 5.3

Systematic Planning Process: Generalized Prototype

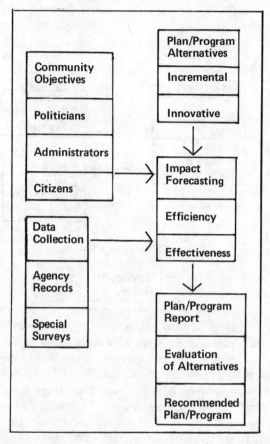

and community groups. The role of the planner here will lie in assuring that all affected parties have properly voiced their concerns, and in attempting to devise or derive measurements of how well objectives are or are not being achieved.

This key need for the quantitative assessment of objectives wherever possible again represents a major role for urban indicators. For broader planning processes (such as Model Cities or land-use/transportation planning) it has been observed that major emphasis in applying the systems approach should lie with the first two steps (see Chapter 3), enhancing even further the need for meaningful quantification and the use of urban indicators. At this level, special attention should be given to the broadest type of indicator, those dealing with general community change. It should be noted, particularly, that at all levels of potential application (including more detailed program and project planning), different quantitative measures for the same objective or objectives will usually be applicable. Quantitative measures and indicators should consequently be under continual refinement.

The second step of the systems approach, identifying alternative plans or programs, also provides a possible role for urban indicators. Experience has shown that meaningful assessment of urban programs is generally possible only when they are themselves measurable in terms of the objectives to which they apply. Consequently, urban indicators of the second two types, relating to both agency effectiveness and efficiency, appear to be relevant here. Experience with PPBS versions of the systems approach has shown that a reorganization of records keeping will often be required, so that program components may be properly identified in relation to the objectives they pursue.

The fact that programs will usually apply to more than one objective, and that they may often overlap among themselves, calls for particularly sensitive measures and indicators of separable accomplishments. As Figure 5.3 suggests, alternatives may be both incremental, in relation to the status quo, and more imaginative and innovative.

The third step, impact or effectiveness forecasting, essentially involves the bringing together of objectives and alternative programs into an analysis format. To the extent that urban indicators will have already been used in the continuing identification and clarification of both objectives and programs, further usage of indicators here is likely to be small. Instead, other types of data are likely to be required to establish programs/objectives relationships. These data have sometimes been referred to as "intervening variables," in that they describe some of the intervening operations or characteristics that influence the use of program resources in eventually relating to "output" measures or indicators (the achievement of objectives). Impact forecasting should probably be undertaken only at more detailed levels of planning application (analysis of urban systems, programs, or problems), so that both public agency effectiveness and efficiency, and the indicators that measure both, are likely to be important. It is at this phase that mathematical modeling and statistical analysis are usually employed.

A final phase of the systems approach can, as suggested by Figure 5.3, involve not only the evaluation of alternative programs, but the recommendation of a preferred plan or program. Depending upon the nature of the planning activity involved, this step may also then involve the preparation of a periodic report (annual or biennial for example) that documents the results of the entire systematic planning process.

It is during this fourth step that comparisons among alternatives in terms of their relative degree of goal achievement should be made.

Both benefit-cost and cost-effectiveness evaluation concepts may be utilized. [13] In either case, benefits and "effectiveness" should generally be expressed in terms of measurable rates or degrees of impact upon each objective. The indicators previously identified may then be used in a comparative or evaluative sense.

Interpretation of some of these indicators in terms of minimum or maximum performance standards or achievement targets can also be important here. In general, the aim should be to identify that program or set of programs that will achieve the highest level of goal achievement for a given cost, or the minimum cost for a given level of goal achievement.

A final element in Figure 5.3, the data-collection activities that underlie and support the entire process, explicitly illustrates the importance of urban indicators and other types of data. As noted in the previous section, urban indicators in particular can be drawn from a variety of sources, including data already collected and available in agency records, as well as those data that require collection via special survey. Systematic planning at various possible levels of application is quite likely to require that urban indicators derived from a variety of sources be employed. This broad level of probable utilization is reinforced by the fact that all three types of urban indicators may well become involved. The resultant need for ongoing, repetitive data collection efforts, providing needed urban indicators on a monthly, quarterly, or annual basis, should be stressed. As part of these ongoing data-collection activities, continuing improvement and refinement of urban indicators in particular can do much to strengthen the systematic planning process.

Experience with the systematic planning process is generally scattered. For example, the land-use/transportation planning programs of six metropolitan areas (Baltimore, Boston, Chicago, San Francisco, Milwaukee, and Minneapolis-St. Paul) were recently examined to determine the degree to which urban goals and indicators had been applied. [14] Though it was found that not all goals had been expressed in specific terms (so that associated indicators were not identified), these examples served to clarify how a particular planning process could begin to become more systematic.

Goal statements were classified into eight functional categories (transportation, residential, open space, etc.), and within each category it was found that three types of goals were evident—those dealing with societal characteristics, activity characteristics, and facility characteristics. These three goal classifications correspond roughly to the three types of urban indicator (social, impact, performance), indicating the considerable potential such indicators (or "performance characteristics," as defined in the article) possess. In addition, the

partial use of criteria and standards (or indicators, with a standard
representing a minimum or maximum desired value) in these six
examples is stressed.

Systematic Plan and Program Evaluation

In recent years, the emergence of a variety of federally-assisted
social-action and community-improvement programs, many aimed at
deteriorating inner-city neighborhoods, has seen an accompanying
need for meaningfully evaluating the results of those programs. These
programs and projects have been enacted in many functional areas,
for example, in education, job training, preschool education, criminal
justice, day care services, and environmental services. Attempts to
evaluate them systematically have seen a need for clearly articulated
objectives, meaningful alternatives to form a basis for comparison,
and analyses of both efficiency and effectiveness. In particular, urban
indicators can play a vital role in this increasingly important planning
activity.

The systems approach to plan/program evaluation appears to be
gaining increasing acceptance. It also appears to be something significantly different from a systems approach to planning, as outlined
above. While the same four steps—objectives, alternatives, analysis,
and evaluation—are still involved, they are typically oriented in different directions. The main difference is, of course, that planning
precedes the actual implementation of programs and projects, while
evaluation occurs after these programs and projects have been enacted.
Differences in methodology and emphasis appear to occur primarily
in the third and fourth steps of the systems approach. Predictions of
impacts and effectiveness are usually replaced by analysis of the
results that did, in fact, occur, for any plan or program. Similarly,
evaluation would then deal with actual rather than anticipated accomplishments, though in some cases continuing forecasts might also be
utilized.

A primary example of how program evaluation efforts may be
expedited through the development of an effective array of urban indicators lies with the Model Cities Program. HUD guidelines and
reporting requirements stress an annual evaluation of the accomplishments of the various Model Cities projects within each of the 150
participating cities. [15]

Successes and failures must be sifted out in order to identify the
most promising approaches to improving the quality of life in under-
privileged neighborhoods. A recent series of project evaluations

conducted by the Chicago Model Cities Program demonstrates many of
the key characteristics a systems approach to plan/program evaluation
should probably display.[16] Figure 5.4 illustrates the basic process that
was used to coordinate this evaluation project, providing a basis as well
for developing a continuing evaluation work program.

A brief review of how the four steps of the systems approach were
employed in the Chicago example provides a better background for assessing the role and utility of urban indicators in systematic plan/pro-
gram evaluation.

It was found that the objectives needed for evaluation are, generally, exactly the same objectives used in Model Cities planning. The
goals and objectives typically identified during first-year Model Cities
planning, particularly as depicted in five-year programs/objectives
tables, are the types of effort that begin to provide a framework for
meaningful project and program evaluation.

While, under second- and third-year Model Cities reporting requirements, Model Cities planning has been facilitated by reducing the
effort involved in identifying objectives, it appears vital for effective
Model Cities evaluation to increase correspondingly the effort expended
in more clearly identifying ends. This need to be more precise in
stating and using objectives was one of the major findings and recommendations of the Chicago report.

FIGURE 5.4

Systematic Evaluation Process:
Chicago Model Cities Program

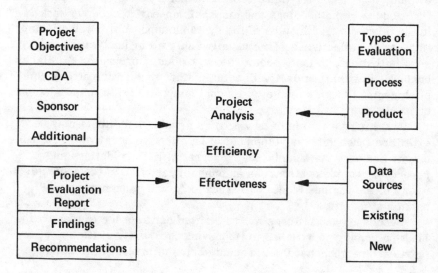

Each of the Chicago project evaluation consultants experienced difficulty in utilizing existing objectives in his evaluation. Meaningful goals and objectives were essential for establishing criteria (indicators, measures) for evaluating all aspects of the Model Cities Program, including, but not limited to, each individual project. In some cases, however, adequate objectives had not yet been identified.

This need for greater sensitivity in stating desired ends appears to offer, therefore, a major initial opportunity for utilizing urban indicators. The goals of such major social-action efforts as the Model Cities Program are likely to be reflected in urban indicators of all three types—general community change, public-agency effectiveness, and public-agency efficiency. The degree to which such indicators are available and measurable will thereby influence the degree to which objectives may be quantitatively refined.

The need to identify alternatives for specific Model Cities projects was particularly critical for evaluation purposes. In general, each Model Cities project should be compared with other attempts to solve the same problems, to determine relatively how good it is. None of the Chicago evaluation consultants was able to use alternatives in this way, largely because none was presented to them as a part of their evaluation assignment. In actuality, it would be very difficult to uncover either ongoing or newly initiated projects that were sufficiently similar to each Model Cities project to warrant evaluative comparisons. Some chance exists that comparison of similar projects in different Model Cities Programs could be applicable here.

In the course of the Chicago project evaluations, an additional utility for the concept of alternatives emerged. This has to do with the idea of process of administrative evaluation, as distinguished from product or impact evaluation (see Figure 5.4).

Process evaluation involves the administration and management of a project—its meeting of targets, schedules, budgets, and so forth. Product evaluation has to do with achieving change in the model neighborhood—change in project participants, overall change in the neighborhood, and institutional change. In the course of process evaluation some of the evaluation consultants ended up suggesting major improvements in project administration that themselves amounted to the identification of project alternatives. These changes were significant enough to amount to the proposal of a new project(s). Many such needed improvements were defined through the use of performance indicators.

Prediction/analysis of effectiveness also has begun to mean something significantly different under the systems approach to evaluation. Here, the concept of evaluative research design enters the picture. [17] Under this concept, projects should be organized in such a way that they can be treated as "experiments." Persons receiving project services should be matched against a group of persons not receiving these services, but sufficiently similar in all other respects to the "test" group. Any changes or improvements in the characteristics of the test group, which are not displayed by the control group, can be validly attributed to the receipt of project services. This provides a means for systematically and rigorously documenting project successes and failures.

These experimental results could then be used to develop mathematical equations or models for forecasting the future impact of Model Cities projects. These models would permit us to predict how much improvement could in the future be achieved by how much delivery of the social services in question—and, in turn, to assess the relative costs of different levels of effectiveness.

Experimental evaluative research designs are extremely difficult, and only one of the Chicago consultants attempted to use such an approach. More typically, some sort of compromise with this "ideal" design for evaluative data collection must be made. Of considerable influence is the degree to which various indicators of the well-being of both the test and control groups are available—as well as the ability to define and isolate these groups in the first place. The indicators most relevant here would primarily involve public agency effectiveness in stimulating participant change.

As in the case of the systems approach to planning, the systems approach to evaluation should accomplish the final step in the process-evaluation—in terms of measuring the achievement of stated objectives. In the course of the Chicago evaluation project, it was found useful to distinguish between process and product categories of evaluation, as noted above. These categories serve to distinguish between four different important aspects of project success or goal achievement: project administration, institutional change, participant change, and neighborhood change.

Note particularly that these four categories of evaluation appear to be quite compatible with the three basic categories of urban indicators. Analysis of project administration relates primarily to performance or efficiency indicators, while analysis of neighborhood change relates primarily to social or community-change indicators. Institutional change and participant change in turn relate primarily to impact or effectiveness indicators. Our ability to generate urban indicators of all three types will consequently relate strongly to the thoroughness with which such an evaluation typology may be carried out.

As Figure 5.4 suggests, urban indicators enter the project-evaluation process as data resources. A wide range of data was collected in the Chicago evaluation, including project documents and reports, the CDA information system, sponsoring-agency performance records, the CDA resident-attitude survey (all of these representing existing data), and agency and staff interviews, participant case records and interviews, site visits and direct observations, and miscellaneous data sources (all representing newly collected data).

Many of these data were secondary or supportive in nature, while others could be properly classed as urban indicators. These latter included comparisons against previously established work programs; interpretation of descriptive statistics describing project and agency changes; subjective interpretation of change in agency, staff, and neighborhood attitudes and opinions; and the analysis of time-series data on neighborhood and participant conditions, where such data were available.

RESPONSIBILITY FOR URBAN INDICATORS

Many different public and private agencies could make good use of urban indicators. An increasing number of these agencies, including state, regional, and municipal planning agencies, have expressed interest in the development of these types of measures. In cities where several agencies may become involved, it should be recognized that there is likely to be a good deal of overlap in the data items that are utilized.

This considerable degree of overlap among the social, economic, and environmental data items that such agencies are likely to be interested in, from one time to another, suggests strongly that a centralized responsibility for collecting, coordinating, processing, disseminating, and reporting key urban indicators be delineated.

Within individual urban areas a regional or local planning agency might well assume this responsibility. Not only would it be able itself to make considerable use of urban indicators, since planning agencies have been traditionally concerned with the programs and activities of many other local agencies, but in the process could effectively serve interagency indicator needs with minimum duplication of effort. The broad charge of metropolitan and municipal planning agencies to coordinate the continuing growth and regrowth of urban areas reinforces the logic of their responsibility for urban indicators that document that growth.

Because, as noted at the outset of this chapter, urban indicators are in an early stage of development, urban planning agencies interested in developing an indicators capability should probably proceed on an incremental, staged basis. They should start on a relatively small scale, perhaps investigating and undertaking the development of indicators in a single functional area. Gradually, the indicators developed in this area could be refined and expanded, while similar beginnings are made in other functional areas. Since urban indicators are closely allied with the use of more systematic planning processes, it is likely that the agency should also begin to reorganize its activities in these functional areas along more rigorous, goals-oriented lines.

This means that objectives should be more clearly identified and elaborated, in concert with the indicators that help define them. At the outset, perhaps only social indicators would be utilized. Alternative plans and programs would in turn begin to be more carefully delineated in terms of how they may be expected to impact upon relevant objective Impact indicators might then come into play. Over the long run, these should probably receive highest priority.

Some agencies may wish to concentrate early on state of the city or region reports. Others, depending on staff and budget resources, might wish to consider integrating the use of indicators within a more systematic, goals-oriented planning process. Building from a modest, feasible start, these planning agencies could perhaps adopt a three-to-five-year work program for increasing objectivity, both along more systematic planning lines and through the use of associated urban indicators. In this way, urban indicators might even be used as catalysts for agency reorganizing.

Effective use of urban indicators may call for a revision of the more traditional, intuitive modes of planning-agency operation. How should an effort to begin the development of urban indicators be incorporated within a planning agency's existing work program? How should urban indicators relate to the other ongoing activities of the agency? Though these decisions will depend largely upon local circumstances, a brief, hypothetical example might be helpful.

Adopting the incremental strategy just outlined, a planning agency might choose the area of housing quality as an initial line of study. A first step might then involve an inventory of all locally collected data regarding the distribution and quality of the local housing stock—such as data involving assessments, rental levels, occupancy, vacancy patterns, substandardness, rehabilitation investments, dwelling-unit size, and similar features. Statistics that describe the quantity of local housing are now collected and processed by various public agencies.

A second step would involve the identification of stated goals and objectives in the area of housing supply. Importantly, these goals should be not only those stated by public agencies but also those expressed by local community groups, at public meetings and hearings, through the news media, by political representatives, and in other participatory ways. The goals and objectives of other cities might also be examined for locally relevant insights. It may be necessary to devote considerable effort to the clarification and reconciliation of goals that may initially appear inconsistent or even in conflict.

Step 3 would then involve a rough matching of existing data with these stated goals and objectives. Which pieces of information serve to indicate how well a particular objective is being achieved? In other words, which data "indicate" current conditions within the community? This, of course, is the essence of the urban-indicators concept. This step essentially involves a sifting of existing data to isolate those that are most useful—by depicting critical aspects of the quality of local housing, and how those aspects have changed.

Step 4 would then involve an identification of indicator gaps—those goals and objectives that are not adequately measured. These might particularly include subjective data regarding citizen perceptions of and satisfactions with their own housing situation. A need for selected community surveys of citizen-perceived housing needs and goals might then be identified. In addition, opportunities for revising ongoing administrative data to make it more revealing in relation to housing goals might also be indicated. Any efforts to outline additional data collection needs (for indicator purposes) reflect a clear relationship with housing goals—in other words, what will these new data indicate?

With these beginnings, a planning agency could then begin to utilize existing and pending housing-quality indicators in the preparation of an annual state of the region report. The systematic planning and evaluation processes mentioned in previous sections might also begin to be pursued. When sufficient progress had been made in the housing area to demonstrate the utility of urban indicators, other functional areas might then be similarly attacked.

In addition to such efforts by urban planning agencies, other public agencies, notably school boards, health departments, and environmental protection agencies, are also likely to become increasingly interested in the use of urban indicators in their own agency programming. These efforts should, of course, be encouraged, and the planning agency should make every attempt to coordinate its evolving capability with the possible gains made by these other agencies.

Any effort to develop urban indicators should be especially sensitive to the need for considerable improvement in both the agency records and community surveys from which they may be derived. Many of the serious problems associated with these data sources have been mentioned earlier. These involve both the costs and procedural difficulties involved in making appropriate data available—at the right time and in the proper form. Anything approaching a comprehensive set of urban indicators will only be possible if the many federal, state, and local agencies within urban areas that collect pertinent data can be

convinced of the desirability and importance of revising and augmenting
their administrative and monitoring procedures to generate indicator-
oriented data—data relating to the goals and objectives directly and indirectly pursued by these agencies.

It should be stressed again that most governmental statistics are
by-products of administrative processing, and are not well-suited for
use as measures of well-being or as indexes of progress in relation to
urban goals. Major steps, therefore, lie ahead in the development of
procedures for collecting and/or adapting both objective and subjective
urban data resources for use as urban indicators.[18] The costs of these
improved procedures may be high, and the economics of better data wil
present major stumbling blocks for expanding the use of urban indicators.

Because of possible cost problems, different planning agencies
will be able, initially at least, to employ indicators at widely varying
levels. Much will also depend on the cooperation of other agencies in
voluntarily improving their own data files. The development and use
of urban indicators in urban planning should consequently involve at
least five different dimensions: (a) identification and more effective
utilization of those indicators that already exist, (b) the continued improvement and refinement of these indicators, particularly through
interagency coordination and cooperation, (c) revision or reorganization of current record-keeping procedures, particularly within public
agencies involved with the direct delivery of services, in order to uncover "buried" urban indicators, (d) the establishment of data-
collection procedures, including procedures for efficiently conducting
regular community surveys, for generating entirely new types of urban
indicators, and (e) continuing research into the validity of various indicators to determine whether they accurately reflect the conditions
they are purported to measure.

A final comment involving the political sensitivity or touchiness
of many urban indicators may be in order. Just as there is a reluctanc
on the part of many political decision makers and public administrators
to define governmental and agency objectives precisely, thereby entail-
ing a degree of commitment that may restrict political maneuverability
a parallel reluctance and even fear of potentially damaging indicator-
type information will all too often appear.

The fact is that many urban indicators, particularly impact and
performance indicators, can sometimes be used for blatantly political
purposes, serving to condemn outrageously the efforts of one adminis-
trator/decision maker (in the eyes of his opponents), while gloriously
affirming the accomplishments of others (in the eyes of their suppor-
ters). The real threat that urban indicators pose to traditional modes
of political operation is quite likely to mean that there will be often a

good deal of difficulty associated with generating many of the urban indicators discussed in this report. This does not negate their potential
value, of course, but perhaps only serves to accentuate the political
sensitivity of urban planning itself.

APPENDIX: POTENTIAL AGENCY DATA INDICATORS

Much of the data from which urban indicators may be derived are
already collected and processed by a wide variety of public and private
agencies. In some cases such data may be utilized directly, without
further processing. In other instances additional computations or transformations (such as ratios or percentages) will be necessary. In still
other cases, and all too frequently, agency data may be reported in
such a way that important pieces of information are inaccessible. This
is particularly true in instances where records are aggregated for large
geographic areas (cities or large districts), so that important characteristics of smaller neighborhoods cannot be determined. Reorganization of such record keeping will thereby be required.

This need for considerable improvement in existing agency data
files has been stressed by two recent preliminary studies of urban indicators (primarily social indicators) conducted in San Antonio and
Detroit.[19] Though both reports acknowledge that much work lies ahead
in strengthening the types of agency data available (and in developing
additional sources for urban indicators, such as community surveys),
they go on to identify initial lists of data items now available and possibly suitable for use as urban indicators. These are classified by area
of public concern—education, health, economic welfare, etc.

This appendix briefly lists specific data items processed by public
(and, in some cases, private) agencies, in four functional areas—
health, education, economy, and housing. These data are intended
merely to illustrate the kinds of agency records that may be pertinent
and are drawn from the two reports mentioned. (In some cases, specific items may be only potentially available from existing agency files.)
Specific agency data sources are not indicated, however, since these
would often be multiple, and would vary from city to city. Because they
are not matched against specific objectives, which would also vary
from city to city and which must be locally determined, these data are
not yet indicators. As noted in the text, urban indicators are best used
as measures of the degree to which specific objectives are achieved.
Many of these data could serve as both social and impact indicators,
depending on context and geographic area of reporting. The more ad-
ministratively-oriented performance indicators are generally not
included.

Agency Health Data

1. Birth rate: births annually per 1,000 population
2. Total infant (first year of life) mortality rate: percent of live births annually
3. Neonatal (first four weeks of life) mortality rate: percent of live births annually
4. Late infant mortality rate: total infant mortality minus neonatal mortality: percent of live births annually
5. Low birth rate: percent of live births annually
6. Congenital defects rate
   a. Birth injury: percent of live births annually
   b. Others: percent of live births annually
7. Age at death: mean, range, standard deviation
8. Age-group mortality rate: deaths annually per 1,000 population, per age
9. Mortality rate due to certain common causes, preferably by individual chief common causes, but may be reported by groups, e.g., heart disease, respiratory disease, etc.
10. Absence rate by school and grade: pupil days annually per 1,000 students
11. Neonatal deaths by specific cause
12. Maternal age-parity relations
13. Viable-age fetal deaths
14. Tuberculosis rates
    a. New active cases of tuberculosis by race and ethnic group and sex
    b. New active cases by extent of disease
    c. New active cases by age groups
    d. Deaths by age groups
15. Mental illness rates, by type, race, age, and sex
16. Disability days annually by category (accidental, chronic disease, acute disease) per 1,000 population

Note: Wherever possible, all of the above should be identified by geographic subarea (place of residence, street address, block, census tract, neighborhood area, city, etc.).

Agency Education Data

1. Attainment—level of schooling completed
2. Postgraduate education—percent of graduates enrolled in a four-year college, two-year college, technical school, etc.

3. Illiteracy rate—percent of students in each grade performing below a specific reading level
4. Potential earnings value—differential productivity (earnings) over time, by number of years of school completed
5. Unemployment index—percent of students 16 and over who are unemployed for X months after leaving school
6. Absenteeism/truancy index—rate of absenteeism directly attributable to truancy per X number of pupils
7. Underemployment index—ratio of underemployed (based on aptitude test results) to suitably employed (based on aptitude test results) for each class of 15-year-old children for the past X years
8. Socialization—results of tests designed to measure internalization of specific norms
9. Educational aspirations—relationship between educational aspirations of students leaving school (excluding transfers) and actual educational experiences
10. Achievement/males—results of testing for induction in armed services
11. Achievement—standardized achievement-test results, by grade and type (reading, writing, calculating, problem solving)
12. Teacher-student ratio, by school and by school district
13. Administrator-teacher ratio, by school and by school district
14. Number of years of education of teachers, by subject matter
15. Rate of functional illiteracy
16. Proportion of dropouts (those who leave school before completion of high school)
17. Proportion of high school graduates as against population total
18. Proportion of college graduates as against population total
19. Proportion with graduate training, by type, against population total
20. Past and present enrollments in all kinds and types of educational and training activities, by grade and age groups

Note: Wherever possible, all of the above should be identified by geographic subarea (place of residence, street address, block, census tract, neighborhood area, school district, city, etc.).

Agency Economic Data

1. Median family and individual income, by age, education, occupation, race, sex of the head of the household, and if full-time or part-time members of the labor force
2. Distribution of income by tenths of population (i.e., top 10 percent of population have X percent of income, second 10 percent have Y percent of income, and so forth)

3. Number of households and number of individuals at income levels below national poverty level (this level set by formula, based on family size and location, with regional cost of living adjustments)
4. Number of potential full-time workers in poverty families or households
5. Number covered by federal, state, and local public and private assistance, or "welfare" programs, by household and by numbers of individuals receiving assistance
6. Number of disabled, blind, aged, dependent children, crippled children, and others receiving public or private assistance
7. Average payment per household and per individual by category of payment and program
8. Labor-force participation rates, by age, educational attainment, race, sex, occupation, marital status, and income of the head of the household
9. Labor-force participation rates for members of the households, by sources of income other than wage and salary income of the head of the household
10. Labor-force participation rates, by levels and changes in regional income produced for classifications listed in 8
11. Labor-force participation rates, by geographic units: state, counties, SMSA, central city, and municipalities for categories listed in 8
12. Unemployment rates, by race, age, sex, marital status, education occupation, residential location, and by industry last employed
13. Cross-classification of above groups
14. Peak-to-trough and trough-to-peak unemployment rates in classification of 11
15. Duration of unemployment by groups used in 11 and 12; frequently of unemployment by cross-classification used in 12
16. Changes in labor-force participation rates
17. Peak-to-trough differences in unemployment rates for occupationa groups, based on age, sex, race, and location
18. Trough-to-peak differences in unemployment rates for age, sex, race, and location

Note: Wherever possible, all of the above should be identified by geographic subareas (place of residence, street address, neighborhood city, county, etc.).

Agency Housing Data

1. Dwelling-unit size (number of rooms) and type of construction
2. Parcel size and dwelling-unit density

3. Assessed value, by dwelling-unit type
4. Building-code violations, by type and dwelling-unit type
5. Housing-code violations, by type and dwelling-unit type
6. Housing starts, by construction cost and dwelling-unit type
7. Market value and rental level, by dwelling-unit type
8. Building permits, by type and value (repairs and rehabilitation)
9. Housing conversions and demolitions, by dwelling-unit type
10. Age of housing, by dwelling-unit type
11. Vacancy rates
12. Turnover rates (housing succession)
13. Household size (persons/dwelling unit)
14. Overcrowding index (persons/room)
15. Cost of housing index (computed as part of the consumer price index)
16. Percent substandard or lacking adequate plumbing

Note: Wherever possible, all of the above should be identified by geographic subarea (street address, block, census tract, neighborhood area, city, etc.).

NOTES

1. Major references include Raymond A. Bauer, ed., Social Indicators (Cambridge, Mass.: MIT Press, 1966); Bertram M. Gross, ed., Social Intelligence for America's Future: Exploration in Societal Problems (Boston: Allyn and Bacon, 1969), also appearing as "Social Goals and Indicators for American Society," The Annals of the American Academy of Political and Social Science (May and September 1967); Bertram M. Gross and Michael Springer, eds., "Political Intelligence for Ameria's Future," The Annals of the American Academy of Political and Social Science (March 1970); Eleanor B. Sheldon and Wilbert E. Moore, eds., Indicators of Social Change: Concepts and Measurements (New York: Russell Sage Foundation, 1968).

2. For an annotated bibliography listing 85 references, see Thomas McVeigh, "Social Indicators: A Bibliography," Council of Planning Librarians Exchange Bibliography 215 (Monticello, Ill.: September 1971). Further discussion of the differences between national indicators and urban indicators is provided in Eugene D. Perle, "Urban Indicators: Editor's Introduction," Urban Affairs Quarterly (December 1970): 135-44.

3. U.S. Department of Health, Education and Welfare, Toward a Social Report (Washington, D.C.: Government Printing Office, 1969). See also Daniel Bell, "The Idea of a Social Report," The Public Interest

(Spring 1969): 72-84; Walter F. Mondale, "Reporting on the Social State of the Union," Trans-Action (June 1968): 34-38; Mancur Olson, "An Analytic Framework for Social Reporting and Policy Analysis," The Annals of the American Academy of Political and Social Science (March 1970): 112-26; Mancur Olson, "The Plan and Purpose of a Social Report," The Public Interest (Spring 1969): 85-97; Mancur Olson, "A Social Report in Practice: The Official Summary," The Public Interest (Spring 1969): 98-105; Mancur Olson, "Social Indicators and Social Accounts," Socio-Economic Planning Sciences (April 1969): 335-46.

4. Martin V. Jones and Michael J. Flax, The Quality of Life in Metropolitan Washington, D.C.: Some Statistical Benchmarks (Washington, D.C.: The Urban Institute, 1970). See also "Developing Urban Indicators: Some First Steps," Search: A Report from the Urban Institute (May-June 1971): 3-6.

5. Barton-Aschman Associates, Inc., An Evaluation of Selected Projects: A Design Framework and Work Program for Social Action Project Evaluation, a study prepared for the Chicago Model Cities Program, February 1971.

6. James S. Coleman et al., Equality of Educational Opportunity (Washington, D.C.: HEW, Office of Education, 1966).

7. See Kenneth J. Dueker, "Urban Information Systems and Urban Indicators," Urban Affairs Quarterly (December 1970): 173-78. For a general introduction to urban information systems, see Chapter 8, this work.

8. Joan E. Jacoby, "The Neighborhood Early Warning System: Design and Development," Socio-Economic Planning Sciences (March 1970): 123-30; Joan E. Jacoby, "DEWS: District Early Warning System for Neighborhood Deterioration," Urban and Regional Information Systems for Social Programs (Kent, Ohio: Kent State University, 1967), pp. 35-44.

9. Robert Richard, Subjective Social Indicators (Chicago: National Opinion Research Center, University of Chicago, September 1969). See also Raymond A. Bauer, "Social Indicators and Sample Surveys," Public Opinion Quarterly (Fall 1966): 339-52.

10. For a planning-oriented discussion of the 1970 Census, see George McGimsey, "The 1970 Census: Changes and Innovations," AIP Journal (May 1970): 198-203; Lenore R. Siegelman, The 1970 Census: A Resource for Housing and City Planning Studies, Planning Advisory Service Report No. 267 (Chicago: American Society of Planning Officials, March 1971); U.S. Bureau of the Census, Data Uses in Urban Planning, Census Use Study Report No. 9 (Washington, D.C.: Government Printing Office, February 1970).

11. Center for Urban Studies, Wayne State University, Social Reporting in Michigan: Problems and Issues (Lansing: Michigan Office of Planning Coordination, January 1970). See also Alamo Area Council

of Governments, Social Indicators and a Social Accounting System for the AACOG Region: A Preliminary Statement (August 1969); Matthew McDevitt and Thomson McGowan, New York State's Central Social Environment Study (Albany: New York State Office of Planning Coordination, January 1970).

12. See Frank Beal, Annual Reports, Planning Advisory Service Report No. 217 (Chicago: American Society of Planning Officials, December 1966).

13. For further discussion of these concepts, see Richard S. Bolan, "Emerging Views of Planning," AIP Journal (July 1967): 233-45; Morris Hill, "A Goals-Achievement Matrix for Evaluating Alternative Plans," AIP Journal (January 1968); Michael B. Teitz, "Cost-Effectiveness: A Systems Approach to Analysis of Urban Services," AIP Journal (September 1968): 303-11.

14. David E. Boyce, "Toward a Framework for Defining and Applying Urban Indicators in Plan-Making," Urban Affairs Quarterly (December 1970): 145-72. See also David E. Boyce, Norman D. Day, and Chris McDonald, Metropolitan Plan Making (Philadelphia: Regional Science Research Institute, 1970).

15. U.S. Model Cities Administration, How to Design a Work Program for Continuing Planning and Evaluation, 2 vols. (Washington, D.C.: HUD, 1970); "Evaluation: A Management Tool," Model Cities Service Center Bulletin (June 1971): 25-29.

16. Barton-Aschman Associates, Inc., op. cit.

17. Edward A. Suchman, Evaluative Research: Principles and Practice in Public Service and Social Action Programs (New York: Russell Sage Foundation, 1967); Robert S. Weiss and Martin Rein, "The Evaluation of Broad-Aim Programs: A Cautionary Case and a Moral," The Annals of the American Academy of Political and Social Science (September 1969): 133-42.

18. For further discussion of the need to improve public agency data, see Doris B. Holleb, Social and Economic Information for Urban Planning, 2 vols. (Chicago: Center for Urban Studies, University of Chicago, 1969); Doris B. Holleb, "Social Statistics for Social Policy," Planning 1968 (Chicago: American Society of Planning Officials, 1968), pp. 80-85. See also "Department Hosts Social Indicators Conference," Plans and Progress (Chicago: Chicago Department of Development and Planning, December 1970).

19. Alamo Area Council of Governments, op. cit.; Center for Urban Studies, Wayne State University, op. cit.

6

URBAN IMPROVEMENT
PROGRAMMING
MODELS

One of the most intuitively attractive methods for evaluating alternative urban plans is the use of a programs-objectives matrix. Such a matrix would balance a set of alternative public investment programs (as columns, perhaps) against a group of goals and objectives (as the corresponding rows) that these programs are intended to achieve. Entered in each cell of the matrix would be some measure of how well program x, contributes to the achievement of goal y. This might be nothing more than a zero or one entry, indicating whether or not that particular program is relevant. Alternatively, the number of actual goal-units to be achieved might be shown. Such a matrix enables us to compare how alternative plans or combinations of programs serve to accomplish the overall goals of an urban area. If possible, the summing of the rows will indicate the level of attainment for each goal or objective, while the summing of columns may provide some measure of the investment level required for each program.

Complications are introduced, however, when we use different units of measurement for different objectives and programs. Unless we can establish trade-off rates among these different units, we will not be able to sum every row and every column. We will have to settle for partial, selective comparisons of individual cells and groups of cells, for each of the alternative plans under consideration. As Hill notes, a complete analysis will require the development of transformation functions that reduce each outcome to a single measurement scale. In his "goals-achievement matrix," three levels of comparison and measurement are distinguished: ordinal (single rankings), interval

Reprinted with permission from Socio-Economic Planning Sciences vol. 4 (London: Pergamon Press, January 1970).

(relative scales) and ratio (absolute scales). In his proposed weighted index of goals achievement these three types of measurement would be somewhat arbitrarily combined to yield a single evaluation rating.

The concept of a programs-objectives matrix can be more rigorously structured in the form of a mathematical programming problem. Such a mathematical model will require that we do establish a common unit of measurement for goal achievement, because the summing of matrix rows and columns is essential. The key feature of mathematical programming lies in the use of an objective function, a combination of program variables we wish to optimize. In general, we will want either to minimize overall cost (given some specified minimum level of goal achievement) or to maximize goal achievement (given some maximum overall budget). In addition to an objective function, the basic programs-objectives matrix will usually be augmented by various constraints indicating minimum and maximum limits on certain programs and program combinations.

This chapter explores the potential application of mathematical programming in the evaluation of alternative urban plans and improvement programs. After a brief review of past modeling efforts of this type, an examination of the problems likely to be encountered in identifying and measuring specific objectives and programs is presented. The Model Cities Program is used as an example. A simple linear programming model is subsequently developed, built around a matrix of relative effectiveness coefficients, a set of performance standards and appropriate program budgets. Supporting analytic techniques and information systems are also discussed. Finally, potential applications of the model are surveyed, and examples of its use in testing and evaluating basic Model Cities Programs and objectives presented.

PAST MODELING EFFORTS

Mathematical programming offers the very powerful advantage of being able to theoretically examine all possible, feasible combinations of program variables, selecting finally the one that minimizes cost or maximizes goal achievement. In effect, the model itself generates alternative plans and programs, in a much more efficient and thorough way than we could ourselves. Because this advantage is such an important one, a number of attempts have been made to apply mathematical programming in urban public investment and plan evaluation contexts. Perhaps the most well known example is Schlager's Land-Use Plan Design Model, which attempts to minimize total public and private investment costs, subject to various design standards and

constraints regarding multiple land-use mix ratios and interrelationships.[2]

Other examples are more directly concerned with multiple urban
goals and objectives.[3] In Boston, for instance, a simple model has
been developed to evaluate transit link alternatives in relation to four
objectives: increased or decreased operating/capital cost ratio, total
passenger volume, percent seated during the peak hour, and peak-hour
auto users diverted. Subject to a budget constraint, the model selects
that system of links that maximizes the value of a weighted linear sum
of the objectives. In another example, a proposal has been made for
developing a programming model that would utilize a matrix of effectiveness probabilities. This matrix would define the probability that
objective j can be achieved if alternative metropolitan plan component
i is adopted. Empirically determined utility values would be assigned
to each of 30 objectives. The model would select that overall plan that
achieves the highest total utility (sum of individual probabilities times
utilities).

Primarily at a conceptual, organizational level, other thinking on
the potential of mathematical programming models includes the paper
by Coughlin.[4] An analytic framework for formulating a capital improve
ment program is set forth, anticipating possible treatment as a programming problem. The objective would be to complete as much as
possible of the comprehensive plan, within a given budget limit. This
early work was subsequently refined to permit community goals (upon
which a comprehensive plan would be based) to appear in an objective
function directly. In this conceptual model the need to distinguish
between independent and interdependent contributions of programs to
goals is recognized, as well as the need to identify the indirect effects
of the achievement of goals upon each other. In a third attempt at
clarifying the problems of public-investment programming models,
Peterson distinguishes three basic matrices necessary in balancing a
vector of community goals against a vector of public investment
opportunities: a programs interdependency matrix, a unit effectiveness
or production matrix and a goals interdependency matrix.

The information requirements of this kind of urban-oriented
programming model are large—so large in fact, that we are only
beginning to scratch the surface of its potential applicability and
usefulness in urban and regional planning. In order to develop models
detailed enough to yield nontrivial results, we must know a great deal
about how different programs affect, in some quantitative way, the
achievement of different objectives; how different objectives themselves can be most meaningfully expressed; and how we can best
predict the future impacts of programs upon objectives. At present,
we are ill-equipped to provide these kinds of inputs for the development

of sensitive programming models. Adequate information resources
are in short supply, and the development of supporting impact and
effectiveness models is itself only just beginning.

This chapter attempts only to structure how the continuing development of urban goal-programming models might proceed. Though two
operational linear programming models are developed, they are based
upon a series of hearty assumptions concerning unavailable or inappropriate data, and hypothetical values are assigned to unknown variables
and parameters. These models are not presently intended for actual
application. Rather, their purpose is to demonstrate how such models
could be constructed, given the necessary data and supporting predictive models. It is anticipated that these needed inputs can (and, hopefully, will) realistically and eventually be made available. The two
models are developed in terms of the goals, objectives, and programs
of the Model Cities Program, which is aimed at the coordinated
improvement of living conditions within the poverty neighborhoods of
our central cities.

MODEL CITIES OBJECTIVES

What kinds of specific objectives should be pursued by comprehensive programs designed to alleviate poverty conditions within model
neighborhoods? Further, what quantitative indexes should be used to
measure how each objective is being achieved? Basic goals for the
Model Cities Program have been established by federal legislation,
and these can be used in turn to identify more detailed socioeconomic
conditions and objectives. The basic goals of the program are to
rebuild or revitalize large slum and blighted areas, to expand housing
opportunities, to expand job and income opportunities, to reduce
dependence on welfare payments, to improve educational facilities and
programs, to combat disease and ill health, to reduce the incidence
of crime and delinquency, to enhance recreational and cultural opportunities, to establish better access between homes and jobs, to improve
general living conditions, and to foster greater citizen participation
in the development of neighborhood improvement programs.[5]

These general, abstract goals carry with them certain implied
performance measures or indexes—for example, the number or
proportion of substandard housing units, the number or proportion of
low-income families living under inadequate conditions (deteriorating
or dilapidated housing, overcrowding), the number or proportion of
families with income under the $3,000 poverty level, the annual
number or rate of high school dropouts, the annual number or rate of

TABLE 6.1

Hypothetical Model Neighborhood: Basic Performance Objectives

Type	Objective variable	Socio-economic condition	Reference group	No. present	% of reference group	Five-year performance standard	% of reference group
Housing	Y_1	Substandard housing units	Total housing units	6580	16	2060	5
	Y_2	Other deficient housing units	Total housing units	6170	15	2060	5
	Y_3	Inadequately housed L–I elderly households	HH 65 and over, income less than $3000	900	45	300	15
	Y_4	Inadequately housed L–I families	Family income less than $5000	7840	70	2240	20
	Y_5	Inadequately housed M–I families	Family income $5000–$8000	3200	38	1010	12
Employment-Income-Education	Y_6	Unemployed persons	14 and over, civilian labor force	4030	8	1510	3
	Y_7	Underemployed persons	14 and over, civilian labor force	5040	10	1510	3
	Y_8	Families with income less than $3000	Total families	5600	20	2240	8
	Y_9	ADC cases	Persons under 18	11,130	30	2600	7
	Y_{10}	Annual high school dropouts	Persons age 14–17	1880	30	1250	20
	Y_{11}	Annual college or jr. college enrollment	Persons age 18–24	1300	15	2170	25
	Y_{12}	Adults with grade school education or less	Persons 25 and over	29,620	44	20,190	30
	Y_{13}	Net new industrial jobs lying within 3/4-hr travel time via public transit	None	—	—	1000	—
Health-Safety-Environment	Y_{14}	Annual infant mortality	Live births	180	6	75	2.5
	Y_{15}	Annual new tuberculosis cases	Total population	700	0.7	70	0.07
	Y_{16}	Annual juvenile arrests	Persons under 18	2020	5	1010	2.5
	Y_{17}	Annual criminal arrests (excl. minor misdemeanors)	Total population	9000	9	2000	2
	Y_{18}	Persons unserved by adequate local recreation facilities	Total population	35,000	35	5000	5
	Y_{19}	Persons expressing satisfaction with general environmental living conditions (excl. housing)	5% sample survey	1000	20	2500	50
	Y_{20}	Persons attending local community planning meetings (annual)	Total population	1000	1	2000	2

Note: total population = 100,000; total families = 28,000; total housing units = 41,150.

new tuberculosis cases, the number or rate of juvenile arrests, etc.
In each case, these kinds of socioeconomic conditions enable us to
tell whether a basic goal is being achieved. Are the appropriate numbers, proportions, and rates increasing or decreasing? A set of basic,
measurable objectives for the Model Cities Program (or for other
public programs) can be developed simply as a set of desired changes
in such numbers, proportions, and rates.

Table 6.1 illustrates a set of performance objectives for a hypothetical model neighborhood containing 100,000 persons.* These
objectives fall into three basic groups: housing, employment-income-
education, and health-safety-environment. This is not a complete set
of objectives, of course, and other important considerations, such as
school integration and the relative quality of inner city schools, mental
health, air pollution, or residential density might easily enter such a
table. The only requirement for additional objectives is that they be
quantifiable, expressed in terms of some neighborhood-wide reference
group. In this case, they should also be related to one or more of the
broad Model Cities goals mentioned above.

Also appearing in Table 6.1 is a five-year performance standard
for each of the 20 basic objectives. Identifying these standards is one
of the important clarifying steps in the potential use of both programs-
objectives matrices and mathematical programming models. Such
standards commonly reflect a desire to bring the appropriate rates
and proportions in line with the rates and proportions exhibited by the
rest of the city or metropolitan area.[6] In other cases more arbitrary
achievement levels may be set, based upon experience and/or judgment. Both kinds of standards are represented in Table 6.1.

MODEL CITIES PROGRAMS

What kinds of public improvement programs are available for
achieving Model Cities objectives? What quantitative measures of
investment or intensity for each program should be used? Most
important, how can we go about analyzing and predicting the level
of impact each program will have upon the objectives to which it is

---

*The hypothetical figures shown in both Tables 6.1 and 6.2 are,
for the most part, generalized from actual data, and are intended to
be reasonably realistic. They are based upon the 1960 U.S. Census
and various municipal agency annual reports and plans, principally
from Chicago, Illinois.

TABLE 6.2

Hypothetical Model Neighborhood: Basic Improvement Programs

Type public improvement program	Output unit	Cost/ unit ($) (000)	Output units /$1000 expenditure	Assumptions
Housing				
Clearance, existing housing	H.U.	5.0	0.20	
Private redevelopment, new housing (clearance subsidy)	H.U.	4.0	0.25	
Public housing, elderly	H.U.	3.5	0.29	Includes clearance of existing housing
Public housing, family	H.U.	4.5	0.22	Includes clearance of existing housing
Housing rehabilitation, sub standard units	H.U.	1.8	0.55	
Housing rehabilitation, other deficient units	H.U.	1.2	0.80	
Moderate-income housing	H.U.	0.1	10.00	
Receivership rehabilitation, substandard units	H.U.	1.3	0.75	
Receivership rehabilitation, other deficient units	H.U.	0.8	1.25	
Rent supplements (5-yr)	H.U.	3.5	0.29	
Code enforcement, substandard units	H.U.	0.4	2.50	
Code enforcement, other deficient units	H.U.	0.2	5.00	
Employment-Income-Education				
Community action job training, unemployed	Persons	4.2	0.24	$500/referral; 1/3 of referrals are placed; 1/3 of placements keep jobs
Community action job training, underemployed	Persons	3.4	0.29	Somewhat better performance
Manpower development and training, unemployed	Persons	5.2	0.19	$1300/referral; 1/2 of referrals are placed; 1/2 of placements keep jobs
Manpower development and training, underemployed	Persons	4.0	0.25	Somewhat better performance
ADC job training, unemployed	Persons	3.0	0.33	Similar to community action job training; somewhat lower referral costs
ADC job training, underemployed	Persons	2.4	0.42	
Day care centers, reduce unemployment and underemployment	Persons	0.2	5.00	Partially self-supporting
Industrial redevelopment, new jobs nearby	Persons	1.5	0.67	$90,000/acre; 60 jobs/acre
Industrial redevelopment, reduce unemployment and underemployment	Persons	15.0	0.07	10% of new jobs for unemployed; 10% for underemployed
Industrial promotion, private development, new jobs nearby	Persons	0.1	10.00	Highly variable, but costs/job would be low
Industrial promotion, private development, reduce unemployment and underemployment	Persons	1.2	0.83	10% of new jobs for unemployed; 10% for underemployed
Basic adult education, unemployed	Persons	13.8	0.07	$275/person; 2% gain employment who otherwise would not
Basic adult education, underemployed	Persons	11.2	0.09	Somewhat better performance

Type public improvement program	Output unit	Cost/ unit ($) (000)	Output units /$1000 expenditure	Assumptions
Employment-Income-Education (continued)				
Basic adult education, grade school level	Persons	1.6	0.61	$275/person; 1/6 receive grade school diplomas
Neighborhood youth corps, unemployed	Persons	3.0	0.33	$750/referral; 1/2 of referrals are placed; 1/2 of placements keep jobs
Neighborhood youth corps. stay in school	Persons	1.2	0.83	$600/referral; 1/2 stay in school who otherwise would drop out
Vocational education, unemployed	Persons	1.8	0.56	$450/student; 1/2 students are placed; 1/2 of placements keep jobs
Vocational education, stay in school	Persons	0.9	1.11	$450/student; 1/2 stay in school who otherwise would drop out
Upward bound, stay in school	Persons	2.8	0.36	$275/member; 10% stay in school who otherwise would drop out
Upward bound, college enrollment	Persons	0.7	1.43	$275/member; 40% go on to college who otherwise would not
Elementary school construction, stay in school	Persons	36.0	0.06	$1800/pupil; 5% stay in high school who otherwise would drop out
High school construction stay in school	Persons	35.0	0.03	$3500/pupil; 10% stay in school who otherwise would drop out
High school construction, college enrollment	Persons	70.0	0.01	$3500/pupil; 5% go on to college who otherwise would not
Jr. college construction, college enrollment	Persons	70.0	0.01	$3500/pupil; 5% of high school students go on to college who otherwise would not
Health-Safety-Environment				
Health center construction	Persons	a,b	—	
Parks and recreation facilities, adequate local recreation	Persons	0.8	1.2	$80,000/acre, each acre serving 10 persons adequately
Parks and recreation facilities, juvenile delinquency	Persons	b	—	
Parks and recreation facilities, environmental improvement	Persons	c	—	
Rodent-vermin control, environmental improvement	Persons	b,c	—	
Police community relations, juvenile delinquency and criminal arrests	Persons	b	—	
Business renewal, environmental improvement	Persons	c	—	
Urban beautification, environmental improvement	Persons	c	—	
Community organization activities, publications	Persons	c	—	

(a) Investment in this program does not clearly vary with output units (TB cases, infant mortality)' but is determined mainly by feasible facility size.

(b) Outputs related to this program are closely dependent upon other programs (above) aimed at improving housing and family income conditions. Estimates of cost parameters are thereby very difficult.

(c) Very little data is presently available to relate these programs to appropriate output units (citizens satisfied with environmental conditions, citizen participation).

related? Table 6.2 provides a start in cataloging the improvement
programs that might be made part of a coordinated Model Cities effort.
Most of them represent existing citywide programs administered by
various agencies—urban renewal departments, community action
agencies, building departments, public housing authorities, boards
of education, welfare agencies, state employment services, public
health agencies, park and recreation districts, planning and development departments. In addition to coordinating existing programs, the
Model Cities agency itself is free to design new, innovative programs
to fill gaps and provide additional facilities and services. The programs in Table 6.2 are also divided into the three basic groups used
in Table 6.1

Though it may sometimes be desirable to express program inputs
or investments in terms of different units (number of building inspectors, acres developed, or job-training referrals), the need for a single
common input unit almost inevitably forces us to use a monetary one.
In terms of mathematical programming, our chief concern is then
with achieving an optimal allocation of dollars among the various program alternatives available. The programs in Table 6.2 are consequently described in dollar terms, in general relating the cost required
to achieve or generate one unit of output, with outputs expressed in
terms of the objective units in Table 6.1 (persons, families, or housing
units). These cost figures would usually be determined on a citywide
basis, though some might be peculiar to the particular model neighborhood under study. Most programs are distinguished by the basic
objectives or groups of objectives they affect. Because objectives are
expressed in terms of measurable socioeconomic conditions, this
amounts to the identification of different target areas or populations
for each program

The key to the development of useful urban-improvement programming models lies in our ability to make reasonable estimates of
these cost-per-unit-output figures. Such figures can subsequently be
converted to reciprocal output units per $1,000 expenditure, a more
useful parameter for further use in actually constructing a programming model. The assumptions listed in Table 6.2 give some indication of the difficulty involved in developing effectiveness parameters
of this type. Improvement programs generally have a number of
important characteristics or features whose variability can affect
program performance. Some knowledge of these features must be
gained, and reasonable values assigned or assumed for them. One
particularly crucial assumption is that costs are linearly related to
output, for each of the programs listed. Another is that the programs
operate with relative independence, and that one program does not
depend upon an investment elsewhere in order to be effective.

The programs and cost parameters in Table 6.2 are consequently quite simple in nature. Most of the cost figures are rough approximations, others are purely hypothetical. Complex programs are described as if they could easily be reduced to a single dimension, which, of course, is usually not the case. A great deal of data collection and analysis, carefully structured to yield results expressed in a consistent, usable form, using the input and output units called for by such a matrix approach, will be required in order to generate an expanded, realistic table of this type. A difficult question will lie in deciding how much detail should be (or can be) included. For example, should the various housing programs be further stratified by the age, density, and neighborhood location of the housing units involved? Will cost parameters vary significantly with these factors? Similarly, should the various job-training programs be distinguished according to the age, experience, education, or background of the individuals referred?

DEVELOPING PROGRAMMING MODELS

The basic tool of mathematical programming involves the bringing together of Tables 6.1 and 6.2 to develop a programs-objectives matrix. The relative effectiveness coefficients entered in this matrix (see Table 6.3) indicate how the different Model City Program alternatives in Table 6.2 will affect the particular objectives of the hypothetical model neighborhood described in Table 6.1. The coefficients will vary with different model neighborhoods, and depend upon the magnitudes of specific quantitative objectives. Each coefficient simply tells how much (what percentage) of objective Y_j can be achieved by investing one input unit ($1,000) in program X_i.

This percentage of goal achievement constitutes the basic common unit of measurement or transformation for the matrix. An essential kind of program stratification occurs when it is seen that certain programs contribute to more than one objective, and it becomes necessary, where feasible, to distinguish separate program alternatives accordingly. This amounts to a more detailed extension of the identification of target areas and populations mentioned earlier. For instance, in applying the code enforcement of substandard housing units (programs X_{24}-X_{27}) to the four objectives to which such a program is relevant, we may focus upon substandard units that house (a) moderate-income families, (b) low-income families, (c) low-income elderly households, or (d) none of these. Such a distinction clarifies just what this program is capable of accomplishing, and forces us to analyze more rigorously the potential impacts of each program upon each objective.

Not all programs can be fully stratified in this way, however. As a simple example, in the public rehabilitation of other deficient housing units (programs X_{10}, X_{12} and X_{14}) it is not possible to separate the achievement of objective Y_2 from Y_3, Y_4, or Y_5. A reduction in the number of other deficient housing units (Y_2) will simultaneously result in a reduction in the number of inadequately housed low-income elderly households (Y_3), low-income families (Y_4), or moderate-income families (Y_5). The needs and possibilities for this kind of objective-oriented stratification of programs will be an important factor in introducing additional objectives into such an effectiveness matrix.

PREDICTING RELATIVE IMPACTS

The programs-objectives effectiveness matrix, together with the cost parameters upon which it depends, form the central elements in developing programming models for urban improvement. What techniques could be used to develop the impact and effectiveness predictions of Table 6.2, upon which the success or failure of this approach to plan design and evaluation so closely hinges? The first requirement, of course, and one so basic that its importance is often overlooked, is the development of an adequate information system. Normal administrative records for the various programs in Table 6.2 may need restructuring so that data in terms of appropriate output units will be generated. In other cases special interview sample surveys within a model neighborhood may be necessary. In general, it will be necessary to disaggregate citywide information files and administrative records, including the products of the U.S. Census, at least to the model-neighborhood level. Ideally, all spatially distributed data should be referenced to a common block-face address-coding guide, such as that being instituted for the 1970 Census, to permit maximum flexibility in subsequent analyses.

The simplest kinds of analyses needed to make effectiveness predictions would involve basic cost-accounting statements and records keeping, preferably on a monthly basis. A number of programs, particularly those in the housing area, are generally straightforward in terms of relating inputs (dollars expended) to outputs (demolished, new, or rehabilitated housing units). By simply recording the net public costs required to clear, build, manage, rehabilitate, inspect, or take legal action against segments of a city's housing supply, on a unit-by-unit, month-by-month basis, an information resource can be built from which appropriate average cost parameters can be drawn.

However, in order to make relatively accurate predictions, we may wish to perform additional statistical analyses (such as multiple regressions or factor analyses) that relate average costs to basic intermediate factors, such as construction methods and costs, building types, or housing markets. Our cost parameter predictions would then be based upon prior predictions for these factors (assuming we can predict them more confidently, rather than dealing directly with average costs), or we might make other appropriate adjustments to account for them.

Effectiveness predictions in the employment-income-education (EIE) and health-safety-environment (HSE) areas are likely to cause considerably more trouble, and require a good deal more analytic effort. In general, intermediate factors will demand much more attention, since inputs (dollars expended) for various social-service and capital-improvement programs will not be clearly related to outputs (persons finding employment, staying in school, enjoying better health, avoiding criminal activity, or more satisfied with their environment). These inputs and outputs will interact within complex socioeconomic contexts, and some account must be taken of the many intervening variables that might influence results (such as economic health and growth of an area, housing segregation, civil rights movements, neighborhood and family factors, and even national or regional trends and issues).

In addition to basic univariate and multivariate statistical analyses (supplemented by appropriate cost-accounting procedures), impact and effectiveness predictions in these areas are likely to call for the development of more elaborate socioeconomic simulation models. One of the basic features of such models, which may be built around microcosmic decision-making sequences or around stochastic sampling procedures, lies in describing socioeconomic interrelationships so that input or program variables can act as levers. By varying the level of investment in these variables, we are able to simulate how other variables in the system modeled, including appropriate output variables, will be affected. Simulation models might be designed to describe employment markets (perhaps by industrial sector), educational services, medical services, housing markets, the use of community facilities, neighborhood or intrametropolitan migrations, or other socioeconomic systems and activities.[7]

LINEARITIES AND INTERDEPENDENCIES

Developing these kinds of supporting analytic techniques and information systems is a vital, first-phase assignment, preceding any operational use of urban improvement programming models. However, two potentially limiting characteristics of a mathematical programming framework must also be dealt with—linearity assumptions and goal/program interdependencies.

In general, those programs that are found to display nonlinear input/output curves can be approximated by a series of linear segments or can be handled by assigning appropriate program minimums and maximums. In either case, such programs can be manipulated to fit within a linear framework. For example, consider a program that exhibits steadily increasing costs per unit of output. Simply break this curve into several appropriate linear segments; assign a special subvariable to represent each segment; determine the maximum input permitted over each segment; and let this set of subvariables represent the program in the programming problem. These subvariables will compete with each other and with the other variables in the problem, with, in general, the lower-cost variables entering the solution in ascending order.

A program with steadily decreasing costs per unit of output could be represented similarly, except that minimums would be assigned to each segment to represent the cumulative input preceding it, and only one subvariable would be permitted in solution. Linear cost coefficients for each segment would be adjusted to include the output generated by its preceding minimum program. For a program with high initial start-up costs, and/or high costs to achieve full implementation, but with an essentially linear curve in between, a single program variable can continue to be used. Program minimums and maximums would be set to exclude both tails of the input/output curve from solution, while the linear cost coefficient would again be adjusted to account for the fixed, required minimum preceding it.

The potential problem represented by program interdependencies is, in contrast, a particularly thorny one. The problems and difficulties involved in trying to distinguish dependent and independent (or controlled and uncontrolled) statistical and simulation variables, and in stratifying the effects and interrelationships of one from another, are of considerable magnitude. Attempts to identify an explicit programs interdependency matrix may well prove fruitless. The cost will be high, the period of analysis lengthy, and the temporal stability of such an interdependency matrix unlikely. However, without the formal use of such a matrix, the known dependence of one program upon another can be roughly approximated by specifying appropriate minimums and maximums for the second or required program. It will be necessary, however, to ensure that all program or solution variables operating within a programming model are independent, as reflected in their respective effectiveness coefficients. Overlapping impacts

TABLE 6.3

Programs–Objectives Effectiveness Matrix: Housing

	Housing programs		Housing objectives					Total
Type	Description	Program variable	Y_1	Y_2	Y_3	Y_4	Y_5	impact
Redevelopment	Clearance for M–I housing	X_1	0.30				0.62	0.92
		X_2		0.32			0.62	0.94
	Clearance for other land-uses	X_3	0.30					0.30
		X_4		0.32				0.32
Public housing	New construction, elderly	X_5	0.44		3.22			3.66
		X_6		0.47	3.32			3.69
		X_7	0.33			0.28		0.61
	New construction, family	X_8		0.36		0.28		0.64
Rehabilitation	Public housing, elderly	X_9	0.84		6.11			6.95
		X_{10}		1.30	8.89			10.19
	Public housing, family	X_{11}	0.84			0.70		1.54
		X_{12}		1.30		1.02		2.32
	Moderate-income housing	X_{13}	0.84				1.72	2.56
		X_{14}		1.30			2.50	3.80
M–I house	Public non-profit corp.	X_{15}					31.25	31.25
Receivership	Substandard units, L–I and M–I housing	X_{16}	1.14		8.33			9.47
		X_{17}	1.14			0.96		2.10
		X_{18}	1.14				2.34	3.48
	Other deficient units, L–I and M–I housing	X_{19}		2.02	13.89			15.91
		X_{20}		2.02		1.59		3.61
		X_{21}		2.02			3.91	5.93
Rent suppl.	Low-income families	X_{22}			3.22			3.22
		X_{23}				0.37		0.37
Code enforcement	Substandard units, L–I and M–I housing	X_{24}	3.80					3.80
		X_{25}	3.80		27.78			31.58
		X_{26}	3.80			3.19		6.99
		X_{27}	3.80				7.81	11.61
	Other deficient units, L–I and M–I housing	X_{28}		8.10				8.10
		X_{29}		8.10	55.55			63.56
		X_{30}		8.10		6.38		14.48
		X_{31}		8.10			15.62	23.72

Note: Each entry represents the fractional reduction/increase (multiplied by 10^4) in the number of objective units present (substandard housing units, other deficient housing units, etc.) which can be achieved by investing $1000 in a particular program. For example, in applying clearance of existing housing as a means to reduce the number of substandard housing units, the relative effectiveness coefficient is obtained by dividing the output per $1000 (Table 2) by the number of substandard units present (Table 1): 0.20/6580 = 0.00003 × 10^4 = 0.30.

cannot be permitted, because the overall sum of program impacts
upon each objective must be matched against a performance standard.

Goal interdependencies, on the other hand, are not particularly
crucial, especially if no attempt is made to define a strictly independent set of objectives. Independence among objectives is not really
required. Effectiveness coefficients relate objectives to programs
only, and not to other objectives. The only independence requirement
is that the coefficients for each objective (each row) are individually
and consistently determined. The summing of rows will consequently
have meaning, while the summing of columns will not. Adding or
deleting objectives will not unduly bias a solution, nor will the fact
that one objective might mean practically the same as another. It
makes no real difference, for example, whether the desire to reduce
unemployment overlaps with the desire to raise family incomes, or
whether the achievement of one is likely to result in achieving the
other.

LINEAR PROGRAMMING EXAMPLES

Using the data presented in Tables 6.1 and 6.2, together with
information about appropriate program budget constraints, it is
possible to construct simple, hypothetical mathematical programming
models for both the housing and EIE areas. Both models use a basic
effectiveness matrix, such as that shown for housing in Table 6.3.
Both are set forth as standard linear programming problems, capable
of utilizing the canned solution algorithms available for most computers (such as the IBM 1130, used here). Other mathematical
programming techniques might also be applicable in an urban
improvement planning context, but are not developed here. The
Boston model mentioned earlier, as an example, used an integer
programming formulation, while Schlager's work has been built
around dynamic programming variations. Other eventual possibilities
include parametric programming, stochastic programming and nonlinear programming. [8]

Both linear programming models may be stated as follows:

$$\text{Minimize } \sum_i x_i \qquad \text{or} \qquad \text{Maximize } \sum_i \sum_j d_j a_{ij} x_i$$

$$\text{Subject to } \sum_i a_{ij} x_i \geq y_j \qquad\qquad \text{Subject to } \sum_i a_{ij} x_i \geq y_j$$

$$\sum_i x_i \leq m_j \qquad\qquad\qquad \sum_i x_i \leq b$$

$$\sum_i x_i \geq n_j \qquad\qquad\qquad \sum_i x_i \leq m_j$$

$$\sum_i x_i \geq n_j$$

where x_i = Model City Program alternatives, in dollars
       y_j = performance standards for each objective
       a_{ij} = relative effectiveness coefficients
       d_j = relative weights for each objective (optional)
       b   = total budget available
       m_j = maximum program budgets
       n_j = minimum program budgets

In translating this formal mathematical structure into a practical, operational problem (see Tables 6.4 and 6.5), a number of clarifications are necessary. First, it should be observed that the budgetary constraints m_j and n_j are actually represented as a series of program budgets, either recombining program variables stratified according to potential target objectives, or combining different programs into functional bundles (such as job-training programs). In some cases individual minimums and maximums are also set for specific program (column) variables. The performance standard minimums represent the percent reduction desired in the appropriate socioeconomic condition shown in Table 6.1 (multiplied by 10^4). If objective function A (maximization) is chosen, an overall budget limit b should be assigned to the total budget row, and maximum performance standards (say within 2 or 3 percent of the minimums) should be set.* Minimum standards may be reduced or eliminated altogether. If objective function B (minimization) is chosen, the total-impact row may be ignored, while both minimum and maximum standards are set for each objective.

POTENTIAL APPLICATIONS

The results of running both models are shown in Tables 6.6 and 6.7.†
In both cases a sensitivity analysis of all variables and parameters

---

*These maximums are necessary to ensure that objectives are not achieved beyond practical limits. The maximum allowable limit for each y_j is 10,000.0 (or 100 percent of goal achievement), but, in general, realistic levels of percentage goal achievement must be set at a lower figure.

†In developing these simple operational examples, a number of liberties with data and with complex improvement program interrelationships were taken. Some of the problems and assumptions regarding data and supporting analysis have already been reviewed in preceding sections. A series of additional major simplifications and assumptions

TABLE 6.4

Basic Linear Programming Model: Housing

		Redevelopment				Public housing								M–I housing		
		X_1	X_2	X_3	X_4	X_5	X_6	X_7	X_8	X_9	X_{10}	X_{11}	X_{12}	X_{13}	X_{14}	X_{15}
Objective function A	IMPACT	0.92	0.94	0.30	0.32	3.66	3.69	0.61	0.64	6.95	10.19	1.54	2.32	2.56	3.80	31.25
Objective function B	BUDGET	1.0	1.0	1.0	1.0	1.0	1.0	1.0	1.0	1.0	1.0	1.0	1.0	1.0	1.0	1.0
	Y_1	0.30		0.30		0.44		0.33		0.84		0.84		0.84		
	Y_2		0.32		0.32		0.47		0.36		1.30		1.30		1.30	
Performance standards	Y_3					3.22	3.22			6.11	8.89					
	Y_4							0.28	0.28			0.70	1.02			
	Y_5	0.62	0.62											1.72	2.50	31.25
	REDEV	1.0	1.0	1.0	1.0											
	PUB H					1.0	1.0	1.0	1.0	1.0	1.0	1.0	1.0			
	PUB ELD					1.0	1.0									
	PUB FAM							1.0	1.0							
Program budgets	REHAB									1.0	1.0	1.0	1.0	1.0	1.0	
	RECEIV															
	RENT SUP															
	COD ENF															
		V	V	V	V											/\
		375.0	275.0	425.0	375.0											50.0

---

were also made. These dealt in part with the stratification of program variables to correspond with individual objectives, the undiscriminating use of average cost figures for each basic program variable, the relative investment life or timespan of effectiveness for different programs (here assumed to be equal at five years), the treatment of those community objectives not represented directly in the model (some can be indirectly acknowledged by setting minimums on certain programs), and the setting of program budget constraints. Further discussion of these simplifications, together with additional details on the methodology of model construction, is presented in Darwin G. Stuart, "Strategy Analysis in Urban Planning: Evaluating Model Cities Alternatives," Ph.D. dissertation, Northwestern University, 1969.

| | Receivership | | | | | | Rent suppl. | | Code enforcement | | | | | | | | |
X_{16}	X_{17}	X_{18}	X_{19}	X_{20}	X_{21}	X_{22}	X_{23}	X_{24}	X_{25}	X_{26}	X_{27}	X_{28}	X_{29}	X_{30}	X_{31}	
9.47	2.10	3.48	15.91	3.61	5.93	3.22	0.37	3.80	31.58	6.99	11.61	8.10	63.65	14.48	23.72	Max.
1.0	1.0	1.0	1.0	1.0	1.0	1.0	1.0	1.0	1.0	1.0	1.0	1.0	1.0	1.0	1.0	Min.
1.14	1.14	1.14						3.80	3.80	3.80	3.80					⩾6869.4 ⩽7000.0
			2.02	2.02	2.02							8.10	8.10	8.10	8.10	⩾6661.3 ⩽7000.0
8.33			13.89			3.22			27.78				55.55			⩾6666.7 ⩽7000.0
	0.96			1.59			0.37			3.19				6.38		⩾7142.8 ⩽7300.0
		2.34			3.91						7.81				15.62	⩾6843.7 ⩽7000.0
																⩽3050.0
																⩽4200.0
																⩾525.0
																⩾1800.0
																⩾2175.0 ⩽6400.0
1.0	1.0	1.0	1.0	1.0	1.0											⩽1400.0
						1.0	1.0									⩾84.0 ⩽280.0
								1.0	1.0	1.0	1.0	1.0	1.0	1.0	1.0	⩽750.0

is conducted for the "minimize-budget" solution. A "maximize-impact"
solution, with relaxed performance standards and a smaller permitted
total budget than the one achieved in the minimum-cost solution, is also
given. To show how the basic model can be used to test various kinds
of alternatives, four revised solutions of the minimum-budget problems
are also shown: the introduction of a new program, the revision of
program budget constraints, the revision of performance standards,
and the improvement of existing programs. In addition, one of the
maximum-impact solutions is revised to account for a relative weighting
among the objectives. In general, because the exercise of a total
budget constraint, carrying across established program and agency
lines and funding procedures, is a somewhat unrealistic feature of

TABLE 6.5

Basic Linear Programming Model: Employment-Income-Education

| | | Industrial promotion | | | | | | |
		X_{63}	X_{64}	X_{65}	X_{66}	X_{67}	X_{68}	X_{69}
Objective function A	IMPACT	102.06	103.54	105.78	101.65	103.13	105.37	103.89
Objective function B	BUDGET	1.0	1.0	1.0	1.0	1.0	1.0	1.0
	Y_6	2.06	2.06	2.06				
	Y_7				1.65	1.65	1.65	1.65
	Y_8		1.48	1.48		1.48	1.48	
Performance standards	Y_9			2.24			2.24	2.24
	Y_{10}							
	Y_{11}							
	Y_{12}							
	Y_{13}	100.0	100.0	100.0	100.0	100.0	100.0	100.0
	CAJOB							
	MDTJOB							
	ADCJOB							
Program budgets	JOBTRAIN							
	DAYCARE							
	INDRED							
	INDPROM	1.0	1.0	1.0	1.0	1.0	1.0	1.0
	NYCORPS							

Note: The relative effectiveness coefficients for objectives Y_{10} and Y_{11} are adjusted to account for the actual number of students attending high school over five years—roughly, double the number attending in any one year, as each class is carried through its own annual sequence. The coefficients for objective Y_9 assumes that 3.0 children will be taken off ADC for every job provided to an ADC parent.

	Adult education							N.Y.C.		Voc. Ed.		Up. Bd.	E.S. Con.	H.S. Con.	J.C. Con.	
X_{70}	X_{71}	X_{72}	X_{73}	X_{74}	X_{75}	X_{76}		X_{77}	X_{78}	X_{79}	X_{80}	X_{81}	X_{82}	X_{83}	X_{84}	
0.38	0.50	0.69	0.39	0.51	0.70	0.58		0.82	2.21	1.39	2.95	6.46	0.08	0.12	0.04	Max.
1.0	1.0	1.0	1.0	1.0	1.0	1.0		1.0	1.0	1.0	1.0	1.0	1.0	1.0	1.0	Min.
0.17	0.17	0.17						0.82		1.39						⩾6253.1 ⩽6500.0
			0.18	0.18	0.18	0.18										⩾7004.0 ⩽7200.0
	0.12	0.12		0.12	0.12											⩾6000.0 ⩽6200.0
		0.19			0.19	0.19										⩾7664.0 ⩽7800.0
									2.21		2.95	0.96	0.08	0.08		⩾3351.0 ⩽3500.0
												5.50		0.04	0.04	⩾6692.3 ⩽7000.0
0.21	0.21	0.21	0.21	0.21	0.21	0.21										⩾3183.6 ⩽3300.0
																⩾10,000.0 ⩽10,200.0
																⩾2300.0
																⩾1700.0
																⩾750.0 ⩽1250.0
																⩽6400.0
																⩽100.0
																⩾600.0 ⩽900.0
																⩽55.0
								1.0	1.0							⩾750.0
												$\stackrel{\wedge}{206.2}$	$\stackrel{\vee}{82.5}$	$\stackrel{\vee}{7200.0}$	$\stackrel{\vee}{14,000.0}$	$\stackrel{\vee}{7000.0}$

(continued)

		Community action job training							Manpower development and training						
		X_{32}	X_{33}	X_{34}	X_{35}	X_{36}	X_{37}	X_{38}	X_{39}	X_{40}	X_{41}	X_{42}	X_{43}	X_{44}	X_{45}
Objective function A IMPACT		0.60	1.03	1.68	0.58	1.10	1.88	1.36	0.47	0.81	1.32	0.50	0.95	1.62	1.17
Objective function B BUDGET		1.0	1.0	1.0	1.0	1.0	1.0	1.0	1.0	1.0	1.0	1.0	1.0	1.0	1.0
Performance standards	Y_6	0.60	0.60	0.60					0.47	0.47	0.47				
	Y_7				0.58	0.58	0.58	0.58				0.50	0.50	0.50	0.50
	Y_8		0.43	0.43		0.52	0.52			0.34	0.34		0.45	0.45	
	Y_9			0.65			0.78	0.78			0.51			0.67	0.67
	Y_{10}														
	Y_{11}														
	Y_{12}														
	Y_{13}														
Program budgets	CAJOB	1.0	1.0	1.0	1.0	1.0	1.0	1.0							
	MDTJOB								1.0	1.0	1.0	1.0	1.0	1.0	1.0
	ADCJOB														
	JOBTRAIN	1.0	1.0	1.0	1.0	1.0	1.0	1.0	1.0	1.0	1.0	1.0	1.0	1.0	1.0
	DAYCARE														
	INDRED														
	INDPROM														
	NYCORPS														

ADC job training			Day care centers							Industrial redevelopment						
X_{46}	X_{47}	X_{48}	X_{49}	X_{50}	X_{51}	X_{52}	X_{53}	X_{54}	X_{55}	X_{56}	X_{57}	X_{58}	X_{59}	X_{60}	X_{61}	X_{62}
2.30	2.71	1.96	12.41	21.34	34.82	9.92	18.85	32.33	23.40	6.87	6.99	7.18	6.84	6.96	7.15	7.03
1.0	1.0	1.0	1.0	1.0	1.0	1.0	1.0	1.0	1.0	1.0	1.0	1.0	1.0	1.0	1.0	1.0
0.82			12.41	12.41	12.41					0.17	0.17	0.17				
	0.83	0.83				9.92	9.92	9.92	9.92				0.14	0.14	0.14	0.14
0.59	0.75			8.93	8.93		8.93	8.93			0.12	0.12		0.12	0.12	
0.89	1.13	1.13			13.48			13.48	13.48			0.19			0.19	0.19
										6.70	6.70	6.70	6.70	6.70	6.70	6.70
1.0	1.0	1.0														
1.0	1.0	1.0														
			1.0	1.0	1.0	1.0	1.0	1.0	1.0							
										1.0	1.0	1.0	1.0	1.0	1.0	1.0

TABLE 6.6

Alternative Housing Model Solutions

| | | Minimize budget | Sensitivity analysis | | | | Maximize impact | Introduce new program | Revise program budgets | Weighting of objectives |
			Cost/unit increase	Cost/unit decrease	Increase limit	Decrease limit				
Objective function A	Impact	34,682.3	—	—	—	—	32,940.3	34,830.7	34,689.2	39,650.1
Objective function B	Budget	11,373.2	—	—	—	—	9600.0	11,373.2	9166.4	9600.0
Performance standards	Y_1	6869.4	1.19	−1.19	6886.68	6810.37	5230.8	6869.4	6869.4	5230.8
	Y_2	6661.3	0.67	−0.67	6672.75	6622.20	7000.0	6661.3	6661.3	7000.0
	Y_3	7000.0	0.00	0.00	7384.32	6016.03	7000.0	7000.0	7000.0	7000.0
	Y_4	7186.9	−0.00	−0.00	7188.50	7184.89	6709.5	7300.0	7158.5	6709.6
	Y_5	6964.6	0.00	−0.00	7073.07	6686.71	7000.0	7000.0	7000.0	7000.0
Program budgets	REDEV	1450.0	0.64	—	1646.75	1450.00	1450.0	1450.0	895.0	1450.0
	PUB H	4200.0	−0.00	0.00	4270.27	4179.42	2939.0	4200.0	4200.0	2939.0
	PUB ELD	525.0	0.48	−0.48	568.20	377.44	525.0	525.0	95.0	525.0
	PUB FAM	1800.0	0.61	−0.61	1833.89	1684.26	1800.0	1800.0	310.0	1800.0
	REHAB	5264.2	0.26	0.91	5284.74	5241.53	3541.0	5264.2	3932.4	3541.0
	RECEIV	1400.0	−0.36	0.36	1451.78	1384.84	1400.0	1400.0	3100.0	1400.0
	RENT SUP	84.0	1.00	−1.00	389.43	0.00	84.0	84.0	84.0	84.0
	COD ENF	750.0	−4.44	4.44	754.83	748.59	750.0	750.0	750.0	750.0
	PUB NEW	—	—	—	—	—	—	100.0	—	—
Programs in solution	X_1	375.0	0.64	−0.64	1975.00	−1075.00	375.0	375.0	55.0	375.0
	X_2	275.0	0.78	−0.78	602.37	179.15	275.0	275.0	40.0	275.0
	X_3	425.0	0.64	−0.64	621.75	367.39	425.0	425.0	425.0	425.0
	X_4	375.0	0.78	−0.78	497.18	339.23	375.0	375.0	375.0	375.0
	X_5	525.0	0.48	0.21	568.20	306.02	525.0	525.0	95.0	525.0
	X_7	1800.0	0.61	0.15	1833.89	1523.51	1800.0	1800.0	310.0	1800.0
	X_9	0.0	−0.00	0.00	868.98	−5949.75	0.0	0.0	0.0	62.1
	X_{11}	1875.0	—	−0.00	1875.00	1006.01	614.0	1775.0	3795.0	551.9
	X_{13}	3389.2	0.00	0.14	3409.74	3319.65	2927.0	3489.2	137.4	2927.0
	X_{15}	0.0	1.00	−1.00	1.13	−3.87	50.0	0.0	0.0	50.0
	X_{16}	0.0	−0.00	0.00	637.39	−4364.10	0.0	604.9	0.0	0.0
	X_{17}	1212.7	0.20	−0.00	1246.56	575.33	1045.0	353.2	10.2	1045.0
	X_{18}	0.0	0.00	−0.00	15.12	−51.65	0.0	254.5	2865.3	0.0
	X_{19}	0.0	−0.00	0.00	30.91	−9.05	355.0	0.0	224.5	355.0
	X_{20}	0.0	−0.00	0.00	30.91	−9.05	0.0	187.3	0.0	0.0
	X_{21}	187.3	0.23	−0.00	195.50	156.37	0.0	0.0	0.0	0.0
	X_{22}	0.0	0.00	0.00	84.00	−11,289.75	0.0	84.0	0.0	0.0
	X_{23}	84.0	1.00	0.00	280.00	−1564.91	84.0	0.0	84.0	84.0
	X_{28}	0.0	0.00	0.00	6.92	−17.71	0.0	4.0	0.0	0.0
	X_{29}	95.6	—	−0.00	95.58	87.85	6.8	0.0	64.4	0.0
	X_{30}	654.4	−0.00	0.00	662.15	647.50	743.2	746.0	685.6	750.0
	X_{33}	—	—	—	—	—	—	100.0	—	—
Programs not in solution	X_6		0.21	−0.21	218.98	−64.12				
	X_8		0.15	−0.15	276.49	−80.95				
	X_{10}		0.13	−0.13	52.58	−15.40				
	X_{12}		0.13	−0.13	52.58	−15.40				
	X_{14}		0.13	−0.13	79.59	−23.30				
	X_{24}		0.92	−0.92	2.05	−7.00				
	X_{25}		0.92	−0.92	2.05	−7.00				
	X_{26}		0.92	−0.92	2.05	−7.00				
	X_{27}		0.92	−0.92	1.41	−4.82				
	X_{51}		0.00	−0.00	2.26	−7.74				
	X_{32}									

TABLE 6.7

Alternative EIE Model Solutions

			Sensitivity analysis						
		Minimize budget	Cost/unit increase	Cost/unit decrease	Increase limit	Decrease limit	Maximize impact	Revise performance standards	Improve existing programs
Objective function A	Impact	5043.3	—	—	—	—	4640.3	4337.6	5043.3
Objective function B	Budget	172,502.4	—	—	—	—	55,000.0	169,547.7	171,789.8
Performance standards	Y_6	6253.1	0.72	−0.72	—	1085.91	6500.0	5000.0	6253.1
	Y_7	7004.0	0.90	−0.90	7289.86	6297.86	7200.0	5000.0	7004.0
	Y_8	6000.0	0.92	−0.92	6633.09	5772.69	6200.0	5000.0	6000.0
	Y_9	7800.0	0.00	0.00	8777.21	5896.81	7800.0	5000.0	7800.0
	Y_{10}	3500.0	0.00	−0.00	11,330.35	1893.95	3500.0	3500.0	3500.0
	Y_{11}	6692.3	25.00	−25.00	—	2777.12	1974.1	6692.3	6692.3
	Y_{12}	3183.6	3.46	−3.46	3581.38	1882.93	3028.7	3183.6	3183.6
	Y_{13}	10,000.0	0.11	−0.11	11,530.00	9520.00	10,200.0	10,000.0	10,000.0
Program budgets	CA JOB	2737.1	0.30	0.16	3458.28	0.00	3285.1	2300.0	2300.0
	MDT JOB	1700.0	0.14	−0.14	2205.12	0.00	1700.0	1700.0	1700.0
	ADC JOB	1250.0	−0.44	0.44	1553.07	0.00	1250.0	750.0	1050.1
	JOB TRAIN	5687.1	—	—	—	—	6235.1	4750.0	5050.1
	DAY CARE	100.0	−16.14	16.14	125.45	29.10	100.0	100.0	100.0
	IND RED	671.6	0.76	—	701.49	671.64	701.5	671.6	671.6
	IND PROM	55.0	−13.24	13.24	59.80	39.70	55.0	55.0	55.0
	NY CORPS	750.0	0.41	−0.41	7051.45	−0.00	750.0	750.0	750.0
Programs in solution	X_{34}	0.0	0.17	−0.17	596.02	−1472.30	0.0	922.9	0.0
	X_{37}	2737.1	0.30	0.00	3458.27	1484.28	3285.1	1377.1	2300.0
	X_{42}	0.0	0.41	−0.41	1406.87	−505.12	0.0	455.6	0.0
	X_{44}	1700.0	0.14	0.00	2205.12	241.46	1700.0	1244.4	1700.0
	X_{47}	1250.0	—	0.30	1250.00	811.25	1250.0	750.0	1050.1
	X_{50}	28.8	−0.02	0.00	37.96	−112.37	28.1	0.0	0.0
	X_{51}	0.0	0.00	0.00	28.82	−72.49	0.0	100.0	46.4
	X_{54}	71.2	0.26	−0.02	80.66	62.04	71.9	0.0	53.6
	X_{57}	0.0	0.00	−0.00	671.64	−5043.86	0.0	671.6	0.0
	X_{60}	0.0	0.00	−0.00	671.64	−10,016.74	0.0	0.0	671.6
	X_{61}	671.7	0.76	0.00	900.00	−4471.62	701.5	0.0	0.0
	X_{65}	55.0	—	−0.00	55.00	−372.96	55.0	55.0	0.0
	X_{68}	0.0	−0.00	0.00	55.00	−173.25	0.0	0.0	55.0
	X_{74}	5143.3	0.00	−0.00	5859.05	4494.22	6733.5	14,246.6	6634.8
	X_{75}	10016.7	−0.00	0.00	10,665.78	9300.95	7688.9	0.0	8525.2
	X_{76}	0.0	0.11	−0.11	5275.76	−1894.19	0.0	913.4	0.0
	X_{77}	0.0	0.59	−0.59	726.72	−3543.14	726.7	0.0	0.0
	X_{78}	750.0	0.41	−0.59	7051.45	23.28	23.3	750.0	750.0
	X_{80}	3717.4	1.00	−1.00	3780.45	3717.24	4329.8	1700.8	3641.8
	X_{81}	206.2	−136.50	136.50	986.12	—	206.2	206.2	206.2
	X_{82}	7200.0	1.00	−1.00	27,275.60	−90,679.40	7200.0	7200.0	7200.0
	X_{83}	34,075.6	11.38	−0.00	—	32,213.10	14,000.0	34,075.6	34,075.6
	X_{84}	104,879.4	−0.00	—	106,741.90	104,879.40	7000.0	104,879.4	104,879.4
Selected programs not in solution	X_{32}		0.57	−0.57	8611.98	−437.12			
	X_{36}		0.00	−0.00	1252.84	−2439.98			
	X_{39}		0.52	−0.52	1700.00	−502.12			
	X_{40}		0.21	−0.21	757.63	−1871.52			
	X_{51}		0.00	0.00	28.82	−72.49			
	X_{52}		8.21	−8.21	35.52	−25.45			
	X_{58}		0.00	−0.00	671.64	−5043.86			
	X_{63}		1.36	−1.36	55.00	−153.58			
	X_{73}		0.11	−0.11	5692.88	−1894.19			

211

the maximum-impact problem, emphasis is given here to the alternative minimum-budget formulation.

OPTIMAL SOLUTIONS

Perhaps the most unsettling aspect of the various linear programming solutions presented lies in the fact that, as the models are presently constructed, no single optimal solution exists. Rather, each solution is one of a family of optimal allocations, each with the same minimum budget or maximum impact value. The differences in these solutions lie in shifts among potential programs where even-cost trade offs may be made. In general, these shifts will be between programs whose corresponding cost/unit increase and decrease figures are zero. For example, compare X_{60} and X_{61} in the "minimize-budget" and "improve-existing-programs" solutions (Table 6.7). The sensitivity analysis for the minimum-budget problem reveals that X_{60} could be increased up to 671.6, while X_{61} could be decreased by up to 4,471.6, both with no added total budget costs. In the second solution, a full shift is, in fact, made between the two, and any combination totaling 671.6 would also be permissible. There are actually an infinite number of optimal solutions, for these problems and for each of the others.

This is disturbing, however, only if an optimal solution is the chief objective of analysis. At least two reasons can be suggested for de-emphasizing the usual role of an optimal solution, whether a single one is achieved or not. First, the very real limitations of input data and parameters should be recognized. Within this complex plan evaluation context it should be acknowledged that not all important objectives and decision criteria are represented. Some objectives may not be amenable to quantitative measurement, while others may be only partially represented by the performance indexes chosen. The uncertainty or probable forecasting error associated with the coefficients in a programs-objectives matrix should also be recognized. No matter what supporting information systems and analytic techniques are developed, these coefficients, and especially the cost-effectiveness parameters (Table 6.2) upon which they are based, can be regarded only as qualified estimates. Their temporal stability is really unknown. In short, while we may be willing to make limited comparisons among groups of programs and objectives, we are not likely to achieve the level of knowledge implied by a comprehensive optimal solution.

Second, the role of this type of analysis in subsequent decision making should be properly understood. Political decision makers are more likely to be interested in what is "good" or "bad" about particular programs and projects, and in how much it will cost to achieve particular objectives. Because some decision factors will almost inevitably rely upon their judgment and intuition, they are less likely to be interested in multiple-program, multiple-objective recommendations, which ignore these subjective factors. In particular, because of these limitations and the uncertainties mentioned above, the notion of an "optimal" solution to difficult public investment problems will seem premature and even presumptuous. Perhaps the finality of an optimal solution is crucial here—this kind of final allocation among investment alternatives is what decision makers themselves wish to accomplish.

This line of thinking suggests that the principal value of mathematical programming lies with the identification of marginal differences or trade-offs among alternative program variables. These trade-offs would be cast in terms of relative deviations from an optimal solution, but the solution itself would stay in the background. It would represent an essentially simple-minded, hypothetical ideal, useful mainly for facilitating relative program, objective, and budget comparisons. These comparisons and trade-offs would be made using the sensitivity analysis of the mathematical programming problem. Since the optimal solution actually identified is not only likely to be an arbitrary one but also subject to serious limitations and uncertainties, primary attention would be focused upon the results of such sensitivity analyses. They are discussed in the following section.

An optimal solution will, however, illustrate the importance of identifying program variables in relation to their specific target populations. For example, the Table 6.6 housing-model solution states that, in order to achieve at least the minimum desired level of improvement for each of the five objectives, an expenditure of some $11.3 million will be required. In this particular solution, the redevelopment and public housing (new construction) programs (X_1-X_5, X_7) are achieved at their minimum levels, with both of the latter (elderly and family public housing) replacing existing substandard units. The sum of $1.9 million should be spent in rehabilitating substandard units for family public housing (program X_{11}), while $3.4 million should be spent to rehabilitate substandard units for moderate-income housing (program X_{13}). In addition, receivership programs should be allocated $1.2 million for the upgrading of substandard units for family public housing and $0.2 million for the improvement of other deficient units of moderate-income families. The sum of $0.08 million in rent supplements should be used to gain better housing for low-income families. Finally, $0.1 million in code enforcement activity should be aimed at other deficient units housing low-income elderly households, with $0.6 million aimed at other deficient units housing low-income families.

In practice, of course, whether this or other solutions are actually selected, it would not be possible to make such allocations to the letter.

For example, clearance of poor existing housing for the construction
of new public housing is likely to involve both substandard and other
deficient units, and not just one or the other, as required by the solution, while it may be necessary to find rent-supplement money for a
few elderly households, in addition to low-income families. In general,
programs can rarely be devoted exclusively to a single target populatio:
or group, though programming models tend to result in such all-or-
nothing allocations. However, a potential asset of such models lies in
their ability to tell us, for each program, where to put the emphasis—t
look for public housing sites containing mostly substandard housing, to
concentrate rent supplements upon poorly housed low-income families.
The further we can go in these directions of emphasis, the more effectively and efficiently our public funds will be spent.

SENSITIVITY ANALYSES

A basic method for testing the relative weight or importance of
each variable or parameter in a mathematical programming problem
(in a sense, testing its "pull" toward or away from an optimal solution)
lies in the use of a sensitivity analysis, as shown in Tables 6.6 and
6.7. * The "cost" in the cost/unit figures is expressed in terms of the
units used in the objective function—dollars, or, more specifically,
thousands of dollars. The "units," of course, represent the appropriate performance standard, program budget, or program variable units.
(In a sensitivity analysis of the "maximize-impact" solution, costs
would be expressed in terms of percentage points of goal achievement.)
These cost/unit figures simply say that the value of the objective
function will be raised or lowered, for every unit of increase or decrease in the element at hand, by the amount shown. This raising or
lowering will take place over the range shown by the increase and decrease limits. The marginal sensitivity of all variables (programs) or
parameters (standards, budgets) can be tested in this way.

This kind of analysis for the performance standards of the housing
model (Table 6.6) indicates, for example, that Y_1 is the most costly
or difficult to achieve, followed by Y_2, with the cost/unit figures to

---

*Sensitivity analysis makes use of the dual problems associated
with each of these linear programming examples. For a discussion
of the basic primal-dual relationships involved, see Darwin G. Stuart,
"Strategy Analysis in Urban Planning: Evaluating Model Cities Alternatives," Ph.D. dissertation, Northwestern University, 1969.

raise or lower these standards varying over a relatively short range. The zeros shown for Y_3, Y_4, and Y_5 do not mean that it costs nothing to achieve them (absolutely), but rather that, because they are tied to Y_1 and Y_2, and for this particular optimal solution it would cost nothing to increase or decrease them over the ranges shown. They are achieved, in a sense, simultaneously with the achievement of Y_1 and Y_2. (In general, standards and other row parameters could be extended beyond the ranges shown, but the cost/unit figures and the values for selected other variables and parameters would change.)

An examination of performance standards in this way can reveal which constraints are particularly binding or difficult to meet (for instance, Y_{11} in Table 6.7), so that we will know in turn which standards can best be reduced in order to reduce total expenditures. We can also determine how much the budget will have to be increased in order to achieve a higher level for some objective, though the permitted increase level may not be very large. For example, to increase Y_8 from 60 percent to 66 percent would require an added expenditure of $0.6 million. We do not know which program will absorb this expenditure, however, or what it would cost to go up to 70 percent. Revising the problem and running it again would, in general, permit us to obtain this additional information.

In a similar way, program budgets can be reviewed to find those that are more or less costly. In the cost/unit increase column, a plus sign indicates a budget minimum that, if reduced, would permit an improved optimal solution (such as REDEV, PUBELD, and PURFAM in Table 6.6), while a minus sign indicates a maximum constraint that should be increased in order to improve the solution (ADCJOB, DAYCARE, and INDPROM in Table 6.7, with DAYCARE the most promising choice).

The sensitivity of program or solution variables can be interpreted in much the same way. In Tables 6.6 and 6.7 alternative programs have been distinguished according to whether they appeared in at least one of the solutions tested. Plus or minus signs in the cost/unit increase column again indicate variables that could be profitably increased or reduced. For example, X_3 (clearance of substandard housing) could be increased up to $0.6 million, but the cost (increased total budget) for each $1000-unit of increase will be $640. This cost/unit figure (or net cost) reflects shifts in the values of other variables that would also take place. If X_3 were decreased, however, the total budget could also be decreased, at a rate of $640/unit of reduction. Where the objective is to minimize the total budget, solution variables with a minus cost/unit figure should consequently be sought.

A program variable not currently accepted by either model could also be entered into solution at the cost/unit increase figures shown.

X_{12} (rehabilitation of other deficient housing units for low-income
family public housing) could enter the housing solution at a net cost of
$130 per unit of investment, while X_{40} (Manpower Development and
Training for unemployed, low-income family persons) could enter the
EIE solution at a net cost of $210 per unit of investment. In some
cases, within similar program groups or programs aimed at the same
objective, we can also directly identify equal-cost (or zero net-cost)
trade-offs among variables. For instance, X_9 can enter the housing
solution (up to a value of $869,000), as long as X_{11} is correspondingly
reduced (up to a value of $1,006,000), and as long as compensating
shifts among other variables take place. These additional shifts can
be identified by fixing X_9 or X_{11} at a desired level and running the
model again.

REVISED SOLUTIONS

What if an overall budget limit has been specified, and we wish to
maximize the effectiveness or impact of all funds expended? Tables
6.6 and 6.7 show the results of such a "maximize-impact" solution,
with a maximum housing budget set at $9.6 million and a maximum
EIE budget at $55.0 million. Minimum performance standards are not
set, so that, in effect, money will be spent upon the most easily realized objectives, until the budget constraint is reached. Y_1 and Y_{11},
for example, become the least well-achieved objectives and are correspondingly the hardest to achieve.

Comparisons with the original minimum-budget solution reveal a
number of significant shifts in allocation and the introduction of new
variables into solution. In the housing model, X_{11} (rehabilitation of
substandard housing for low-income-family public housing) and X_{12}
are both substantially reduced; X_{15} (moderate-income housing, with
a high impact coefficient of 31.25) and X_{19} (receivership proceedings
against other deficient housing for low-income elderly households) are
new variables; and X_{21} is deleted. In the EIE model similar reallocations take place. In general, these shifts in allocation are to variables
with higher total-impact coefficients, so that, for example, in the
housing model total impact is kept at nearly the same level, while the
total budget is reduced by some 15 percent.

Similar allocation shifts are likely to occur when basic changes in
column vectors or constraint parameters are made. Such shifts will
generally be toward a more optimal solution, either in terms of minimum budget or maximum impact. The remaining portions of Tables
6.6 and 6.7 give examples of the shifts generated by introducing alter-

native programs, standards and program budgets into the original model solutions. Multiple optimal solutions also exist for each of these examples, and sensitivity analyses should also be performed. In general, sensitivity analyses will show which reallocations are simply equal-cost trade-offs, and which are an actual improvement on the previous solution.

The effects of a new housing program—the construction of prefabricated public housing units, mainly on scattered vacant lots—are tested (shown as X_{32} and X_{33} in the housing model), as well as the effects of improved services and delivery for two existing programs—Community Action job training and the promotion of new industry providing jobs for the unemployed and underemployed—in the EIE model. In general, the housing alternative is found to be sufficiently attractive (in terms of its relative-effectiveness coefficients) to draw investment away from other programs, while the EIE alternatives (X_{34}, X_{37}, X_{65}, and X_{68}) fall short.

"Revised Performance Standards" in Table 6.7 shows the effects of reducing the performance standards for the four employment-income objectives (Y_6, Y_7, Y_8, Y_9) to a fixed level of 50 percent. Significant shifts include the entry of Community Action job-training programs (X_{34} and X_{35}) into the solution, a change in emphasis among Neighborhood Youth Corps programs (X_{77} and X_{78}) from staying in school to unemployment, and a substantial increase in vocational education programs (X_{80}).

Alternative program budgets in the housing model are also evaluated, with the clearance programs (X_1, X_2, X_3, X_4) set at lower minimums, public housing construction (PUBELD, PUBFAM) set at lower minimums, and the budget for potential receivership programs substantially increased. The results show, in addition to the expected decreases in X_1-X_7, major increases in X_{11} (rehabilitation of substandard dwelling units as public housing for low-income families) and X_{18} (receivership action against substandard housing for moderate-income families) and a major decrease in X_{13} (public rehabilitation of substandard housing for moderate-income families).

Finally, the significance of assigning weights to the objectives in the housing model, for the maximize-impact solution, is also considered. Table 6.6 shows the results of assigning a weight of 2.0 to Y_4, while remaining objectives receive a weighting of 1.0. In effect, this amounts to doubling the effectiveness coefficients for the Y_4 row when computing the row of total impact coefficients (objective function A). The effectiveness coefficients in the performance standard remain the same. In this example, shifts among the allocations resulting from the weighting are not significant.

CONCLUSIONS

These potential applications of mathematical programming in a plan/program design and evaluation context illustrate its versatility as a plan evaluation tool. These results should not, of course, be considered as actual recommendations for the various Model City Programs concerned—the data base is far too sketchy for that. However, they are representative of the kinds of insights and findings that mathematical programming models could produce, once given appropriate data and supporting analysis inputs. It is hoped that a simple framework for continuing research and development in these supporting areas has been outlined. Whether mathematical programming is explicitly used or not, the information systems and analytic studies called for here are the types most likely to be useful in constructing basic programs-objectives matrices. Parallel research should continue to explore how such matrices might best be recast as urban-improvement and public-investment programming models.

In short, much work remains to be done before viable urban-improvement programming models can actually be developed. This exploratory study indicates that several basic guidelines for continuing research efforts can be drawn.

1. Identifying objectives

Though the need for quantitative measures of goal achievement is clear, options are still open regarding the choice of specific objectives and measurable indexes. If these indexes are consistently designed to reflect community-wide socioeconomic conditions and characteristics (in terms of persons, families, housing units, acres, or other basic units), then objectives can be expressed in terms of desired changes in terms of desired changes in the numbers, rates, and proportions associated with these socioeconomic conditions. This will permit the establishment of performance standards for each index, and the development of consistent methods for matching programs against objectives.

2. Identifying programs

Alternative programs and policies must be expressed in terms of three essential characteristics—the objectives to which they are related, the impact or effectiveness they will have in achieving each objective, and the costs associated with varying levels of effectiveness. This will permit the development of cost-effectiveness accounts for each objective, comparing the costs encountered by different programs in achieving a given level of effectiveness (or performance standard), or comparing the different impact levels that can be achieved for a given budget, if assigned to each of the program alternatives. For maximum flexibility, costs should be measured in terms of dollars.

3. Measuring effectiveness

In order to permit comparisons and trade-offs among different programs and groups of programs, a common measure is also essential for the development of mathematical programming models. If objectives are represented as changes in various measurable socioeconomic conditions, and programs are expressed in dollars, then basic cost-per-unit-output parameters can be developed, using appropriate persons, family, housing, or other units of output or impact. These cost-per-unit-output parameters can then be utilized to develop a matrix of relative effectiveness coefficients. One way to define the common measure of goal achievement needed in such a matrix is to let each coefficient represent the percentage of objective j that can be achieved by each dollar invested in program i.

4. Predicting effectiveness

Programs-objectives effectiveness matrices of this type will require a prodigious amount of supporting research and analysis. Basic cost-effectiveness parameters cannot be estimated without considerable research into the impacts of alternative programs and policies upon their target populations. Unanticipated consequences must also be investigated. These supporting activities will rely upon major progress in the coordinated development of data resources and information systems. Predicting program effectiveness will involve improved cost-accounting and records-keeping procedures, the continuing application of various univariate and multivariate statistical analyses and, in some cases, the development of more elaborate socioeconomic simulation models. Identifying and dealing with program interdependencies will present particularly crucial problems for analysis.

5. Sensitivity analyses

Because the level of knowledge implied by an optimal solution is likely to be unrealistic, and because political decision makers are likely to be unreceptive to such an overall allocation, the primary value of mathematical programming may well lie with the identification of marginal differences among alternative variables and parameters. The sensitivity analysis of all elements—standards, budgets, or programs—within a programming problem can provide a good deal of information on relative costs, effectiveness, and trade-offs. Comparison of these marginal sensitivities will, in general, tell us how important each variable or parameter will be in attempting to achieve our overall objective (minimum cost or maximum impact). Revised solutions for a programming problem can also test the relative effects of specific standard, budget, or program alternatives.

ACKNOWLEDGEMENTS

This chapter is based upon the author's doctoral dissertation in Civil Engineering at Northwestern University. The advice and encouragement of Professors George L. Peterson, Walter D. Fisher, and Arthur P. Hurter are gratefully acknowledged.

NOTES

1. Morris Hill, "A Goals-Achievement Matrix for Evaluating Alternative Plans," Journal of the American Institute of Planners 34 (January 1968): 19-29. See also Morris Hill, "A Method for the Evaluation of Transportation Plans," Highway Research Record, no. 180 (Washington, D.C.: Highway Research Board, 1967), pp. 21-34. A matrix method for plan evaluation is also proposed in Edward L. Falk, "Measurement of Community Values: The Spokane Experiment," Highway Research Record, no. 229 (Washington, D.C.: Highway Research Board, 1968), pp. 53-64.

2. Kenneth J. Schlager, "A Land-Use Plan Design Model," Journal of the American Institute of Planners 31 (May 1965): 103-17. Other attempts at applying mathematical programming in a metropolitan planning context have focused upon the aggregate behavior of residential developers and consumers, rather than upon achieving a set of community-wide objectives. See Kenneth J. Schlager, "A Recursive Programming Theory of the Residential Land Development Process," Highway Research Record, no. 126 (Washington, D.C.: Highway Research Board, 1966), pp. 24-32; John Herbert and Benjamin J. Stevens, "A Model for the Distribution of Residential Activities in Urban Areas," Journal of Regional Science 2 (Fall 1960): 21-36.

3. For accounts of the two models mentioned here, see William Jessiman, Daniel Brand, Alfred Tumminia, and C. Roger Brussee, "A Rational Decision-making Technique for Transportation Planning," Highway Research Record, no. 180 (Washington, D.C.: Highway Research Board, 1967), pp. 71-80; Charles G. Schimpeler and W. L. Grecco, "Systems Evaluation: An Approach Based upon Community Structure and Values," Highway Research Record, no. 238 (Washington, D.C.: Highway Research Board, 1968), pp. 123-52. Mathematical programming models have also been proposed for evaluating low-cost housing alternatives in A. L. Silvers and A. K. Sloan, "A Model Framework for Comprehensive Planning in New York City," Journal of the American Institute of Planners 31 (August 1965): 246-51, and

for evaluating urban renewal alternatives in Wilbur A. Steger, "The
Pittsburgh Urban Renewal Simulation Models," Journal of the American
Institute of Planners 31 (May 1965): 144-49.

4. The more abstract interpretations described here may be found
in Robert E. Coughlin, "The Capital Programming Problems," Journal
of the American Institute of Planners 26 (February 1960): 39-48;
Robert E. Coughlin and Benjamin H. Stevens, "Public Facility Pro-
gramming and the Achievement of Development Goals," paper prepared
for the Seminar on Land-Use Models, University of Pennsylvania,
Philadelphia, October 1964; George L. Peterson, "Complete Value
Analysis: Highway Beautification and Environmental Quality," Highway
Research Record, no. 182 (Washington, D.C.: Highway Research
Board, 1967), pp. 9-17.

5. U.S. Department of Housing and Urban Development, Improving
the Quality of Urban Life: A Program Guide to Model Neighborhoods
in Demonstration Cities (Washington, D.C.: Government Printing
Office, 1966).

6. This use of performance standards is discussed in U.S. De-
partment of Housing and Urban Development, Measures of Living Qual-
ity in Model Neighborhoods, Technical Assistance Bulletin No. 2
(Washington, D.C.: HUD, Model Cities Administration, July 1968);
U.S. Department of Housing and Urban Development, "Comprehensive
Program Submission Requirements," CDA Letter No. 4 (Washington,
D.C.: Model Cities Administration, July 1968).

7. For reviews of the problems and procedures of urban model-
building and analysis in general, see Willard B. Hansen, "Quantitative
Methods in Urban Planning," in Principles and Practice of Urban Plan-
ning, William I. Goodman and Eric C. Freund, eds. (Washington, D.C.:
International City Managers' Association, 1968); Ira S. Lowry, "A
Short Course in Model Design," Journal of the American Institute of
Planners 31 (May 1965): 158-166; William A. Steger, "Review of Ana-
lytic Techniques for the CRP," Journal of the American Institute of
Planners 31 (May 1965): 166-71. Examples of specific simulation
models are described in Ira M. Robinson, Harry B. Wolfe, and Robert
L. Barringer, "A Simulation Model for Renewal Programming,"
Journal of the American Institute of Planners 31 (May 1965): 126-34;
F. Stuart Chapin, Jr., "A Model for Simulating Residential Develop-
ment," Journal of the American Institute of Planners 31 (May 1965):
120-25.

8. For a brief discussion of these programming techniques, see,
for example, John D. C. Little, "Mathematical Techniques: Mathematical Programming," in Operations Research for Public Systems,
Philip M. Morse and Laura W. Bacon, eds. (Cambridge, Mass.: MIT
Press, 1967).

7

INTERACTIVE
SENSITIVITY ANALYSIS
IN TRANSPORTATION
PLAN EVALUATION

Increasing attention is being focused on the transportation plan evaluation process, as perhaps the pivotal point in the continuing transportation planning process. Fewer regional-system plans are being implemented and heeded; too many route-location controversies embroil corridor planning; environmentalists point toward a shallow consideration of indirect effects; citizens tend to distrust the technical planner; statewide planners seek a meaningful framework for expanded activity; and, in general, at all levels of transportation planning—state, regional, corridor—the need for more carefully defined and elaborated alternative plans has become apparent. A more rigorous and thorough evaluation of these alternatives is necessary, based upon broad community and public official participation strategies.

A major theme in the development of improved plan evaluation techniques lies in the use of "cost-effectiveness" frameworks.[1] Effectiveness is measured in terms of relative levels of goal achievement, moving beyond dollar-valued benefits to consider and include other quantitative as well as qualitative measures. Figure 7.1 depicts the basic elements contained within a transportation-plan evaluation process recently designed for the Southern California Association of Governments (SCAG).[2] It emphasizes the use of a wide range of effectiveness criteria for evaluation; distinguishes between corridor, system, and design scales of planning and evaluation, with an emphasis on the system scale; and suggests that evaluation should proceed through at least two major cycles. The development of comparative

---

Reprinted from Transportation 3 (1974): 280-310, with permission of Elsevier Scientific Publishing Company, Amsterdam.

FIGURE 7.1

Basic Elements in Regional Transportation Plan Evaluation: SCAG

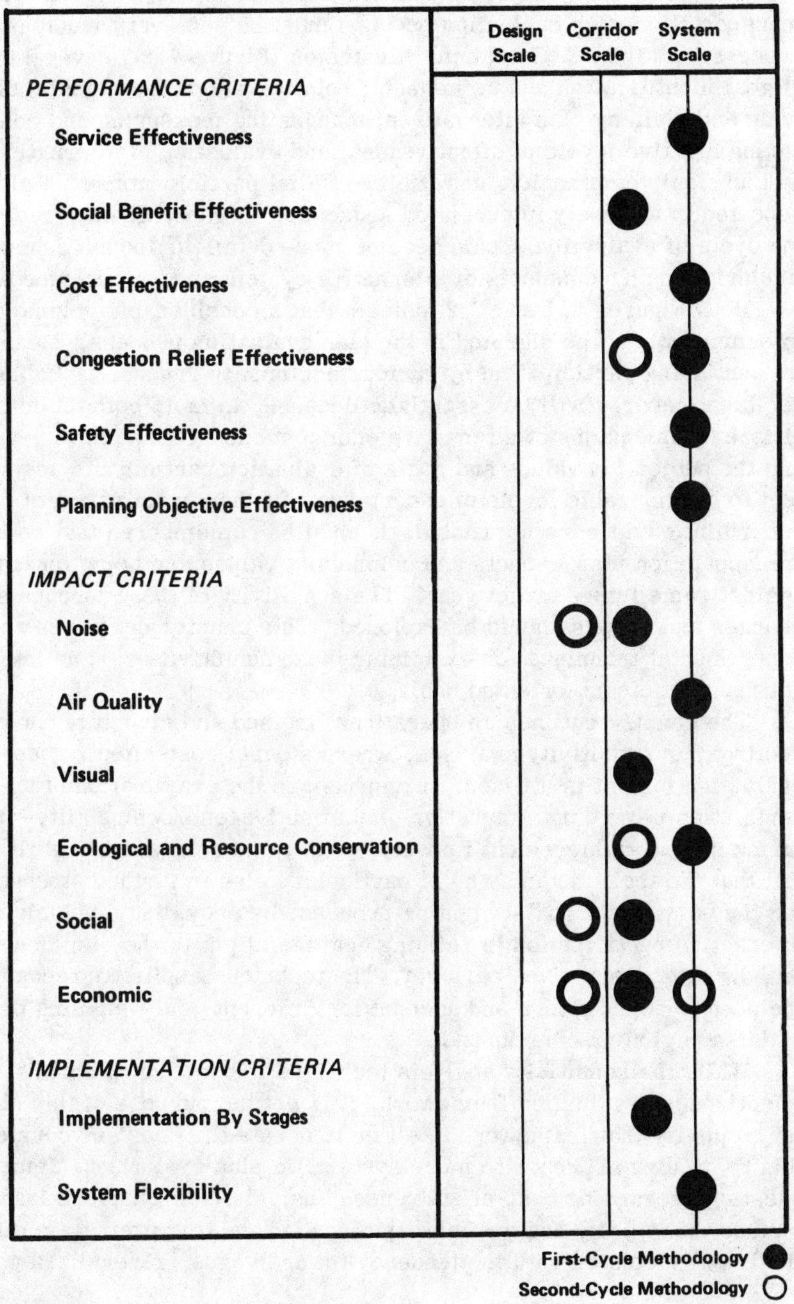

	Design Scale	Corridor Scale	System Scale
PERFORMANCE CRITERIA			
Service Effectiveness			●
Social Benefit Effectiveness		●	
Cost Effectiveness			●
Congestion Relief Effectiveness		○	●
Safety Effectiveness			●
Planning Objective Effectiveness			●
IMPACT CRITERIA			
Noise	○	●	
Air Quality			●
Visual		●	
Ecological and Resource Conservation		○	●
Social	○	●	
Economic	○	●	○
IMPLEMENTATION CRITERIA			
Implementation By Stages		●	
System Flexibility			●

First-Cycle Methodology ●
Second-Cycle Methodology ○

effectiveness measures that can then be subjectively "traded off" among alternatives by decision makers and others, is a basic underlying evaluation strategy.

Because of its complexity and critical participatory elements, the transportation-plan evaluation process must be seen very much as a process. As the SCAG example illustrates (Figure 7.2), several cycle of goal identification and refinement; relative weighting of goals; clarifying and refining plan alternatives; forecasting measuring and comparing relative levels of effectiveness; and evaluation of alternatives by technical, community, and public-official participants; must all be repeated in a loosely interrelated sequence. In general, each succeeding cycle of evaluation should become more detailed, focusing on particularly sensitive aspects of alternative system and/or corridor plans

Both Figures 7.1 and 7.2 indicate that a considerable volume of information must be digested in the plan evaluation process. Meaningful continuing participation by various community groups, including decision makers, will be essential. Because, in fact, both the many different dimensions of alternative plan costs and goal achievements and the subjective values and goals of evaluation participants are subject to considerable levels of uncertainty, further examination of these uncertainties appears warranted. It must be remembered that both transportation plan impacts and community values are being forecasted against some future target year. The sensitivity of these forecasts to changes and errors should be explored. This chapter describes an experimental technique for examining these sensitivities on an interactive, participant-oriented basis.

The chapter outlines an operational method and structure for conducting plan sensitivity analyses, where a basic cost–effectiveness evaluation format is utilized. It emphasizes the examination of uncertainties regarding alternative plan effectiveness/desirability—in terms of goal–achievement impacts, costs, and goal weighting. It is felt that the technique may be of particular value in further strengthening the community goal–weighting process, by providing a vehicle for interactive participation in refining goals, in light of their influence on how plan alternatives perform. The technique explicitly recognizes the need to acknowledge and account for different goal weighting profile within a region or community.

While the sensitivity analysis technique is based upon a cost–effectiveness evaluation framework, it is not the purpose of this chapter to justify that framework itself or to debate the pros and cons of this particular approach to more systematic plan evaluation. Important questions regarding cost–effectiveness analysis (see Chapters 2 and 4) include the validity and workability of goal–weighting exercises; difficulties associated with the tendency toward vague, generalized goals,

FIGURE 7.2

Basic Process for Regional Transportation Plan Evaluation: SCAG

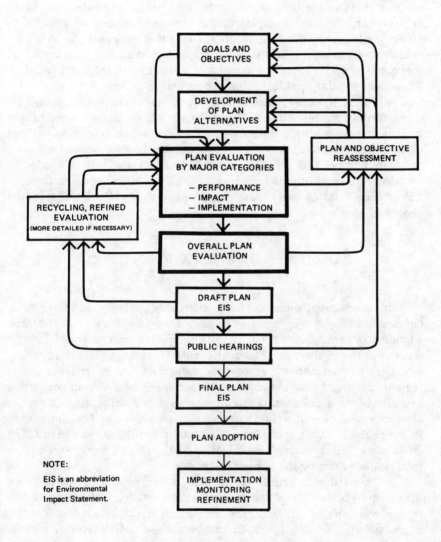

NOTE:

EIS is an abbreviation for Environmental Impact Statement.

with implicit assumptions, interdependencies, and overlaps; problems
with the availability of data for use as criteria of goal achievement, as
well as with the suitability of such criteria in fully measuring each
goal; the dangerous tendency for summary weighted scores to hide important plan differences; the often serious limitations of forecasting
models in providing the kinds of data most useful as goal-achievement
criteria; and the often complex difficulties of assigning weights to abstract goals, without a clear picture of what these goals (as well as
relatively abstract, generalized plan alternatives) mean, in terms of
more specific, localized circumstances familiar to the participant.
These and similar problems are not investigated here.

It is felt, however, that sensitivity analysis can soften some of
these limitations by better defining the variations in goal weights and
impact forecasts within which many plan evaluation outcomes will not
change significantly. In any event, whatever the evaluation framework,
the main point of this chapter is that sensitivity analysis is needed to
acknowledge explicitly and deal with plan evaluation uncertainties.
These uncertainties will exist regardless of the evaluation framework
chosen.

SAN DIEGO PLAN EVALUATION CONTEXT

An interactive, computerized sensitivity analysis technique is
currently under development by the San Diego Region Comprehensive
Planning Organization (CPO). It will be applied over the next few
months in the evaluation of four alternative regional plans. These
plans are currently being elaborated using a series of land-use and
transportation simulation models. Other measures of plan performance
are also being generated. Delphi techniques are being used to generate
alternate sets of goal weights among citizen groups and decision makers
in the region. Plan costs, for major public facilities, are also being
calculated. After extensive evaluation, selection of a preferred plan
is anticipated during the spring of 1974.

A few additional details on the San Diego plan evaluation process
may help to better define the context within which sensitivity-analysis
procedures will be utilized. The four alternatives under consideration
are based on traditional plan-form concepts—existing trends, radial
corridors, multiple centers, and controlled trends.[3] Each of these
is being advanced as an "idealized" target. After preliminary rounds
of evaluation, it is expected that additional composite alternatives,
combining the best features of each initial alternative, will be generated and further evaluated. The initial alternatives simply provide

basic organizing principles around which to structure different regional growth and distribution patterns.

A full set of urban system simulation models are currently being applied. Foremost among these is the Projective Land-Use Model (PLUM), which has recently been adapted and calibrated specifically for the San Diego Region.[4] This model will provide the greatest variety of plan characteristics, covering the distribution of 11 different types of land use, 12 different family income levels, five different types of employment, and related socioeconomic characteristics. It will provide detailed, small-area inputs for the operation of the traditional battery of transportation models (trip generation, trip distribution, modal split, traffic assignment, and transit assignment), as well as other models involving flood control and drainage patterns, regional park attractiveness, and water and sewer facility requirements. Additional forecasting or simulation models are anticipated or under development in air quality and housing market analysis. In general, all models will be applied to provide different forecasts under each of the four basic plan-form concepts.

It was acknowledged early in the San Diego plan evaluation process that a separate identification of regional goals and objectives, and quantitative and qualitative criteria to be applied against them, would be essential. Consequently, under a Regional Goals Program involving intensive levels of community participation, a set of some 45 different regional goals were identified.[5] These goals fell into 10 different categories, with a further stratification into about 200 more detailed objectives accomplished in most goal areas. Criteria and measures that might be applied against each goal were also considered concurrently. Special efforts were made to identify measures to be generated by regional simulation models that might be converted into criteria. Other sources for criteria, and other important plan characteristics to be forecasted, were also identified. An initial listing of nearly 400 criteria was further reviewed and reduced to a list of some 65, and subsequently 25, criteria to be emphasized in plan evaluation. This key list is intended to provide a capsule picture of the differences between alternatives. All goals and criteria are under continuing review and revision.

The San Diego plan evaluation procedure recognizes that the assignment of weights among different goals will be essential in clarifying the differences between alternatives.[6] Consequently, an ongoing activity within the process has involved the preliminary assignment of weights to the goals identified in the goals program, by citizen groups, local government officials, special-interest groups, and by members of CPO advisory committees. In particular, elected officials on the CPO Board of Directors (Policy Committee) have been involved. Several versions of a Delphi technique have been applied in this exercise, with the clear understanding that these goal-weighting exercises are intended to clarify differences between goals. They will be subject to further review, and all participants may revise their weightings as the plan evaluation process continues.

The costs of the different alternative plan-form concepts are also being estimated, at both regional and local levels. Regional costs will cover major region-level systems and facilities, including highways, transit, major water and sewer lines and facilities, major recreation facilities, etc. It is expected that differences in these costs will be stressed in comparing plan alternatives. In addition, methods for analyzing variations in local governmental service costs, covering such facilities/services as education, police and fire protection, local streets, and related municipal services, may also be important. These may be matched against the relative tax revenues to be generated by each alternative.

Regional transportation plan analysis and evaluation will represent a major element within the CPO plan evaluation process. In particular, the impact of transportation facilities and services upon both transportation and nontransportation goals will be emphasized. Consequently, many of the data to be produced from or built upon transportation simulation model outputs will be converted to goal-achievement criteria, in a number of different goal areas. These include transportation impacts upon the environment, physical form of the region, growth and economy, housing, and related areas. The transportation cost and benefit data traditionally utilized in transportation planning, including user operating costs, travel-time savings, accident costs, system capital and operating costs, and related direct and indirect consequences, will still be utilized but set within this broader land-use/transportation planning framework.

Though the San Diego sensitivity analysis technique is still in an experimental stage, under further development and refinement, the eventual need for a carefully designed "user environment" is being anticipated. It is expected that a special room will be set aside for plan evaluation purposes, with a wide variety of wall-mounted charts, maps, tables, and graphs used to depict the key differences between alternative plans. This room would be used for continuing work on elaborating these alternatives, including application of the sensitivity analysis procedure. Graphic displays would be used to reinforce many key areas of plan impact, including transportation impacts, and to suggest some of the important differences between plans that should be tested further. The "Plan Evaluation Room" would be the central repository for all data, computer model outputs, maps, studies, special reports, goal-weighting analyses, and related efforts pertinent to plan evaluation.

Within this context, it is hoped that use of the sensitivity analysis technique might become routine. A remote computer terminal would be located in the room, used for other analysis purposes as well. Through appropriate wall-mounted instructions and background information, individuals and groups working in or visiting the room would be encouraged to utilize the interactive sensitivity analysis technique. Special demonstrations and orientation sessions are anticipated. In the course of the several-month plan evaluation effort both individuals and groups would be encouraged to utilize the technique, either with or without supplementary technical assistance from CPO staff.

STRUCTURING A SENSITIVITY ANALYSIS TECHNIQUE

The San Diego sensitivity analysis technique attempts to capitalize on potentials for developing an "online" processing capability. Using a remote computer terminal, it will be possible to allow immediate testing of different goal weights or impact forecasts, simply by key-punching them in for direct computer processing. In this case, the appropriate cost-effectiveness tables and relationships would be stored within the computer, and the results could be reported in any form desired. For example, effects on a particular group of objectives or on a summary cost-effectiveness index, for each alternative, could be printed out.

In fact, with appropriate programming, online sensitivity analysis could be linked with a computer graphics capability. Graphic goal-achievement profiles could be printed out, or various computer mappings of relative plan differences could be generated. Visual displays on a cathode ray tube (similar to a TV screen) could even be produced. All of the computer hardware and software necessary for such online analysis and display capabilities are currently available within the computer industry.[7] Some, including computer mapping techniques, are currently being utilized by CPO. These features are also being carefully reviewed as to their applicability and desirability in connection with further development of the sensitivity analysis methodology.

The "interactive" or "online" feature of the San Diego technique is one of its major characteristics. It emphasizes, through a coordinated series of printed computer instructions, the offering of a full range of user options. These options involve opportunities for altering or manipulating the results of an initial comparison of plan alternatives. Because of the complexity of the plan evaluation process, and the many different types of goals and objectives that must be

considered, these user options must be well-coordinated and systematically communicated to the user. In addition to online plan analyses
at a computer terminal, it is also suggested that a variety of graph-
ical devices, pertinent to the user's areas of interest, also be used.
These would illustrate, in a supplementary way, the results of basic
forecasts and goal achievement analyses for each alternative.

The key to the sensitivity analysis procedure involves a goal-
achievement or cost-effectiveness matrix, comparing the plan alternatives, that is stored within the computer.[8] A preliminary, hypothetical example has been developed to illustrate the structure of such
a matrix, as well as the need for and potential complexity of sensitivity analyses. The example also shows how the interactive features
of the procedure can be approached sequentially, carrying the user
stage by stage through a series of analysis options, any one of which
he may repeat as often as he wishes. Figure 7.3 and Tables 7.1-7.4
summarize this example, and illustrate the types of sensitivity testing
and cost-effectiveness analysis output that may be generated by the
San Diego sensitivity analysis program. It should be stressed that
this program is under continuing development and refinement and is
currently regarded as in an experimental stage.[9] Hypothetical data
have been entered to show how the technique might work. Total costs
for a complete run, making numerous sensitivity tests, average about
$4.00. Several important elements of the technique are described
below.

1. User Instructions. Figure 7.3 illustrates the instructions that, if
   needed, may be printed out for the user's orientation. These instructions provide a quick summary of the purpose of the procedure,
   its general capabilities, and requirements to be made of the user.
   The simplicity of the procedure is stressed. On a step-by-step
   basis, the user is then presented with the series of output options
   and sensitivity analyses among which he may choose.

2. Cost-Effectiveness Analysis Format. Three different options are
   available to display cost-effectiveness analysis output. First, a
   complete printout of all goals used in the evaluation, along with
   their relative weights, applicable criteria, forecasted impacts,
   and weighted scores, is available (Table 7.1 shows an excerpt from
   one of nine goal areas). Second, summary scores for each goal
   area are available, and finally a summary over all goal areas is
   available (both shown in Table 7.2).

   Table 7.1 summarizes several of the key features of the cost-
   effectiveness evaluation framework that is being employed. Note
   that several different criteria may be applied against a single
   goal. Only one of these measures, or an average of them, however,
   can be used to represent goal-achievement. Forecasted impacts

FIGURE 7.3

User Instructions for Sensitivity Analysis

E
#Running 5807

This is the cost effectiveness-sensitivity analysis procedure used in the CPO Plan Evaluation and Selection Process. Do you need instructions? Answer yes or no.

YES

   The purpose of this procedure is to determine goal achievement scores and cost-effectiveness ratios for alternative regional plans. This is accomplished by matching the goal weights assigned by any group to the various projections generated for the different plans. Each goal has specific criteria associated with it which will allow the proper measurement to take place.

If you are not familiar with these goals, objectives, and criteria refer to the report, GOALS AND OBJECTIVES OF THE SAN DIEGO REGION. If you are not familiar with the four alternative regional plans, refer to the CPO reports which describe each plan.

Although the ensuing, step-by-step instructions are self explanatory, the list below describes the options available.

1. You can specify which community group's set of goal weights you wish to analyze.
2. You can obtain a complete analysis goal by goal.
3. You can obtain a summary analysis of individual goal areas only.
4. You can obtain a summary analysis over all goals.
5. You can change weights, impacts, or costs to test sensitivity.

You will now be presented with a simple series of questions asking which of these analysis options you wish to explore. All you will be required to do is to type a YES or NO answer to each question. When an opportunity to make changes in weights, impacts, or costs is presented, you will then be required to type a few numbers decribing the sensitivity changes you wish to examine.

The sequence of instructions has been designed to allow you to explore a wide range of sensitivity tests, singly or in combination. The computer will automatically print out the results of each sensitivity test you request.

GOOD LUCK --- ---

TABLE 7.1

Cost–Effectiveness Reporting Excerpt

Cost-effectiveness analysis Del Mar
Physical form goal area
Alternative plan scores

Goal	Relative weight	Forecasted Impact				Weighted Score			
		Existing trends	Control trends	Radial corr.	Multi center	Existing trends	Control trends	Radial corr.	Multi center
2. Preserve and enhance the pattern of distinct identifiable communities throughout the region. Criterion: Population within currently urbanized areas. Criterion: Population within currently unincorporated areas. Criterion: Population within 30 minutes travel time of major centers.	9.0	0.67	0.69	0.75	0.69	6.0	6.3	6.7	6.3
3. Adopt and implement a regional development plan characterized by a series of well planned, economically balanced communities, encompassing a wide variety of residential densities and housing types.	6.0	0.42	0.53	0.60	0.57	2.5	3.2	3.6	3.4

Cost-effectiveness analysis Del Mar
Physical form goal area

Alternative plan scores

Goal	Relative weight	Forecasted Impact				Weighted Score			
		Existing trends	Control trends	Radial corr.	Multi center	Existing trends	Control trends	Radial corr.	Multi center
Criterion: Multi-family dwelling units, by sub-area.									
Criterion: Residential densities, vicinity of rapid transit stations.									
Criterion: Basic employment jobs per household, by sub-area.									
Criterion: Commercial and non-basic jobs per household, by sub-area.									
4. Maintain and enhance the position of central San Diego as the administrative-financial-cultural center of the region in addition to subregional centers.	7.0	0.57	0.56	0.60	0.63	4.0	3.9	4.2	4.4
Criterion: Population growth, Center City San Diego.									
Criterion: Employment growth, Center City San Diego.									
Summary score — Physical form goal area						12.5	13.4	14.5	14.1

233

TABLE 7.2

Cost-Effectiveness Summary Analysis

Cost-effectiveness Analysis
Del Mar

Goal Areas	Weighted Score			
	Existing trends	Control trends	Radial corr.	Multi center
Summary score – human resources	15.3	8.0	11.2	13.4
Summary score – human resources – last run	15.3	8.0	11.2	13.4
Summary score – education	0.0	0.0	0.0	0.0
Summary score – education – last run	0.0	0.0	0.0	0.0
Summary score – growth and economy	6.3	8.7	7.8	6.8
Summary score – growth and economy – last run	6.3	8.7	7.8	6.8
Summary score – physical form	12.5	13.4	14.5	14.1
Summary score – physical form – last run	12.5	13.4	14.5	14.1
Summary score – transportation	7.4	15.6	11.5	15.4
Summary score – transportation – last run	10.2	18.0	9.2	15.4
Summary score – housing	2.3	4.6	0.9	1.2
Summary score – housing – last run	2.3	4.6	0.9	1.2
Summary score – open space	5.7	7.5	12.7	13.0
Summary score – open space – last run	6.8	8.5	10.0	11.0
Summary score – environment	18.8	29.6	16.7	17.9
Summary score – environment – last run	18.8	29.6	16.7	17.9
Summary score – government	1.1	5.6	5.3	1.8
Summary score – government – last run	1.1	5.6	5.3	1.8
Summary score – total	69.4	93.0	80.7	83.6
Applicable costs, in $ million	7.0	6.0	5.0	8.0
Cost-effectiveness ratio	9.9	15.5	16.1	10.5
Summary score – total – last run	73.3	96.4	75.7	81.6
Applicable costs, in $ million	7.0	6.0	5.0	8.0
Cost-effectiveness ratio – last run	10.5	16.1	15.1	10.2

will be handled on a normalized basis; that is, actual measures of criteria will be converted to percentages of a high-low range of possible impacts for each criterion. (For completeness, both the actual impact and its normalized conversion might be shown on a supplementary tabulation.) Relative weights assigned to each goal are used to calculate weighted goal-achievement scores.

While a simple linear summary score over all nine goal areas is then shown in Table 7.2, it might be desirable to assign weights to the goal areas themselves, as well as to individual goals within each area. This possibility is under further study at CPO. Depending upon the procedure used to assign weights across all goals, this kind of double-weighting might be redundant. The goal-weighting procedure presently being utilized by CPO is described further below.

3. Goal Weighting. Note that both Tables 7.1 and 7.2 depict the cost-effectiveness analyses that result from applying only one set of goal weights—in this case, those of the suburb of Del Mar. A total of 34 different community groups, in addition to the CPO Board of Directors and a Regional Goals Committee, in the San Diego region participated in a series of Delphi-like goal-weighting exercises. The goal weights of any one of these groups, or an average over all groups, may be selected for each sensitivity analysis. (The average or composite weighting is being further studied, and different ways to combine various weightings are being explored. It may be desirable to weight different groups themselves.)

Many options will actually be available for conducting the goal-weighting exercises that underlie the cost-effectiveness approach.[10] The San Diego procedure provides an illustrative example. Each of 45 basic goals was rated on a zero-to-ten priority scale.[11] Each participating group utilized a Delphi-type procedure, where two to three rounds of priority assignment were conducted. After each round, participants were given a chance to revise their ratings, based on the average ratings of the group. Discussion was permitted during these review sessions, but respondents each filled out their own survey form individually and anonymously. The highest average goal weight fell at 8.0, the lowest at 4.3. The overall average goal weight was 6.7.

4. Forecasted Impacts. Twenty-five of the primary 45 goals used in the Delphi goal-weighting exercise appear to be measurable (directly or indirectly) by computer-generated forecast data. These goals will be emphasized by comparing regional plan alternatives, at least initially. A total of around 65 forecast data items appear to be applicable as goal-achievement criteria. As noted above, these criteria will be forecasted by a series of computer-based

simulation models, operated apart from, and providing inputs to, the cost-effectiveness and sensitivity analysis procedure. Many of the 65 criteria will apply to more than one of the 25 key goals.

The "forecasted impact" values shown in Table 7.4 have actually been normalized, as mentioned above. To accomplish this, a normalizing range will be set for each of the 65 criteria. This range will consist of a logical low- and a logical high-impact measure, within which all of the forecasted impacts for the four plan alternatives will fall. This will permit all impact measures to be converted, in effect, to a percentage score. This percentage score will represent relative levels of goal achievement to be compared consistently, as a common ratio measure, regardless of the original units of measurement for impact (acres, minutes of travel time, dollars, etc.). Judgment will necessarily be involved in setting many of these high-low ranges, with "reasonableness" being the target. Because the choice of range will itself affect plan scores, these ranges should also be subject to sensitivity testing. (However, note that, regardless of the range chosen, as long as it brackets all plan scores, the relative ranking of each alternative will remain the same.)

5. Summary Weighted Scores. For simplicity, and to summarize somehow the performance characteristics of the various alternative plans, a series of summary weighted scores are shown in Table 7.2, both within each of the nine goal areas and over all goal areas. Though devised to answer a real need on the part of decision makers for summarization in some form, the danger of oversimplification is recognized. A number of recent studies argue that summary or composite indexes should be avoided altogether, because they conceal too much valuable information, and tend to make the evaluation task look easier than it really is.[12] To help guard against oversimplification, one strategy might be to provide or deal with summary scores only in the presence of a full set of goal-achievement analyses. Visual aids, such as "goal-achievement profiles," which graphically display the relative performance of each alternative against all those under consideration, can be of great assistance here.[13] The organization and effective communication of plan evaluation results will continue to offer a real challenge.

6. Testing Sensitivities. In Tables 7.3 and 7.4 user instructions and operations for two of the basic sensitivity analysis options are depicted. Different combinations of sensitivity analysis may be explored in sequence, and several successive iterations throughout the procedure may be accomplished at any one sitting. Changes in the three basic areas of plan variability—goal weights (Table 7.3),

TABLE 7.3

Goal-Weighting Sensitivity Analysis

The following list represents the weight associated with each goal. An * means that the goal is currently used for evaluation, with one or more measurable criteria applied. Other goals may be included later.

To make changes merely type the goal area #, the goal #, and the new weight, with commas between each. When you are finished type 9,9,9.

Goal Area	Goal #	Goal Weight
1	1	9.0*
1	2	8.0
1	3	9.0*
1	4	8.0
1	5	8.0
1	6	6.0
2	1	9.0
3	1	7.0*
3	2	9.0
3	3	7.0*
4	1	9.0*
4	2	10.0
4	3	6.0*
4	4	7.0*
4	5	7.0
4	6	6.0
5	1	9.0*
5	2	9.0*
5	3	9.0*
5	4	9.0*
5	5	8.0*
6	1	9.0
6	2	8.0*
6	3	8.0*
6	4	6.0
6	5	6.0
7	1	10.0*
7	2	9.0*
7	3	8.0*
7	4	9.0*
7	5	9.0
8	1	10.0*
8	2	9.0

Goal Area	Goal #	Goal Weight
8	3	8.0*
8	4	9.0*
8	5	9.0*
8	6	10.0
8	7	7.0
8	8	7.0
9	1	9.0
9	2	7.0*
9	3	7.0*
9	4	6.0
9	5	8.0
9	6	9.0

PLEASE LIST YOUR CHANGES.

5,1,7.5
5,2,8.0
5,3,9.0
5,4,5.5
5,5,6.3
7,1,7.2
7,2,8.3
7,3,7.0
7,4,9.2
9,9,9

237

TABLE 7.4

Forecasted Impact Sensitivity Analysis

DO YOU WISH TO CHANGE ANY OF THE CRITERIA IMPACTS FOR ANY PLAN? ANSWER YES OR NO.

YES

The following list represents the impact associated with each criterion for each alternative plan. The last two numbers are the logical low and the logical high for that criterion. Criteria numbers indicate the goal area, goal, and specific criterion applied to each goal. See the wall chart for a written statement of goals and criteria.

To make changes merely type the criterion #, plan #, and the new impact with commas between each. When you are finished type 9,9,9. Use the following numbers for each plan.

EXISTING TRENDS = 1
RADIAL CORRIDORS = 2
CONTROLLED TRENDS = 3
MULTI CENTERS = 4

Criterion Number	Existing Trends	Radial Corridors	Controlled Trends	Multi Centers	Logical Low	Logical High
111	7.	7.	7.	7.	1.	15.
132	1100.	1100.	1100.	1100.	8000.	1200.
311	21.	25.	23.	24.	20.	30.
332	1100.	1100.	1100.	1100.	8000.	1200.
414	121000.	85000.	105000.	95000.	50000.	150000.
434	11.	19.	13.	15.	1.	20.
441	35.	31.	33.	32.	25.	45.
512	121525.	55000.	55000.	55000.	50000.	150000.
523	75692.	60000.	60000.	60000.	60000.	100000.
531	76781.	80000.	80000.	80000.	60000.	'0000.
541	1015763.	1300000.	1300000.	1300000.	1000000.	1500000.
554	62.	75.	65.	70.	60.	80.
622	7800.	8000.	7900.	8000.	7200.	9000.
631	20.	22.	23.	24.	20.	30.
711	7.	8.	10.	10.	5.	15.
722	12.	20.	15.	20.	10.	30.
731	55.	80.	75.	75.	70.	90.
743	10500.	12500.	11500.	11000.	10000.	12000.
811	200.	200.	200.	200.	300.	400.
832	18.	31.	22.	28.	15.	35.
841	75.	79.	78.	77.	65.	85.
851	100.	120.	115.	118.	90.	125.
921	1765.	1600.	1600.	1600.	1500.	2000.
931	115934.	117000.	117000.	117000.	100000.	120000.

PLEASE LIST YOUR CHANGES.

512,2,60000
523,2,65000
531,2,85000
541,2,1350000
554,2,70
711,3,12
722,3,20
731,3,70
743,3,10000
9,9,9

forecasted impacts (Table 7.4), and forecasted costs—may all be introduced. In addition, changes in the normalizing range associated with different impacts may also be explored.

    a. Goal Weights. Table 7.3 suggests that not all of the goals important in plan evaluation may yet be included in the cost-effectiveness evaluation framework. Acknowledgement of these more subjective goals will still be carried through the full evaluation process, even though they may not be included quantitatively. In other cases, data useful as criteria may still be under development, and could be included at a later time. Interim use of the sensitivity analysis and cost-effectiveness evaluation technique could still be made, as this figure suggests.

    One of the more important questions for sensitivity testing would be to determine whether a particular change in goal weights would lead to a shift in preference among the alternative plans. Such a change could simply represent the substitution of one community group goal-weighting vector for another, or perhaps a variation of the weights assigned to a few "touchy" or controversial goals might be entered. To illustrate such an output hypothetically, the changes in goal weights requested in Table 7.3 would, with no change in forecasted impacts or costs, produce the modified goal-achievement scores and cost-effectiveness measures shown earlier in Table 7.2. Note that, under this new set of goal weights, a different alternative would be preferred (higher overall cost-effectiveness ratio).

    b. Forecasted Impacts. Table 7.4 depicts changes in forecasted impacts that might be requested. Here the difference between "raw" and normalized impacts must be kept in mind. Raw impacts will be printed out, with the process of normalization conducted internally within the computer. Three-digit codes for each criterion number would reflect both the goal area (digit one) and the goal (digit two) to which the criteria related. Supplementary charts or tables should be used to allow these identifications.

    Again, a particularly useful application of sensitivity testing would be to determine whether one or more changes in forecasted impacts would be sufficient to cause a shift in preference among the alternative plans. Changes in forecasted impacts might be entered to reflect an acknowledged range of uncertainties (such as a 20 percent plus or minus error factor) or to accommodate alternative forecasts provided by other models, researchers, or community groups. To illustrate this possible outcome, the requested impact changes

listed in Table 7.4 would, given no change in goal weights or
costs, yield the same shift in hypothetical goal-achievements
scores, cost-effectiveness ratios, and plan preferences
depicted earlier in Table 7.2.

c. Normalizing Ranges. In association with the instructions
shown in Table 7.4, the user would also be presented with
an opportunity to change the value range (logical low/logical
high normalizing range) for each criterion. If, in Table 7.4,
a change in the value range of any criterion had been requested, the user would have been asked to type the criteria
number, a 1 or 2, to indicate whether a low or high value
was to be changed, and the new value, with commas between
each.

d. Forecasted Costs. Opportunities to alter forecasted plan
costs can also be made available. If, when the appropriate
instruction ("Do you wish to change any plan costs?") were
printed, a change in any plan costs had been requested, the
forecasted costs for each plan would have been printed out,
broken down by major type of costs (highways, transit, sewers, water supply, etc.). The user would have been in-
structed to type the cost category number, the plan number,
and the revised cost estimate, with commas between each,
for every change he wished to make.

e. Parametric Testing. In general, each of the above sensitivit
testing options involves the introduction of certain predetermined or given changes in goal weights, forecasted impacts,
normalizing ranges, or forecasted costs, simply to see what
the effect would be. There is also clearly an opportunity to
explore plan sensitivities on an intuitive, experimental basis
examining different sensitivities in sequence. Other options
would include a parametric testing for the effect upon the
overall cost-effectiveness ratio (or subratios) of a one-unit
change in any of the pertinent cost-effectiveness variables.
As a general strategy, this might become rather laborious,
and emphasis should probably be given to isolating those
goal-weight, impact, or cost variables that, singly or in
combination, are likely to have the greatest effect.

Perhaps a more useful thrust for this kind of parametric
analysis would be to locate those sets or combinations of
newly valued variables (and there would be many such sets)
that would have to be assumed in order for the "second-best"
or "third-best" alternative to equal or exceed the cost-
effectiveness of the currently preferred plan. The credibilit
(or lack of it) of these "break-even" points would help establish levels of confidence in the ultimately chosen plan.

As noted above, applications of the technique have to date been only experimental in nature. When the full results of applying the different system simulation models to each alternative are available, as converted to appropriate goal-achievement criteria, these will be entered in a cost-effectiveness matrix, such as that depicted in Table 7.1. It may be necessary to expand or revise the form of the matrix. When initial goal-weighting activities have been completed, appropriate values will also be entered. When cost analyses for each alternative are completed, these values will be entered. It may be desirable to separate out some types of costs (for example, transportation costs) for stratified analyses in relation to particular goal areas. Other refinements in the preliminary technique described here are also quite likely to be pursued.

It is hoped that refined versions of the technique will be of value to both CPO staff and its Policy Committee in the systematic evaluation of alternative regional plans. Exposure and involvement of staff members to the technique has already begun. While a more careful and systematic use of the procedure on the part of staff is anticipated, with some sort of memorandum on plan sensitivities to be issued, use of the technique by any staff member, citizen, administrator, or public official involved in the planning/evaluation process will be encouraged. Allowing an individual to explore, for himself, changes in his goal-weighting vector will be especially encouraged. Wherever possible, direct involvement of users, at the remote terminal, will be encouraged, in order to gain a greater awareness of the elements involved in sensitivity analysis. However, technicians or staff members should probably also be available to process outside sensitivity analysis requests.

ACKNOWLEDGMENTS

Programming and operationalizing the sensitivity analysis technique was accomplished by Lee Johnston of the Comprehensive Planning Organization, who also assisted in developing Figure 7.3, and Tables 7.1 through 7.4.

NOTES

1. E. N. Thomas and J. L. Schofer, Strategies for the Evaluation of Alternative Transportation Plans, National Cooperative Highway Research Program Report 96 (Washington, D.C.: Highway Research Board, 1970).

2. Gruen Associates, Transportation Plan Evaluation Process (Southern California Association of Governments, July 1973).

3. San Diego Region Comprehensive Planning Organization, Regional Development: Issues and Alternatives, 2 vols. (San Diego, Calif.: CPO, September 1972).

4. San Diego Region Comprehensive Planning Organization, The Regional Model System (San Diego, Calif.: CPO, April 1972).

5. San Diego Regional Goals Committee, Goals and Objectives for the San Diego Region (San Diego, Calif.: The Committee, November 1972).

6. Barton-Aschman Associates, Plan Evaluation and Selection Process (San Diego, Calif.: San Diego Region Comprehensive Planning Organization, June 1972).

7. J. B. Schneider, Interactive Graphics in Transportation Systems Planning and Design (University of Washington, January 1974); Highway Research Board, "Application of Interactive Graphics to Transportation System Planning," Highway Research Record, no. 455 (Washington, D.C.: The Board, 1973) (4 reports).

8. M. Hill, "A Goals-Achievement Matrix for Evaluating Alternative Plans," AIP Journal 34 (January 1968): 19-29.

9. L. Johnston and D. G. Stuart, "Interactive Sensitivity Analyses of Alternative Regional Plans," presented at American Institute of Planners Confer-In 1973, Boston, October 1973.

10. M. Skutsch and J. L. Schofer, "Goals Delphis for Urban Planning: Concepts in Their Design," Socio-Economic Planning Sciences 7, no. 2 (1973): 305-13.

11. San Diego Region Comprehensive Planning Organization, Priorities Among Regional Goals and Objectives (San Diego, Calif.: CPO, November 1973).

12. P. Kamnitzer, "Computer Aid to Design," Architectural Design (May 1969): 507-09; C. H. Oglesby, B. Bishop, and G. E. Willeke, "A Method for Decision Among Freeway Location Alternatives Based upon User and Community Consequences," Highway Research Record, no. 305 (Washington, D.C.: Highway Research Board, 1970), pp. 1-15.

13. Oglesby et al., op. cit.

8

INFORMATION SYSTEMS
IN URBAN PLANNING:
A REVIEW

Planning requires information—information on existing urban conditions, information on problems requiring planned solutions, information on proposed solutions themselves, and information on the relative desirability of different solutions or plans. In the past urban planners have often dealt with these information needs on a disjointed or one-shot basis. Information needs have been considered only in relation to the development of a particular plan or planning component. Severe problems in data availability have frequently been encountered, so that only a partial or incomplete look at problems and proposed solutions has been possible. Interrelationships between problems (and between successive planning efforts) have often been overlooked.

In particular, partly as a result of information difficulties, rigorous development and evaluation of alternative plans have usually been slighted. It has been difficult enough to document and support the need for and characteristics of a single, intuitively preferred plan. If, on the other hand, it were possible to have much of the information required for problem analysis and plan development and testing already available, collected on a continuing basis, kept at a centralized location, and organized so that data from different agencies or sources could be easily compared, considerable time would be saved for actual planning. It would be possible to strengthen the process of planning, by identifying interrelationships between different planning activities and plan components, thereby permitting greater

Reprinted with permission from American Society of Planning Officials, Planning Advisory Service Report No. 260 (August 1970).

attention to examination of alternative solutions to planning problems. For these reasons, "information systems" are of growing importance in urban and regional planning.

Though varying interpretations have appeared in the literature, the term "information system" generally implies that (a) records and information from several agencies have been coordinated and often are maintained at a central location; (b) the data are updated regularly; and (c) data can be quickly retrieved, displayed, and organized for preliminary analysis. In most cases each of these capabilities will call for the supporting use of electronic computers for data processing.

An urban information system is usually conceived as ideally metropolitan in scope, and as largely a method for taking advantage of the considerable information resources lying within the files of diverse public, quasi-public, and private agencies. Coordination and reconciliation of these ongoing files with each other (and, in particular, with a common geographic coding base) can improve tremendously the information available for planning.

There are many types of planning information that may not be computerized or that for some other reason may not be a part of such a system—for example, nonregular or specially collected types of data, such as citizen attitude or perception surveys, which are not likely to be updated regularly. But such data may still be coordinated with various elements of an information system.

Urban information systems and the systems approach to planning are strongly interdependent, largely because of the information demands associated with the "systems approach." Growing support for the systems approach in urban public administration as well as in urban planning has more or less paralleled the development of computer-based urban information systems. The systems approach provides a fundamental method for structuring various planning processes (transportation/land-use planning, comprehensive city planning, community renewal programming, capital improvement programming, Model Cities programming). It thereby also defines the associated information requirements.[1]

Four basic, interrelated steps comprise the systems approach to planning, each with critical information demands:

1. Identifying Community Objectives. Many types of data or information sources are likely to be required. A "richer" supply of regular agency-generated data provided by some sort of coordinated information system will mean that less time, effort, and budget need be expended in quantitatively supporting various community objectives. Greater latitude will be possible in the choice of variables by which to measure the achievement of

different objectives. Greater sensitivity in expressing objectives themselves can be achieved (concerning, for example, housing supply, land-use compatibility, building conditions, education, recreation, crime reduction, or unemployment). A wide variety of data on existing conditions and socioeconomic problems will be needed to match diverse objectives against appropriate measurable indexes.

2. Identifying Alternative Programs and Policies. Once problems and objectives have been adequately (measurably) defined, alternative solutions to those problems must be designed. If achievement of community objectives is regarded as "outputs" of various public plans, programs, and policies, then the plans, programs, and policies, together with the resource expenditures and commitments associated with them, can be regarded as "inputs." They too must be specified in measurable terms. The "costs" of alternative programs and policies should be identified, not only in terms of dollars but in terms of the various resources consumed. Information systems, especially if they include the administrative data of agencies directly involved with alternative programs and policies, can be of great value in properly identifying these alternatives.

3. Predicting Relative Effectiveness Levels. The most difficult phase of the systems approach is forecasting the impact of alternative programs and policies upon a given set of community objectives. Many different mathematical models have been developed for this phase (such as transportation planning models, urban development models, socioeconomic simulation models, regional economic models, programming/budgeting models), though some have met with only limited success. One of the most crucial constraints on model building and impact forecasting has been the lack of needed supporting data. Often the unavailability or improper format of required data will force the use of less satisfactory surrogates. Flexible testing of various assumed program-objective relationships or hypotheses is thereby restricted. Communication between model builders and information system designers should consequently be close and continuing in order to provide data more relevant for prediction and analysis.

4. Evaluating Alternative Programs and Policies. The final step of the systems approach calls for evaluation of predicted effectiveness levels and selection of a preferred plan or program from among the alternatives. Since this step is largely the product of the three previous steps—identifying objectives, identifying programs, and predicting effectiveness—it is not likely to use much further information system support. On the contrary, subjective or judgmental elements are likely to assume importance,

especially in estimating impact upon those objectives that could
not be readily quantified, and in assigning relative importance
to various impacts or objectives.

Against the background of such a systematic approach to planning,
this chapter reviews the development and application of urban information systems as they relate to the needs of urban and regional
planning. It describes the development of general purpose, interagency
information systems, with the planning department as only one of
many participating local governmental agencies. Four actual interagency urban information systems are briefly examined. Several
different applications of data systems in planning—including data
retrieval, report generation, statistical analysis, and computer
graphics—are described. The implications of the 1970 Census for
improved information capabilities are outlined. A number of potential
planning data requirements are discussed in relation to specific examples, and the broad range of plausible data needs is noted. The
design and operation of urban information systems are summarized
in terms of four major phases: data collection, data organization,
data processing, and data maintenance. Finally, the continuing needs
for coordinated urban information resources are outlined.

DEVELOPMENT OF URBAN INFORMATION SYSTEMS

Most of the urban information systems (or "data banks") presently
in operation have been developed to serve day-to-day public administration needs. The rapidly expanding and increasingly complex workload of many municipal, county, school-board, and other local governmental jurisdictions, together with the rising costs of government at
all levels, have led to the use of computer processing to save both
time and money, and frequently to increased accuracy and convenience
A planning department is consequently only one among many local
public agencies, bureaus, and departments likely to be participating
in the development and use of an urban information system. Very
often planning departments use such a system only intermittently, and
in some cases they have been only peripherally involved in system
design and planning.

Most urban and regional planning agencies, especially those
located in smaller metropolitan areas, are likely to find that their
own particular information needs and interests can best be met through
participation in a general-purpose, interagency urban information
system, because much of the local information of interest for planning
purposes is contained in one way or another within the files of other

agencies.[2] Usually only the largest city and metropolitan planning
agencies (including the major urban transportation studies) have successfully launched their own, semiautonomous information systems.

If a general-purpose information system or data bank is to serve
the needs of local planning agencies adequately, local planners must
thoroughly understand the workings of such systems. Much of the
information processed by these systems will be routine, of interest
mainly for internal administrative purposes. Other data, such as
those pertaining to land use or housing, will be of obvious and direct
importance for planners. Still other data may not be immediately
perceived as planning-related but could eventually become extremely
useful once various planning problems and concepts are more carefully analyzed. In any event, it is important to understand the organization and format of each type of administrative data that has potential
utility for planning. The many agencies involved, including the agency
in charge of data processing, should also be made aware of the potential importance of their data for planning purposes.

Among the types of data included in general-purpose information
systems have been the following:[3]

- General Administration: appropriations accounting, purchasing,
  cost accounting, inventory control, monthly financial statements,
  continuing daily audit, cash flow analysis, annual budget administration, capital budgeting, personnel payroll and accounting,
  fixed asset accounting, business licenses and permits, and
  equipment and vehicle maintenance

- Public Safety Administration: emergency vehicle dispatching and
  control, parking violations, moving traffic violations, crime
  reporting and mapping, arrest and conviction records, vehicle
  registration, wanted persons and stolen vehicles, driver registration and driving records, and vehicle inspection

- Property Assessment and Land-Use Controls: assessment rolls,
  reassessment conversions and updating, tax billing, tax collec-
  tions and delinquencies, title searches and tax histories, zoning
  classifications and changes, building permits, building code
  violations, housing code violations, and public property files

- Utility Administration (Water, Sewer, Electric, Refuse Disposal):
  meter reading, billing, cash receipts, and connections and
  disconnections

- Health and Welfare Administration: hospital cost accounting,
  hospital accounts receivable, hospital billing, medical records,
  hospital and health statistics, hospital resource scheduling,
  welfare cost accounting, and welfare records and payments

● School and Library Administration: student class scheduling, attendance reporting, grade reporting, test scheduling and scoring, student information files, library circulation, and library overdue notices

● Street and Highway Administration: street and highway inventory, street maintenance scheduling, traffic accident records, and traffic flow analysis and control

● Voter Registration and Jury Selection

Several specific examples will serve to illustrate the broad scope and capability that any particular general-purpose information system may assume. Examples at four different levels of local government— municipal (Los Angeles), county (Santa Clara), metropolitan (San Francisco Bay area), and regional (San Gabriel Valley)—are described briefly in the following sections. These are among the most advanced systems at each level, and the fact that each is from California documents the leadership of that state in the field. Each example is discussed in terms of system design and history, as well as general data-base characteristics. The role of planning and planning agencies within each system has varied a good deal.

Los Angeles Municipal Information System

The Los Angeles Data Service Bureau was established in 1963 to provide for the centralized administration of most city data-processing activities and services. Many of the city's numerous boards, commissions, and independent departments, including the civil service department, city controller, and city clerk, had previously operated their own data-processing equipment. All general-purpose tabulating and electronic data-processing equipment, including medium-size computers, were consolidated so they could be used with efficiency. The Data Service Bureau now operates two of the medium-size third-generation IBM 360/40 computers as well as one IBM 360/30. New applications of data processing are being systematically coordinated.

A revised master plan for the Los Angeles Municipal Information System (LAMIS) inaugurated in 1967 now guides all operations of the Data Service Bureau. LAMIS distinguishes ten functional subsystems for information processing, each serving one or more departments: library, fiscal, personnel, management, planning, building and safety, public works, traffic, police, and fire. These subsystems permit data sharing across departmental lines as needed. The LAMIS system has been developed in a series of steps, and is expected to be in full operation in the early 1970s. Among the various subsystems already in use are the automated city payroll system, automated library technical services, the sanitation-management information system, the city clerk business-tax system, the traffic-accident information subsystem, the capital-improvements information subsystem, and the fire-suppression-bureau reporting subsystem; others are still being designed.

The bureau's data base contains a wide range of municipal data, the bulk of which is associated with day-to-day governmental operations. Past data processing applications have tended to handle various departmental data files separately (with about 1,000 different computer programs). As LAMIS continues to develop, however, consolidation into master data files crossing departmental lines will increase. All applications will eventually be consolidated under the ten subsystems mentioned above. Coordination and management of the overall data base have been strengthened, and a data dictionary to describe all the information or data elements within the system is contemplated. The annual budget for the Data Service Bureau is in the neighborhood of $3 million.

The planning department has not yet used the bureau's data resources extensively, though it has a close relationship with the bureau. Use is likely to increase with the development of an Automated Planning and Operating File (APOF), which will contain citywide data related to land parcels, and the planning department's recent community analysis program, which relies extensively on community planning-related data acquisition and analysis. It has been observed that "much of the content of the existing data base is involved with day-to-day city operations and is therefore less immediately useful—or accessible—for planning. However, as LAMIS is implemented, it can be expected that the City of Los Angeles will have one of the better information systems to support urban planning."[4]

Santa Clara County Data Processing Department

Santa Clara County (located in the San Francisco Bay area, with San Jose as its county seat and major city) has also had considerable experience with data processing equipment.[5] In 1964 the Data Processing Advisory Committee was created to study computer applications for each county department. This committee, composed of representatives from each major department, then made recommendations for improved and coordinated data processing services and performance. The concept of data processing as a total information system was advanced, with grouping of all available data into various information subsystems and integrated application of data processing across departmental lines. Present computing equipment includes an IBM 360/40 and 360/30.

The overall coordinating concept of the Santa Clara County information system was set forth in 1965, when a plan for Local Government Information Control (LOGIC) was established. Ten major subsystems, encompassing a broad range of county data-processing needs, have been identified under LOGIC: property, people; general, people; law enforcement, people; personnel; supply; accounting; engineering; library; hospital; and advanced analysis. The original system design called for the first seven subsystems of LOGIC to be implemented over the period 1965-71. As various subsystems have evolved, emphasis has been placed upon development of master data files containing data used or required by many county departments as well as upon integrated applications. In addition, the data-processing department has continued to carry out a great many routine, independent data processing applications, using about 1,000 different computer programs. It provides for a full range of typical county applications (taxbilling, payroll, accounting, etc.). Its annual budget is about $2 million.

Among the subsystems already implemented is an administrative services system that combines features of the personnel and accounting subsystems. The department of public works has independently undertaken implementation of the engineering subsystem. A real-time, online welfare department information system has been inaugurated, using remote terminals for direct and immediate communication with "people" information files. This system will be expanded to include hospitals and health data. It enables data to be both entered in and retrieved from a centralized computer from consoles located within the operating agency.

The emphasis of LOGIC upon developing and maintaining master data files organized according to various common entities (e.g., property files organized by individual land parcel, people files organized by individual person) is useful for planning-department purposes. The data collected for the planning department's extensive 1965 land-use survey have, for example, been merged with other parcel data in the master property file and are now available for use by any of the county departments. However, reservations have been expressed about the adequacy of the Santa Clara County information system for urban planning needs, especially concerning the ability of the data processing department to look beyond its extensive commitments to the day-to-day processing needs of many operating departments.

Bay Region Planning Information Support Center

A work program design for a Bay Region Planning Information
Support Center (BRISC) has recently been completed for the Association of Bay Area Governments (ABAG).[6] As currently envisioned,
the center will provide information support for a variety of local
comprehensive planning processes, special studies, development of
the regional plan, and other ongoing planning activities in the nine-
county San Francisco Bay area. It will coordinate regional data
resources that are now overlapping, fragmented, and sporadic. The
center will also provide data processing services to member agencies
and other public and private agencies in the region. It represents an
ambitious proposal for areawide, intergovernmental information
system development.

Since it is likely that areawide planning responsibilities in the
Bay region will continue to be shared by several agencies, BRISC is
seen as a centralized information-handling service for each, func-
tioning as an arm of the ABAG planning program. Cooperating agencies would include the Bay Area Transportation Study Commission
(BATSC), which has already developed a significant information system of its own, the Bay Conservation and Development Commission,
and the sponsors of other regional planning programs. Under an
interagency agreement establishing working relationships between
BRISC and these regional planning programs, ABAG will be eligible
for HUD 701 grants to support the development of the center partially.
It is anticipated that, as the various products of the 1970 Census
become available, BRISC will also function as one of the area's
summary tape-processing centers.

The recommended data-acquisition plan outlines eight major
data categories: geographic base description, population and housing,
land use, employment, transport, mapping and aerial photography,
regional economy, and public investment. Specific work items are
proposed under each category, including, for example, a Continuing
Land Activity Surveillance System (CLASS) as the land-use inventory
element. BRISC staff will also be concerned with regional analysis
and modeling applications, including its own regional demographic,
economic, land-use, and other forecasts, as well as projections
made by other local agencies. It is suggested that an in-house computer installation (such as an IBM 360/40) may prove economically
feasible, and that the annual budget for full system operation will
reach $450,000 by 1973.

The BRISC system will also take advantage of lessons learned
in the operation of the BATSC information system. It is noted that
"the BATSC experience has shown that an information system designed

to support the planning process must meet at least the following
objectives: (1) promote close interaction between the planning analyst
and his data; (2) provide him with a broad range of capabilities for
processing and analyzing data without the necessary intercession of
a computer programmer; and (3) provide for the systematic management of a growing data base containing data from a variety of sources
in a variety of formats." The BRISC system, in order to promote
planning applicability and utility, will employ the BATSC practice of
assigning to a data base coordinator the responsibility for data base
maintenance, documentation, coordination, software application, and
ease of user access.

San Gabriel Valley Municipal Data System

The San Gabriel Valley Municipal Data System (MDS) is another
recent and innovative development of an urban and regional information system.[7] Unlike the BRISC system, which is strongly planning-
oriented, MDS is principally an administrative, operations-oriented
system, similar in design to the Los Angeles and Santa Clara County
examples. Thirteen cities lying east of Los Angeles, with a total
population of 496,000 and covering roughly 40 square miles, have
joined in establishing the San Gabriel Valley MDS as a cooperative,
joint-power agency. Their size ranges from 12,000 to 86,000, the
largest being Pomona. Each city will have relatively sophisticated
data-processing and computer services available that could not be
economically provided on an individual basis.

MDS was officially established in 1967, after nearly two years
of staff and consultant studies had shown that basic data processing
requirements of the cities were very similar. A consultant report
recommended a management-information system that would encompass
four broad areas: general accounting, utility accounting, police statistics, and planning. A medium-sized computer installed at a central
location would provide each city with online, time-sharing services
in each of the four functional areas. All data input, file maintenance
and updating, and limited online response would be made via
typewriter-like terminals or consoles located in each city hall. Volume printing (payroll checks, utility bills, financial statements, etc.)
would be done at the computer center and delivered via courier. This
basic system is now being established, with full operation scheduled
in early 1971.

The four functional areas recommended will be developed in
detail. General accounting applications, for example, will cover
nearly all of the administrative bookkeeping tasks listed earlier. The

planning subsystem will focus mainly upon parcel-oriented data, much of which exists already as a by-product of normal city operations but is usually not easily available for planning purposes. Census data, county assessor data, and other location-based data will be integrated with existing city parcel records. Longer-range goals include an increasing emphasis upon planning-programming-budgeting system (PPBS) concepts and development of a complete management information system. The 30-month development cost of MDS will be about $558,000, and annual operating costs will probably run about $275,000. An RCA Spectra 70/45 computer will be utilized.

APPLYING INFORMATION SYSTEMS IN PLANNING

Though a number of cities and counties across the country have begun to develop coordinated interagency, general-purpose urban information systems, and though countless individual agencies and departments have for some time supported their own independent data processing applications, effective integration into urban information systems is only just beginning. The examples discussed in the previous section represent the exception rather than the rule. Further, the participation of city, county, metropolitan, and regional planning agencies in the design and use of general-purpose data processing systems has been characteristically weak, whether those systems have been partially or more fully developed. Neither have planning agencies been particularly successful in developing their own, semi-independent information systems. These are among the reasons for the recent inauguration of major research and development projects in six cities aimed at the design and implementation of various prototype municipal information systems.* These demonstration projects display considerable potential for general advancement of the field.[8]

---

*Integrated municipal information systems will be developed in Wichita Falls, Texas, and Charlotte, North Carolina; a human-resources-development subsystem will be developed in St. Paul, Minnesota; a public-finance subsystem in Dayton, Ohio; a physical and economic development subsystem in Reading, Pennsylvania; and a public safety subsystem in Long Beach, California. Each city will cooperate with a systems consulting firm and a university research group. The projects, begun in 1970, are expected to be completed in two to three years. A group of nine federal agencies known as the Urban Information Systems Inter-Agency Committee (USAC) has sponsored the research program.

While it is difficult to document the extent to which various urban planning agencies are actually making use of information systems, two 1967 surveys shed some light on the growing number of applications. Hemmens surveyed urban development modeling and related data processing activities in the 25 largest SMSAs.[9] Twenty-six of the 34 agencies that were sent questionnaires responded: 16 metropolitan or regional planning agencies, six city planning departments, two state agencies, a federal agency, and a consulting firm. All reported that they were either using or planning to use computers and data processing in their operations. Table 8.1 lists those agencies that provided details on computer use. Hemmens found that while none of the agencies employed a fully developed data-bank system (that is, one comprised of existing data files, regular data-updating procedures, and existing programming systems for manipulation and retrieval), half indicated the existence of operating systems somewhat short of this ideal.

A second 1967 survey obtained much broader national coverage, but its reported results are more generalized.[10] Questionnaires were sent to 59 state planning agencies; 239 county, metropolitan, and regional planning commissions; 148 transportation study groups; and 63 city-planning departments. The total response was 55 percent. Many, perhaps most, of the nonrespondents probably had no experience with information systems, but the number who had or expected to could not be determined. As of 1967, 16 city, county, metropolitan, or regional planning agencies and 17 transportation studies reported that they were employing operational, computer-based data-processing systems. Two additional urban planning agencies reported joint operation with transportation studies. Forty-two urban planning agencies and ten transportation studies indicated that information systems were currently being developed or designed, and 11 additional agencies reported planned joint undertakings. Finally, 27 urban planning agencies, 12 transportation studies, and 11 joint agency responses indicated that urban information systems were currently under active consideration.

Many of these agencies, which three years ago were developing, designing, or considering data processing systems, may now be involved in operational applications, but it should be kept in mind that in most cases such systems would be only partially developed. And their relationship to general-purpose municipal or county information systems (where these exist) is unknown. Usually only certain data files, most commonly those dealing with selected land-use and/or transportation characteristics, will have been computerized for urban planning purposes. Often such data will have actually been initially automated by operating agencies (such as the county assessor's office),

TABLE 8.1

Planning Agency Experience with Computer Facilities

Agency	Computer	Source	Estimated Current Average Usage (hours per week)
Baltimore Regional Planning Council	IBM 1460 & 1620 IBM 7090 & 360/40, UNIVAC 1005	State operated Service bureau	} 4
Bay Area Transportation Study Commission	Honeywell 120 IBM 7094 CDC 3800	Agency Service bureau Service bureau	50 2-10 1-5
Chicago Area Transportation Study	IBM 1401	Agency	30
Cleveland-Seven County Land Use-Transportation Study	CDC 3200 CDC 360	Agency Service bureau	90 —
Delaware Valley Regional Planning Commission	IBM 360/30 IBM 7094	Agency Service bureau	25 3
Denver Planning Office	IBM 360/30	City operated	less than 1
Eastern Massachusetts Regional Planning Project	IBM 7094 IBM 1401	Service bureau Service bureau	1.2 3.8
Los Angeles City Planning Department	IBM 360/30;/40 IBM 7044; 7094	City operated Service bureau	} 10
Metropolitan Washington Council of Governments	CDC 3600, GE 235	Service bureau	$\frac{1}{2}$-2
New Orleans City Planning Commission	IBM 1401	City operated	4
New York State Departments of Public Works—Subdivision of Transportation Planning and Programming	Burroughs B-5500	State operated	60
Puget Sound Regional Transportation Planning Program	IBM 1401 IBM 7094	Service bureau Service bureau	} $\frac{1}{2}$
Regional Plan Association of New York	IBM 7094 CDC 3600	Consultant Consultant	— —
Southwestern Pennsylvania Regional Planning Commission	Honeywell 200	Agency	90-100
Southeastern Wisconsin Regional Planning Commission	IBM 360/30	Agency	25
Tri-State Transportation Commission	IBM 1460 IBM 7094, IBM 360/65	Agency Service bureau	75 —

even though coordinated local information-system development may
not have been inaugurated.

Only larger planning agencies, such as those surveyed by Hemmens, have begun to think in terms of truly integrated, multiple-file,
interagency information systems—that of necessity will be likely to
require a heavy emphasis upon "practical," day-to-day administrative
applications.

Whether planning agency use of data-processing systems has been
large, small, dependent, or independent, what are the kinds of analytic and planning benefits that have accrued? What are information
systems good for? Beyond the essential feature of rapid access to
large amounts of data, computerized information systems can be
used for four broad planning purposes or tasks: selective data retrieval and display, generation of standardized summary reports,
statistical and modeling analysis, and computer graphics and mapping.
These are discussed and related to the basic steps of the systems
approach in following sections.[11] In addition, the implications of innovations in the 1970 Census for improved planning information and
information systems are briefly reviewed.

Data Retrieval

The simplest level of planning application is retrieval of specific
data items for day-to-day planning operations. A comprehensive
information system will, of course, permit considerable flexibility
in the types of data that might be available at any given time. A multi-
tude of possible applications of this type could be suggested. Many
would be associated with neighborhood or community planning analyses
or specialized problem-oriented (or crisis-oriented) short-range
studies. For example, current information on the number of building
code violations in a particular community may be desired so urban
renewal strategies may be set. The current level and characteristics
of unemployment in a model neighborhood might help establish a
framework for proposed job-training projects. Recent building permit
and assessment patterns in a suburban community might help establish
criteria for zoning revisions.

Often such information is needed quickly, in as much detail as
possible, and as up to date as possible. These are probably the three
most important advantages of computer-based data banks for day-to-
day planning applications. In the past, data on most land-use and
socioeconomic conditions have been typically unavailable in convenient
printed form, in the wrong format if available, often summarized for
large geographic areas only (and not available at the neighborhood

FIGURE 8.1

Data Request Application Form:
Metropolitan Data Center Project

Metropolitan Data Center Project   Demonstration Project
                                         No. Okla. D-1

APPLICATION DESCRIPTION FORM

APPLICATION NUMBER: T-3

List all properties, buildings, and establishments within Community Renewal Project Area 15. Data items to be included in this listing and the order in which they are to appear in the report are as follows:

APPLICATION REQUEST:
1. Parcel Number
2. Building Location Code
3. Establishment Location Code
4. Space Use Code
5. Establishment Name
6. Building Condition
7. Number of Dwelling Units
8. Year Building Built
9. Type of Building Construction
10. Number of Floors
11. Current Zoning Code
12. Attributable Parcel Acreage

Sort by census block within parcel number, within building number, and within establishment number. Summarize the attributable parcel acreage and dwelling unit fields at each census block break.

PURPOSE: To determine the extent of blight in Community Renewal Project 15, and number of families to be displaced on the condition of buildings, existing land uses, and current zoning, in order to develop a Re-use Plan for the area.

USERS: Planning Office
Urban Renewal Administration

FREQUENCY: As Required

FIGURE 8.2

Data Request Computer Printout:
Metropolitan Data Center Project

REQ. NO.   TUL   ANALYSIS OF EXISTING CONDITIONS IN COMMUNITY RENEWAL PROJECT AREA 15

PARCEL NUMBER	BLDG LOC CODE	EST LOC COD	SPACE USE CODE	ESTAB NAME	BUILDING CNDITION	NO. DWLG UNIT	YR. BLT	TYPE CNST	NO. FLR	ZON # 1	PARCEL ACRGE	CFN BLK
023011001	01	01	3000000		4		21	26	1	042	296	011
	02	01	3000000		4		21	01	1	042	56	
	03	01	3000000		3		21	42	1	042	077	
023011002	01	01	3225097	SCTRIC	2		57	42	1	042	233	
023011004	01	01	2625022	SMITHS	1			23	1	042	133	
02301105	01	01	3403432	TESC3T	1			26	1	042	266	
	02		2324212	CONSDE	1			26	1	042	265	
023011006	01	01	3407213	TULLIN	2			26	1	042	612	
023011007	01	01	3404111	MKOLIN	2		58	23	1	042	998	
MAJOR TOTAL	9										2936	
023012001	01	01	2625099	C&JDIS	3		20	26	2	042	21	012
	02		3225099	MARTEC	3		20	26	2	042	44	
023012002	01	01	2625097	ENTERP	3		20	26	2	042	98	
023012006	01	01	2000000		3			26	2	042	100	
	02		2625082	INGRAN	3			26	2	042	30	
	03		2325099	CLARKI	3			26	2	042	129	
	02	01	3102512	RIGGUP	3		24	26	2	042	56	
023012009	01	BB	1210002		4	2	12	01	1	042	47	
	02	BB	1110001		4	1	12	01	1	042	47	
023012011	01	01	3403281	MIDWST	2		35	23	1	042	44	
	02	01	3223281	MIDWST	2		20	23	1	042	378	
	03	01	3403281	MIDWST	2		56	26	1	042	69	
023012013	01	01	2322752	SCOTT	2			03	1	042	64	
023012017	01	BB	1110000		3	1	18	01	1	042	49	
	02	BB	1410001		3	9	13	01	1	042	17	
023012018	01	BB	1110000		4	1	20	01	1	042	25	
023012019	01	BB	1110000		4	1	15	01	1	042	26	
023012020	01	01	3403533	SKINER	2		25	26	2	042	59	
MAJOR TOTAL	19					15					1303	
023042001	AA	01	5644013	MKTRRT						042	590	042
023042002	AA	01	5644013	MKTRRT						042	590	
MAJOR TOTAL	2										1180	
GRAND TOTAL	30					15					5419	

30 ITEMS RETRIEVED FOR THIS REQUEST

level), seriously outdated, extremely difficult or impossible to obtain from operating agencies, and often costly and time-consuming to obtain even if those agencies are willing and able to cooperate. An ongoing, continuously updated, multipurpose urban information system in which operating agencies such as city building departments, state employment services, and county assessor's officers all participate will mean that much planning-related data will be conveniently and routinely available.

Figure 8.1 is an example of such a data request, while Figure 8.2 shows how, after appropriate computer programming, that request might be answered.[12] Note that considerable parcel-level detail can be provided, as long as each of the 12 specific data items has been properly incorporated within the information system (that is, identified and referenced to a particular parcel number). As long as each parcel is in turn referenced to a census block number, and each census block number is referenced to or coded by the renewal project area in which it is located, data requests of this type could be filled for any renewal project area. Required computer programming need be done only once, so that subsequent requests of this type could be easily satisfied.

Report Generation

Data requests and reports such as those shown in Figures 8.1 and 8.2 transacted regularly (for instance, annually or semiannually), especially if they summarize the data by larger geographic areas (for example, for all renewal projects or for the entire city), constitute a standardized type of planning application. For most operating agencies, generation of such regular summary reports is, of course, one of the key applications of data processing. Most of these reports will be concerned with fiscal or budgetary characteristics, while planning-related reports will be concerned with changes in the status of the land and people resources of an urban area. For example, they might summarize building permits, water connections, code enforcements, welfare caseloads, zoning acreage, school enrollments, or renewal acreage on a detailed annual basis, and covering a number of different planning subareas.

Summary reports might be generated to support major planning activities—such as regional transportation/land-use plans, community renewal programs, or comprehensive city plans—and also as part of a regular annual reporting function. Consider, for example, the many planning and development achievements that must be documented annually in HUD-required Workable Programs for Community

FIGURE 8.3

Land-Use Inventory Excerpt:
Indianapolis Regional Transportation and Development Study

ACRONYM*	DISTRICT NUMBER							
	58	59	61	62	63	64	65	66
THUA	1198	4601	1377	1554	1268	2330	2427	378
SFAHU	1194	4546	720	912	1082	2305	2366	376
FA2HU	4	13	570	520	166	22	60	2
FA3MOR		42	77	95	19	3		
GRHU			10	27	1		1	
SFALAN	6760	18430	760	1070	1810	6940	3390	2360
FA2LAN			290	300	100	20	50	
HU3LAN		110	10	50	10	10		
GRLAN				10				
TRNLOD		70						20
SARROW	4720	8670	1430	1310	2240	4790	3410	1730
PARKLO			310	40	240	10	30	
CULACT								
PUASAM	50	210			80			
REREPA	220	1070	80	300	710		60	
CEMETE	230	400			40			10
QUARMI				670		930		
USENUR	132920	159310	740	5240	10210	25640	10690	48000
WATARE	460	150	360	2410	1140	780		20
AUJUNK			40		120	70	10	
TLURU	12724	33800	4667	5748	13793	12572	8763	6832
TLNURU	133380	159460	1140	8320	11470	27420	10700	48020
AREA	146104	193260	5807	14068	25263	39992	19463	54852

*Acronym	Data Item
THUA	Total housing units 1964
SFAHU	Single-family housing units 1964
FA2HU	Two-family housing units 1964
FA3MOR	Housing units three or more family 1964
GRHU	Housing in group quarters 1964
SFALAN	Acres in one-family residential use 1964
FA2LAN	Acres in two-family residential use 1964
HU3LAN	Acres in three or more family use 1964
GRLAN	Acres in group quarters residential use 1964
TRNLOD	Acres in transient lodging use 1964
SARROW	Acres in streets, alleys and R.R.R.O.W.
PARKLO	Acres in parking lots
CULACT	Acres in cultural activities
PUASAM	Acres in public assembly and amusements
REREPA	Acres in recreational use
CEMETE	Acres in cemeteries
QUARMI	Acres in quarrying and mining
USENUR	Acres in vacant and agricultural use
WATARE	Acres in water
AUJUNK	Acres in auto junkyard use
TLURU	Acres in urban use
TLNURU	Acres in non-urban use (vacant, agricultural, mining, water, and auto junkyard use)
AREA	Total acres in zone

Note: Twenty-five additional land-use types, covering industrial, transportation, commercial, services, and other categories are also distinguished. The inventory covered 87 separate planning districts.

Improvement in order for localities to qualify for federal housing and renewal assistance. Monitoring and eventual reporting of many of these community and agency achievements—such as dwelling unit construction, building and housing code enforcement, rehabilitation permits, renewal project dispositions, or relocation housing needs and resources—could be facilitated by an information system. Regular updating of the population, employment, housing, and land-use inventories typically conducted by metropolitan transportation/land-use studies could also be improved. Figure 8.3 illustrates a portion of a summary report of this latter type.

It should be noted that both data retrieval and report generation activities can greatly improve the information available for the first two steps of the systems approach to planning—identifying goals and objectives and identifying alternative programs and policies. Problems, objectives, programs, and policies can all be substantially clarified by local data that are relevant, detailed, recent, and easily available. But the use of much planning-related data for immediate purposes—short-range, localized planning and standardized areawide reporting—should not obscure their value for more thoughtful, penetrating, long-range analyses of basic planning problems and their relationships. The greater objectivity inherent in the systems approach, and in PPBS applied to urban public administration generally, depends absolutely upon improved data resources—in particular upon the increased knowledge provided by sensitive data retrieval and report generation on the part of planning agencies.

Statistical Analysis

The third phase of the systems approach—predicting relative effectiveness levels—depends in large measure upon quantitative analysis of data. This analysis can be greatly facilitated by a computer-based information system, not only because of the quantity and ready availability of needed data but also through the use of a variety of standardized software packages for statistical analysis and modeling, available from computer manufacturers, service bureaus, and governmental agencies. Because of the importance of computer modeling in urban transportation planning, to use a major example, the U.S. Bureau of Public Roads has developed a number of standard computer programs for trip generation, modal split, trip distribution, and traffic assignment analyses. Experimental urban development models have also depended heavily upon computers, and upon associated urban information systems, though many of these models are not well documented and available for ready use in other urban areas.

FIGURE 8.4

Land-Use/Transportation Planning Sequence:
Southeastern Wisconsin Regional Planning Commission

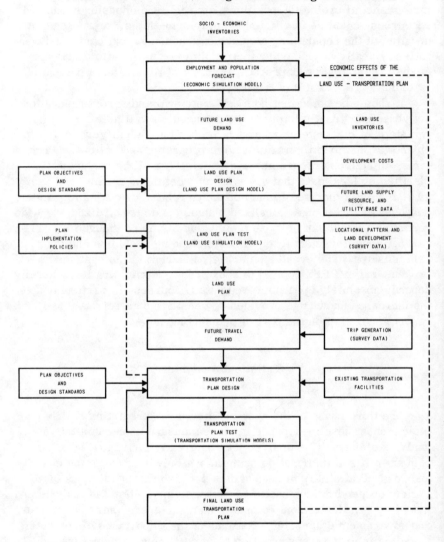

Both standard statistical analyses (using "canned" programs) and experimental or research analyses (requiring original and often time-consuming computer programming) can be conducted in collaboration with and through the use of urban information systems. Because the emphasis is on prediction and forecasting, this level of information system application essentially supports long-range planning activities. It also tends to call for the use of large amounts of detailed data, so that complex social, economic, and environmental relationships can be explored. Statistical analysis activities are likely to represent the "trickiest" and most demanding use of an information system. It should be recognized that there are varying degrees of difficulty or scope in potential analytical applications, ranging from relatively simple two-variable cross-tabulations or linear regression analyses, conducted perhaps in support of some narrowly defined or specialized planning effort, to highly complex multivariate statistical analyses or activity-distribution models, conducted in support of major transportation/land-use planning programs. Figure 8.4 depicts how various data inventories support the use of four different types of mathematical models in Southeastern Wisconsin's transportation/land-use planning program.

A major problem of communication between model developers, data processing specialists, and model users has sometimes been experienced in the use of large-scale urban analysis models.[13] Lessons learned from these innovative attempts at employing more complex analytic techniques should not be lost on other statistical analysis applications. In particular, there is a tendency for the technical aspects of model building to absorb all of the energies of systems analysts and quantitative methods specialists, and for these model developers to become somewhat isolated from nontechnical planning staff and others who will eventually utilize resulting models. Every effort should be made to involve planning agency staffs in initial model design and conceptualization and to make them adequately familiar with the mechanics of model operation. In addition, the limitations of certain types of data—availability, compatibility, coverage, format, and other features—may serve to frustrate and constrain both model builders and users. Information system capabilities, the special province of data processing specialists, must consequently also be clarified early in the process of statistical analysis.

Computer Graphics

One of the more intriguing aspects of computer-based information systems lies in the potential for computer mapping and other graphic

FIGURE 8.5

SYMAP Computer Mapping: New Haven Census Use Study

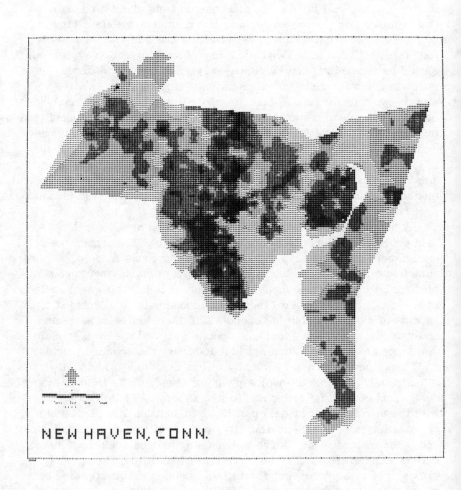

NEW HAVEN, CONN.

POPULATION DENSITY
(PEOPLE PER ACRE)
1967 NEW HAVEN BLOCK DATA
SYMAP IV CONTOUR OPTION

FIGURE 8.6

MAP 01 Computer Mapping: New Haven Census Use Study

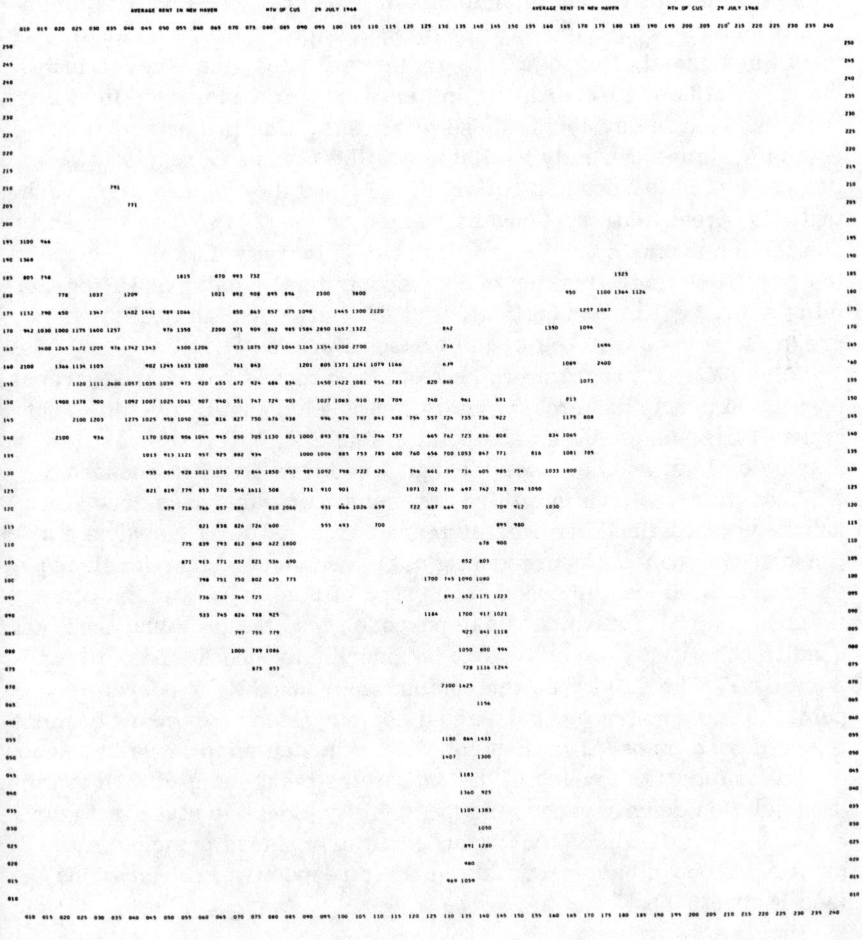

AVERAGE RENT FOR BLOCKS
(AGGREGATED TO GRID CELL)

1967 NEW HAVEN BLOCK DATA

MAP-01

output. Computer mapping is of particular interest because a wide variety of spatially distributed data can be mapped quickly and cheaply, compared with traditional draftsman techniques. Mapped display of data can, of course, depict many planning conclusions and findings more meaningfully than other forms of presentation. Computer mapping requires two basic software packages (computer programs): one to assign data to geographic grid coordinates, the other to print maps from the grid-coordinate information. Considerable effort has been involved in developing these programs. The two principal geo-coding systems presently available are the Census Bureau's Dual Independent Map Encoding (DIME) file,[14] and the University of Washington's Street Address Conversion System (SACS).[15] Two currently available mapping systems are Harvard University's SYMAP[16] and the New York State Division of Transportation Planning and Programming's MAP 01.[17] A modification of the latter, called MAP 360, is presently being developed by the Census Bureau.[18]

The SYMAP program (which can also produce bar charts, graphs, population pyramids, etc.) permits the development of five different types of base maps. One uses points (single X, Y coordinates) for the display of data; another uses straight lines (two or more connected X, Y coordinates); while a third, the most common, uses zones or subareas (as defined by three or more connected X, Y coordinates). Because the symbols representing data are assigned individually to these points, lines, or zones, each type of map is known as a con-formant map. A fourth, special-purpose type, the proximal map, is used to construct geometric zone boundaries around X, Y coordinate-point data. The fifth type, the contour map, used X, Y coordinate-point data to construct equal-valued contour lines. For many of these types of base maps, it is then possible to assign up to 12 value ranges or data categories to each of the data items being mapped. An example of population density ranges mapped by city blocks is given in Figure 8.5. The less flexible MAP 01 program is designed principally to print X, Y coordinate-point data at their respective grid locations (see Figure 8.6).[19]

1970 Census Implications

The decennial census of population and housing has traditionally provided much of the most fundamental data used by urban planners. In order to make the current 1970 census more responsive to the needs and interests of users, the U.S. Bureau of the Census has in the past few years developed, tested, and implemented a number of significant innovations.[20] They will not only make census products themselves much more useful, they will afford major opportunities for improving and integrating other urban data files. They will make it possible for census results to become a key component of multi-purpose urban information systems. The two main innovations—geographic coding guides and the increased availability of small-area data—emerged initially from research conducted by the New Haven Census Study[21] and are being investigated further in the Southern California Regional Information Study (SCRIS).[22]

The potential of geographic coding guides is enormous, and their use will represent a major step forward in urban planning, research, and analysis. The great value of coding guides lies in the fact that nearly all planning-related data (including census data) are spatially distributed, and each item of data is found at a unique location. Many planning questions and problems are in turn concerned with spatial subareas, small sections of the urban community that happen to contain particular groupings of various data items. Other planning questions and subject areas are concerned with the spatial relationship between specific locations and subareas—mainly distances and daily transportation flows. If data items can be associated with a unique location (street address or parcel number), and each location in turn associated with various subareas (blocks, census tracts, city wards, traffic zones), considerable flexibility will exist for aggregating data at different levels and for performing spatial-interchange analyses. This is essentially the purpose of the census geographic coding guides and related techniques.[23]

These geographic base files have four important features:

1. The basic Address Coding Guide (compiled using specially prepared block maps in each Standard Metropolitan Statistical Area) relates each street address range (for example, 400-480 B Street) to a specific block face or street segment number, block, census tract, ZIP code zone, and other census areas. All data reported by street address can then be summed by block and aggregated in turn according to each of the higher levels.

2. Local planning agencies and other users are free to add additional geographic code numbers for subareas of special interest (traffic zones, planning districts, community areas, etc.) by associating them via computer with block face serial numbers. This permits considerable flexibility in analysis, including the ability to aggregate detailed data by newly created geographic areas.

3. In order to permit census returns (as well as any local data file) referenced by street address to be geographically coded, a computer program package known as ADMATCH has been developed to ensure that reported street addresses are compatible with the address ranges in the geographic coding guide. This will permit

TABLE 8.2

Availability of Small Area Data: 1970 Census

	On Summary Computer Tapes[a]		In Published Reports	
Type of Area	Cells of Data[b]	Tentative Completion Dates	Cells of Data	Tentative Completion Dates
City blocks	250	January–July 1971	20	January–July 1971
Block groups and enumeration districts	400	August–December 1970	None	—
Census tracts 100 percent items[c]	3,500	October 1970–April 1971	260	March–April 1971
Sample items[c]	30,000	January–October 1971		
ZIP code areas[d]	800	July 1971	None	—

[a]The anticipated cost per reel is $60 (tape included). UNIVAC and IBM seven-track or nine-track tapes will be available.

[b]The term cell "refers to each figure or statistic in the tabulation for a specific geographic area."

[c]The 100 percent data items cover the questions to which every household must respond. The sample items cover additional questions asked of 15 percent or 20 percent of the households. The 5 percent sample questions will not be tabulated for census tracts.

[d]Within SMSAs, data will be tabulated for five-digit ZIP code areas. Elsewhere data will be tabulated for three-digit ZIP code areas.

other elements within an urban information system to be coordinated with census data.

4. A second program package known as Dual Independent Map Encoding (DIME) has been developed, assigning node numbers to each street intersection, and standardized X, Y coordinates to each node. These coordinates can then be used to calculate distances, areas, and densities and can also be used to define the boundaries of special analysis subareas. They will also permit the use of computer-mapping techniques, as described above.

A second major area of improvement in the 1970 census involves the much greater availability of small-area data. The anticipated availability of data by four different geographic areas is summarized in Table 8.2.[24] Population and housing data for city blocks will be available for the first time for all cities over 50,000 in population, with their environs also tabulated. Twenty data items will be published by block, and 250 will be available on summary computer tapes. Four hundred data items for nearly all urban areas will be available on tape only for enumeration districts and block groups. Both the areal coverage and data content of census tract reporting have been enlarged, with some 30,000 data items available on tape for the detailed sample-survey phase. ZIP code tabulations will also be included for the first time. The census bureau has established a data access and use laboratory to facilitate access to unpublished data and has encouraged local public and private groups to establish summary tape processing centers for the same purpose. (Note that only a small fraction of available data will actually be published.)

PLANNING DATA REQUIREMENTS

With the widening range of concern of urban planning agencies increasingly including social and economic as well as physical problems and issues, the types of planning-related data that might conceivably be contained within an urban information system are quite diverse. In addition to census information on population, employment, and housing, the data might range from assessed valuations to retail sales taxes to public welfare payments to criminal-activity patterns to building permits. The extent to which additional data elements can be referenced by street address and subsequently aggregated via geographic coding guides will greatly influence the flexibility of the resulting data system. In order to illustrate the broad range of possible planning data requirements, three examples of information systems developed or proposed in the Washington, D.C., area are briefly reviewed.

In general, no single list of preferred or recommended planning-oriented data elements for an urban information system can be easily identified. Not only are planning functions and problems structured differently in different urban areas, so that comparability in data requirements between those areas is unlikely, but the planning process within any urban area is continually evolving, so that new or unexpected data demands are likely to emerge periodically. Only very broad categories of planning-related data can presently be identified with any confidence, with the designation of particular desired data items within those categories a matter for local determination. For example, three obvious classes of urban data that are likely to be of interest for planning purposes include physical features (both natural and man-made), socioeconomic characteristics (population, employment, economy), and public-services data (by governmental function). While the specification of an ideal data base for urban planning is probably inappropriate, a number of suggested checklists for potential planning-oriented data have been developed.

Metropolitan Washington Information System

In the Washington metropolitan area an information system has been recently developed that is similar in many respects to the proposed BRISC system discussed earlier. With HUD financial assistance, the project was first initiated by the District of Columbia government, then carried through by the Metropolitan Washington Council of Governments. WCOG now maintains the system on an ongoing basis, with an emphasis upon integrating various data (primarily land-use parcel data) regularly produced by local operating agencies. It is noted that

> although a major purpose of the DC/WCOG project was to
> facilitate metropolitan planning, it was not centered in and
> did not focus on planning agencies. It focused on operating
> agencies in the various jurisdictions, for these are the
> ultimate sources of continuous information. It dealt with
> no data outside those generated by operating programs.
>   It sought to render comparible the definitions and clas-
> sification schemes of operating agencies both intra- and
> inter-jurisdictionally, to give professional assistance to
> the automation efforts of those agencies and while doing
> so, influence them in the direction of data compatibility
> and metropolitan cooperation, to develop a mechanism for
> periodic input of selected and updated information from
> these many different and independent agencies into a

unified metropolitan data system located in WCOG, and to
utilize the information to help solve metropolitan problems.[25]

The major conclusions of the project included (a) the finding that a
successful metropolitan data system requires a permanent, full-time
professional planning and computer systems staff located within a
metropolitan agency and (b) the conclusion that a metropolitan information system should not be involved in carrying out regular governmental operations or the data-processing activities of operating
agencies, but rather should be oriented toward metropolitan planning,
programming, and evaluation.

TABLE 8.3

Comprehensive Land-Use Classification System:
Washington Council of Governments

---

1. Activity (e.g., type of use, such as residential, commercial,
   industrial, church, barber shop, oil refinery, etc.)
2. Ownership (e.g., public, semipublic, private, commercial,
   nonprofit, city, county, state, federal, etc.)
3. Intensity of use (e.g., single-family, two-family, multiple-
   family, high-rise, street classification, vacant, small, large,
   high-density, low-density, medium-density, multistoried,
   three-bedroom units, etc.)
4. Quality of development (e.g., condition of structure, nuisance
   characteristics, health hazards, lack or presence of conven-
   iences, light, heavy, landscaped, park, glare, heat, noise,
   vibration, etc.)
5. Restrictions on use (e.g., governmental and contractual restrictions such as covenants, easements, reserved right-of-way,
   zoning requirements, etc.)
6. Public services (e.g., those utilities or types of access available or being supplied to property)
7. Financial value of land and improvements
8. Location (e.g., in, over, underground, accessory, adjacent,
   central, downtown, rural, suburban, urban district, outdoor,
   indoor, on-site, off-street, etc.)
9. Type of structure (e.g., detached, semidetached, high-rise,
   walk-up, duplex, etc.)
10. Other (any concept that is indicated in the name of the land-use
    category but does not fit under 1-9 above).

TABLE 8.4

Availability of Selected Parcel Data:
Washington Council of Governments

Data Items	Local Jurisdictions									
	Alexandria (1)	Arlington	District of Columbia	Fairfax City	Fairfax County	Falls Church	Loudoun County	Montgomery County	Prince George's County	Prince William County
Premise Address	A	A	I	A	A	A	I	A	I	P
1960 Census Tract and Block	A	A	A	I	I	I	I	I	I	I
1970 Census Tract and Block	COG	COG	COG	COG	COG	COG	COG	COG	COG	COG
Land Use	A	A	I	A	A	A	I	A	A	I
Master Plan Land Use	A	A	I	I	I	I	I	I	I	I
Multiple Land Use Indicator	A	A	P	I	P	I	I	I	I	I
Ownership Code	A	A	A	I	A	A	I	A	I	I
Land Value	A	A	A	A	A	A	A	A	A	M
Total Value	A	A	A	A	A	A	A	A	A	M
Lot Area	A	A	A	A	A	A	P	A	I	I
Gross Floor Area	A	A	M	P	A	A	I	I	P	M
Number of Stories	A	A	I	I	A	A	I	I	I	M
Number of Parking Spaces	A	P	I	I	P	I	I	I	I	I
Number of Dwelling Units	A	A	I	A	A	A	P	I	P	I
Zoning	A	A	A	A	A	A	P	A	P	M

LEGEND: A = Adequate data are available in automated form.
P = Automation of existing data is planned.
M = Data are available in manual form only; there are no immediate plans to automate them.
I = Existing data are inadequate for parcel records.
COG = The Council of Governments will make these data available in automated form as a result of its role as regional coordinator of the 1970 Census Street Address Coding Guide.

The major initial thrust of the system was toward the integration and reconciliation of various land-use information files generated by jurisdictions within the area. Extensive comparison of existing agency files showed that many different definitions, classification schemes, coding techniques, data identifiers, and data-processing procedures were being utilized. A standardized coding system was needed, but one that went beyond the functional activity codes of the URA/BPR Standard Land Use Coding Manual.[26] The ten general dimensions listed in Table 8.3 were eventually defined, and a coding scheme for each of these dimensions was developed. Any given parcel, structure, or establishment may be coded in several, and possibly all, of these usage categories or dimensions. This land-use classification scheme illustrates how one type of planning-related data may be structured, as part of a general-purpose information system.

The difficulty of the coordinating role played by the DC/WCOG information system is brought into perspective when the many differences among multiple data files are considered. For example, ten different jurisdictions (five cities and five counties) are empowered to tax and assess land. The definitions and coding techniques of these assessors' offices must be made compatible with one another, because they will serve as major land-use data sources. Similarly, there are almost 30 jurisdictions in the Washington area that issue building permits, and these additional sources of land activity data must also be coordinated. In the former case, the DC/WCOG project adopted a strategy of encouraging local assessors' offices to continue to improve their own files, to provide assistance where needed, and to explain ways in which their data could be made more useful. Table 8.4 summarizes the current status of selected parcel data items within the system.

Other Washington Experience

One of the early attempts at developing an information system for urban planning was conducted by George Washington University for the Maryland-National Capital Park and Planning Commission.[27] Though a good deal of progress had been made in information-system design generally since that work was completed, the project's final report is still of considerable value. In particular, the recommended planning information system is related to an overall systematic planning process. It is observed that

. . . the planner needs information if he is to:

1) Establish planning goals—because goals depend
first of all upon a knowledge of what standards actually
exist in a city; only with this information can political
decisions be made concerning what the standards ought
to be.

2) Construct realistic models, the basis for the
creation and evolution of designs—because the design
of a plan depends upon an intimate functional and spatial
knowledge of the urban place.

3) Implement the plan—because administration of
a plan by such means as subdivision regulations and
zoning ordinances requires a detailed factual knowledge
of all segments of the city.

It is within this framework that a three-phase information system
is developed in detail. The three elements or files within the system
are defined as (a) the "Land-Use Deck," (b) the "Family Characteristics Deck," and (c) the "Employment Characteristics Deck." (Decks
of punched data cards could today, of course, also be easily transferred to computer tapes, disks, or data cells.) The land-use deck
would contain detailed information on every land parcel within the
planning jurisdiction and would be developed by modifying information
collected by county assessors' offices (see Figure 8.7). Figure 8.8
depicts the information contained within the land-use deck. The
family characteristics deck (Figure 8.9) would consist of information
collected by planning agency personnel, based upon a random sample
of all residential parcels within the land-use deck. The employment-
characteristics deck (Figure 8.10) would be similarly collected.
This proposed system offers an example of the types of data that
might be included within a planning information system, though many
individual data items could conceivably be better provided by a cooperative, interagency information system.

A third urban information system example from the Washington,
D.C., area consists of the District Early Warning System (DEWS)
for neighborhood deterioration developed by the District of Columbia
government.[28] It illustrates how various planning-related elements
within an information system can be organized to support a particular
local planning program. The proposed DEWS system would monitor
various components of physical and social change within neighborhoods
on a block-face level, with aggregation at the block and neighborhood
levels as needed. It would provide data to support proposals and
programs for community renewal, relocation, housing, and related
activities. It is also intended to facilitate the statistical analysis of

FIGURE 8.7

Proposed Assessor's Data Card: George Washington University Project

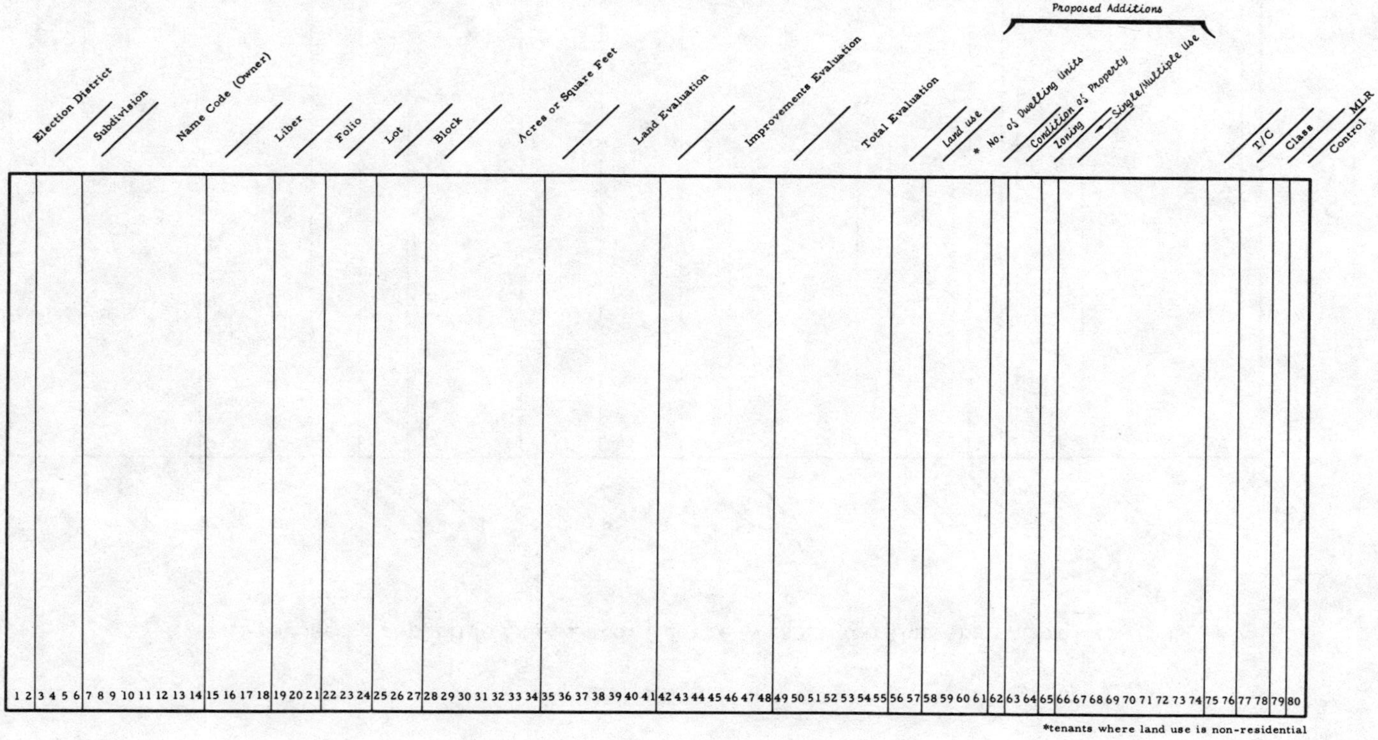

FIGURE 8.8

Proposed Properties Data Card: George Washington University Project

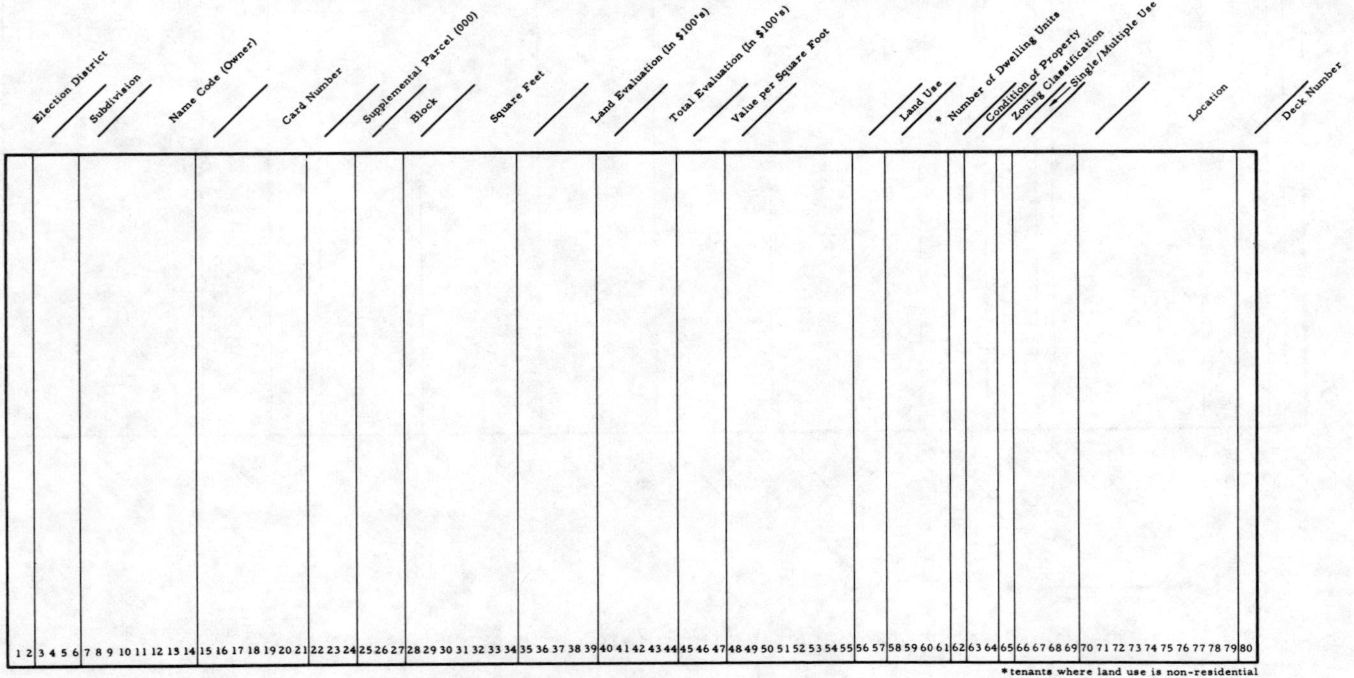

*tenants where land use is non-residential

FIGURE 8.9

Proposed Family Characteristics Data Card:
George Washington University Project

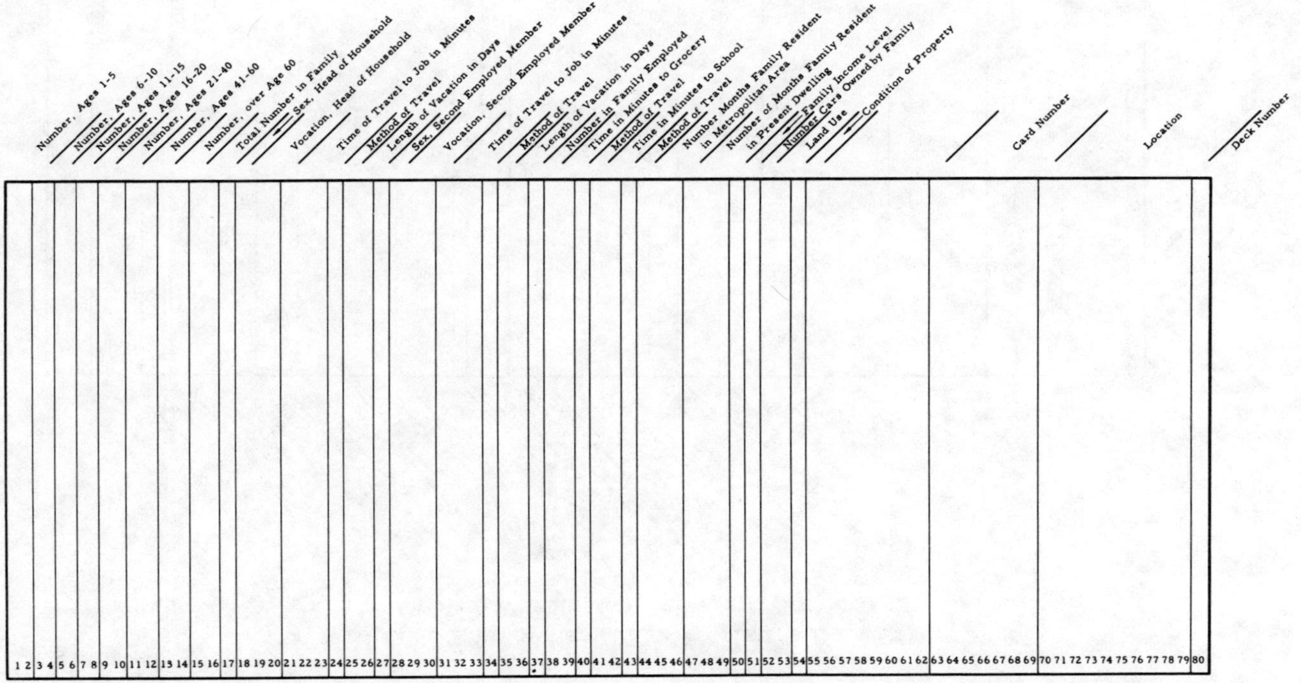

FIGURE 8.10

Proposed Employment Characteristics Data Card:
George Washington University Project

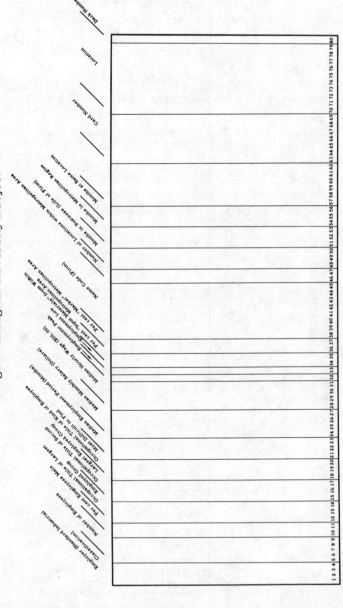

TABLE 8.5

Neighborhood Data Elements: Washington District
Early Warning System

---

1. Real Property Data Bank—contains information concerning the approximately 150,000 parcels of land in the District of Columbia. Presently available are the following:
   - Location identifiers: square and lot, address, census tract, elementary school district, neighborhood code, planning commission planning area, and health department planning area
   - Land information: size of lot (square feet or acres), assessed value per square foot, assessed value of land, zoning, and tax exempt status
   - Improvement information: land use, number of floors, construction material, class (relative to quality of original construction), depreciation index, and assessed value of improvements
   - Space-use information: type of licensed business activities, and number and type of dwelling units for licensed residential properties
   - Ownership information: lending institution holding mortgage or receiving tax bill, name and address of record owner, federal agency ownership, and owner of licensed businesss activity
   - Change information: year of last reassessment, reason for last review of property, and sales information
2. Service Activity Monitoring System
   - Housing code violations: address of property and type of violation
   - Health violations: address of property and type of violation
   - Welfare recipients: address of recipient, type of welfare received, and number of persons receiving welfare
   - Police offenses: address of event and type of offense
3. Block Face Index—includes address range, city square, Carney block, census tract, other locators as deemed necessary, and summary information about land use, density, etc.

---

various physical and social indicators to derive a "deterioration index" so that the need for appropriate public action can be anticipated and the impact of ongoing public programs can be evaluated. Table 8.5 summarizes the data to be contained in DEWS.

SYSTEM DESIGN AND OPERATION

Since urban information systems can be designed to serve a wide variety of purposes over and above the planning-related types of applications discussed earlier, many different forms of structure for such systems can be advanced.[29] In general, however, nearly all information systems (including nonautomated records systems) can be reduced to five basic structural elements or phases: input, processing storage, inquiry, and output.[30] Figure 8.11 illustrates the sequential relationships among these fundamental phases. In the following paragraphs three of these phases are briefly described. Data input in terms of various techniques for data collection and conversion to machine-readable form is discussed. Data storage in terms of various factors important in data organization and compatibility is reviewed.

FIGURE 8.11

Basic Structure of an Urban Information System

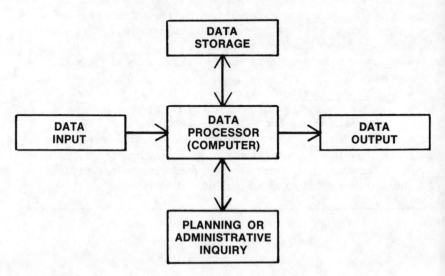

Generally required capabilities for data processing are outlined. In
addition, a number of considerations important in data maintenance
and ongoing system operation are also described. The two remaining
phases, inquiry and output, have already been reviewed (from an
urban planning perspective only).

Data Collection

Data collection activities can generally be divided into two phases:
field collection and conversion to machine-readable form. In some
cases the two can be combined, usually at considerable savings.
Hearle and Mason distinguish four major field collection methods for
governmental data: (a) observation of an event or object by government personnel (such as building code inspections), (b) report of an
event by a citizen or by someone on behalf of a citizen (birth or death
certificate), (c) application or registration by a citizen in connection
with government service or regulation (school enrollments, driver
licensings, building permits), and (d) administrative actions by government agencies (zoning changes, street construction, public land
acquisition).[31] To this list might be added a fifth source, special
surveys (possibly using random sampling techniques), such as transportation origin-destination surveys or comprehensive land-use
surveys.

The "instruments" used for each of these data collection methods
are usually some sort of form or report that is filled out by hand.
These results must then be converted into machine-readable form.
Typically, this calls for the manual transfer of original field data to
computer coding sheets and the keypunching of coding sheet data onto
computer punch cards. Both coding and keypunching are costly operations. Increasingly, the coding-sheet step has been bypassed by utilizing data collection forms that can be read easily by keypunchers.
Techniques have been devised to eliminate the keypunching step as
well. For example, in some instances punch cards themselves can
be used as source documents and the appropriate spaces on each card
marked or punched out in the field. Standardized collection forms,
with predetermined spaces assigned for recording specific data items,
can also be read automatically. For special applications, optical
reading devices have been developed that can automatically read hand-
printed characters (numbers or letters).

To identify multiple-agency data items for potential inclusion
within the system, the data items handled by different governmental
agencies and departments should be inventoried, especially during
the initial stages of data system development. The specific data

items collected via each of the five methods listed above should be
catalogued, as should the uses to which those data are put. Data collection forms should be examined to determine more precisely the
nature and definition of each data item. If possible, the agencies
should be interviewed to determine unmet data needs. Inventories
are likely to uncover many overlapping information interests, inconsistent data definitions, and gaps in desired data. Planning agencies
in particular are likely to learn much about the sources and availability of planning-oriented types of information.

The specific interests of urban planning agencies fall into three
broad categories of local, small-area data: administrative operations,
urban transportation studies, and the decennial census.[32] Data from
the latter two sources need to be coordinated and integrated with those
provided by multiple-agency administrative data files. In many cases
administrative operations data may not be in a form usable for planning purposes, and changes in reporting procedures might be necessary. Since the planning department, perhaps more than any other
local agency, will be dependent upon others for its data requirements,
the concept of data sharing as a means of data acquisition or collection
has special relevance. It should also be noted that in some urban
areas the data collection activities of metropolitan transportation
studies have in fact laid important groundwork for subsequent development of more diversified urban information systems.

Data Organization

Given an inventory or master list of potential data items, which
of those data items should actually be included within an urban information system? Many administrative and political factors cloud the
answer to such a question, and it would largely be a matter for local
determination. There appear to be no easy guidelines or criteria for
data selection, though of course there are bound to be budgetary and
operational constraints on the overall size of any urban information
system. Probably not all data elements desired from a comprehensive
planning standpoint can be included. One of the first factors to be
considered is the degree of interagency participation and the nature
and extent of the existing data files of each participant. What portion
of the costs of data collection, processing, and updating can be borne
directly by each agency involved? How do these costs compare for
different data items? What would be the number of uses to which a
particular data item could be put, as well as the number of agencies
that could utilize it?

Once the particular data items have been selected, with their corresponding variety of collection procedures and reporting formats, the next major phase of information-system design and operation involves data organization. The paramount need is a consistent series of data identifiers. In general, there are two basic units for urban data collection and identification—the individual person and the individual parcel. Though nearly all events and objects in urban areas can be associated with one or the other of these identifiers, and though nearly all source data originate or can be associated with one or the other, frequently the data collected by governmental agencies are stored only in some aggregate form. Even more frequently, these aggregation levels (census tracts, wards, postal zones, police districts) vary among agencies, so that data are incompatible for matching and analysis purposes. A consistent set of data identifiers for each data item in an information system is clearly essential.

Planning-oriented data especially, which are frequently derived from different agencies, require this compatibility. A basic problem lies in settling upon a set of entities (preferably, persons or parcels, but possibly also including small-scale aggregation units, such as households or city blocks, as well as other levels and types of aggregation) to which various items of data are assigned as attributes. At least two different kinds of compatibility problems, both arising from the use of varying classification schemes for different data items (attributes), can be distinguished.[33] The first involves the use of different code numbers or alphanumeric identifiers for the same data item (as applied to the same or a very similar set of entities). These problems can generally be overcome by developing appropriate code-conversion tables. The second problem involves the use of different classification schemes or spatial aggregation levels for dealing with the same set of entities. This type of incompatibility may be more difficult to resolve, unless, as noted above, data entities can be further stratified or disaggregated to some common level (such as, ideally, person or parcel).

A related but separate problem for data organization involves data-item definition. Here the question centers on whether two similar data items really have the same meaning—whether they represent the same type of urban phenomenon. Hence, standardized definitions are necessary in an interagency urban information system. For example, when there are multiple zoning jurisdictions within an urban area, each jurisdiction may continue to use whatever system of land-use zoning categories it wishes, but they must be definable in terms of a common, standardized, master list of zoning definitions. Thus, each jurisdiction's zoning classifications could be translated into standardized equivalents, and compared with those of other jurisdictions. Even more necessary is a set of standardized, detailed land-use codes, as discussed earlier in the Washington Council of Governments example.

A final dimension of data system organization involves the technical aspects of file organization. The manner in which individual data items are logically arranged within a particular data file can influence the cost and time associated with different processing operations to be performed on that data set. It may become necessary to reorder some data sets, and often these new versions are also preserved for future use. The most common method of data storage involves simple data files that are serially organized. That is, any particular data entity file will be ordered according to the sequential numerical values of a particular attribute (such as land parcel number, census tract number, or social security number). Other attributes may also be included in the file (and usually are), but these are not accessible in any easy way. It is possible, however, to develop a serial index for some secondary attribute, indicating with which of the primary attribute values each secondary value is-associated. More complex data file structures involve additional organizational problems.[34]

Data Processing

One perfunctory but essential application of computer processing in urban data systems involves editing data files for errors and consistency before such files are placed in storage or used for analysis or administrative purposes. For example, the attributes assigned to a given set of entities can be checked to see that each attribute has been assigned to the right entity and that all entities and attributes have been accounted for. Computer processing routines can be designed to make many types of checks and comparisons to verify the internal validity and consistency of reported data. This preliminary application of data processing permits correction of human errors in data collection, coding, key punching, and file organization, thus achieving much greater accuracy than under nonautomated records systems.

The data-processing component of an information system is typically seen as having two elements: computer hardware and software. Consideration of computer hardware, or equipment, characteristics, such as computational speed or memory size, is an exceedingly complex topic and lies beyond the scope of this report. The various computer manufacturers have developed a wide variety of equipment and system alternatives, each with a complicated and

often confusing array of technical capabilities and characteristics.[35]
But the crucial importance of supporting software (computer programs) for input, storage, processing, and output operations has
sometimes been overlooked. Local urban information systems and
data processing agencies typically obtain required software from
four major sources, and usually maintain some sort of mix of these
programming packages.

The four major software sources are:[36]

1. Manufacturer supplied or generally available software. These
include programmed routines available directly from computing
equipment vendors, users, organizations, software exchanges, uni-
versities, research laboratories, or other sources operating in the
public domain.

2. Proprietary software. These include leased or purchased computer
programs to which the vendor or supplier retains title, as well as
software provided by a private consulting firm as part of broader support or consultant services, including personnel, experience, etc.

3. Agency-developed software. In general, there will always be a
need for some software to be developed internally, for specialized
agency applications. Computer programming personnel will be required to develop, test, and apply such internally generated programming routines.

4. Federal agency sponsored software. The federal government,
particularly the Department of Defense and, in more recent years,
the Bureau of Public Roads, has also sponsored development of both
generalized and specialized data management packages.

A recent report on planning-oriented urban information systems
has identified a number of broad capabilities the data-processing
system (that is, computer hardware and software) should display:[37]

1. Accept and deliver data in a variety of forms. An interagency
information system will necessarily acquire data from different
sources and agencies. The system should be capable of accepting
and processing files organized in a variety of formats and data structures, and of producing files in a variety of output data formats.

2. Handle large volumes of data. It is likely that some urban data
files will be very large, beyond the normal storage capacity of the
data-processing system. There should be a capability for solving
these problems through file partitioning and recombining of data.

3. Operate on the individual values in a data set. A number of basic
capabilities in handling individual data items must be available, including (a) data transformation, such as addition, multiplication,
trigonometric functions, or other arithmetic or logical conversions,

(b) validation of inputs, as discussed above, (c) text manipulation, such as the handling of uncoded "natural" street names, (d) entity classification, or the automatic grouping of data according to the values of certain attributes, (e) dictionary look-up, or the use of file indexes for rapid access to a particular data item, and (f) entry value modification or updating.

4. Manipulate and alter data-set structures. A number of capabilities for handling data sets, as well as individual data items, must also be available. These include (a) entity selection and data set subsetting, (b) organizing and reorganizing data sets, as mentioned above, (c) combining or merging data sets, (d) data set reduction or summarization, resulting in such measures as sum, mean, median, or standard deviation, (e) processing of hierarchically organized data, (f) file inversion and dictionary construction, and (g) matrix operations on serial data sets, as related to a variety of statistical analysis procedures.

5. Display data. Once data have been processed or manipulated, the results of these operations must be reported to the user. The two most common forms of output display are the printed report (both standardized and special purpose) and graphic display (such as charts, maps, or graphs).

6. Provide for fact retrieval and analysis. In general, these capabilities refer to the data-retrieval and statistical-analysis applications of information systems discussed earlier. Summary report applications are also facilitated by this and the preceding "display data" capability.

7. Provide data base reference service and documentation. Included here are the need for (a) data naming and indexing, to permit the retrieval of data from secondary storage devices (such as disk or tape), (b) adequate data definition and description, and (c) data documentation, which will be discussed briefly in the following section.

8. Provide process management. A series of capabilities for managing the internal operation of the data processing system itself are also needed. These include (a) user/system communication, (b) job-specifications retention and recall, (c) linkage to user-supplied special-purpose functions and programs, (d) procedural control of computer tasks, (e) process monitoring and recording, and (f) data-set access and release protection, control, and auditing.

Finally, the importance of flexibility in data system design should also be acknowledged. Data input and output procedures should not become rigidly fixed, but should be capable of accommodating the as yet unknown information demands of future planning applications. As System Development Corporation has noted:

Information systems designed to support planning and programming must be highly sensitive to data acquisition and
data sharing operations; they must be both flexible and
open-ended. They must permit, to the greatest degree
possible, the incorporation of future data acquisitions,
as well as data from other agencies in a variety of formats,
codings, and media. In contrast, most city and county
files are fixed-length, single-organized files. The present
tendency of cities and counties to develop parcel files, in
which all data from various departments relevant to a
single parcel are brought together into a single record,
is an important step forward. Yet, an even greater degree
of flexibility and open-endedness is essential to the
planner.[38]

Data Maintenance

Once the initial data base for an urban information system has
been established, a continuing process of data updating and maintenance must be set in motion. Many information sources will involve
administrative data generated monthly (for example, building permits
or welfare caseloads), while practically all will (or should) involve
data reported annually. In concert with the various data-collection
tasks and methods outlined above, procedures should be established
for the regular absorption of updated data into the system. As a part
of ongoing data-system maintenance, various types of cooperative,
incremental improvements in data organization, entity definition,
and file compatibility should be sought. Agencies should apprise one
another of contemplated changes in data content and format and of
new or revised data collection activities. In general, the centralized
urban information center or data-processing agency should coordinate
these data maintenance operations.

The interagency, cooperative features of urban information
systems will become especially crucial for effective ongoing data
maintenance. Data systems must be designed so that the updated
files of various administrative agencies contain information used in
their regular operations. File updating should then emerge as a
matter of course, as a consequence of the normal operations of the
agency, so that continuous updating is ensured. If the files within an
information system are seen only as an additional burden to source
agencies, and not of direct value or benefit to them, there is a very
real danger that the information system will eventually break down.

Agencies must not only depend upon one another as sources for various types of interrelated data, they must themselves serve as direct users of the information system for regular administrative purposes—by incorporating their own functionally important data files within the system.

Closely related to the data organization phase of information system design is the parallel and continuing need for data documentation. That is, each type of series of data contained within the system must be adequately identified, described, and classified. Some sort of thesaurus, dictionary, or other reference file must be developed so that potential users of the system (such as the planning department) can quickly determine whether and how particular data needs can be met. These data base descriptions should also include indirect or secondary types of data that have been or could be created by the transformation of original data files, for a variety of possible analytic or administrative purposes. Often these transformations are or could be saved for later use. The data maintenance process is likely to lead to continuing changes and improvements in the overall data base, as new files are added, old ones reorganized, or new transformations created. Systematic and up-to-date documentation of these improvements consequently becomes a key feature of data system maintenance.

Finally, another key aspect of ongoing information system operation involves the problem of confidentiality. Many data files will contain information on persons, families, businesses, or organizations that, in some cases, will be regarded as private and confidential. These types of information will be publicly reported or available only on an aggregated basis (blocks, census tracts, etc.), where the identities of individual respondents are "hidden" within group statistics. Usually, only the source agency will have access to individual records, and then only for established and accepted administrative purposes.

However, for planning and analysis purposes, other agencies, and particularly the planning agency, may require access to individual unit records that will then be cross-tabulated or analyzed individually, with results reported on a group-statistic basis only. (Individual unit records will usually be required, of course, for accurate aggregation and reporting by new geographic subareas.) A consequent concern for the dangers of "invasion of privacy" has in some instances led to unwarranted fears over the misuse of urban information systems. But because the concept of a multipurpose, interagency, integrated information system requires exchange or sharing of data among different agencies, firm policies for control of data access and release must be established. Much guidance can be gained from the disclosure restrictions and procedures presently observed by the U.S. Bureau of the Census.[39]

COORDINATING URBAN INFORMATION RESOURCES

A really effective and workable urban planning information system would probably draw upon most of the information resources coordinated within a multipurpose, interagency urban information system. In general, except for the largest urban areas (which are most likely to be developing multipurpose systems, in any event), planning agencies are likely to find that the problems of independent planning information systems are overwhelming. Both the costs of system development and implementation and the problems associated with data acquisition and maintenance will be severe. Participation in the development and use of a general-purpose information system consequently offers the most practical means for improving planning data bases.

As noted at the outset of the chapter, a number of basic factors lie behind the growing importance of computer-based information systems in urban government. These include problems of data collection, availability, compatibility, updating, retrieval, processing, and analysis. Computerization has reduced the expanding costs associated with many of these problems and has dramatically shortened the time required for most data-processing applications. However, in spite of these gains, there is still considerable room for improvement in the development of integrated urban information systems. A number of fundamental improvements in further coordinating urban information resources should continue to be sought, in order to meet the data needs and interests of both administrative and planning agencies better. These areas of improvement serve to summarize many of the objectives and benefits of urban information systems described throughout this chapter and indicate that these benefits have to date been only partially achieved.

Among the basic areas for continued improvement in urban information resources are:[40]

1. Improving and coordinating existing data files. A wide variety of local, state, and federal agencies currently collect data on transportation, land use, population, and the economy that are of interest not only for administrative purposes but for a variety of urban and regional planning programs as well. Coordination of these data files is a complex assignment, involving many technical problems in collection, coding, and storage. A considerable amount of cooperation among agencies will be required to organize these diverse files into compatible parts of a centralized system. High on the list of desired improvements will very often be a more

detailed spatial disaggregation of reported data according to
common areal units, such as city blocks, census tracts, or other
small-area units.

2. Adopting standardized data-collection procedures. Spatial disaggregation problems could be circumvented in many instances if
the address-reference files and geographic-coding guides developed for the 1970 Census were widely adopted. Where such a
major shift may not be practicable or financially feasible, continued effort should be aimed at reaching agreement upon common
classification boundaries for related data files. Strong advocates
for various geographic-coding systems best suited to the operating
needs of individual agencies may often be found. In general,
standardized collection procedures require that we solve data
identification and matching problems according to person, parcel,
structure, activity, or other unit of observation.

3. Developing administrative records as new data sources. The
various operating programs of both the federal government and
local governments represent substantial sources of data currently
unavailable on a spatially disaggregated basis. Examples include
the federal income tax system, social security system, health
insurance system, and unemployment insurance system, as well
as local record systems such as those for various welfare programs, the public schools, local property taxes, state income
taxes, various licensing records, state sales taxes, and others.
In fact, a considerable amount of urban activity is covered in
government records in one form or another. With the widespread
and growing use of computers to increase the effectiveness of
such administrative records for operating purposes, the development of significant new sources of statistical information should
be sought as a by-product.

4. Coordinating data collection dates and time intervals. Temporal
relevancy represents another area for improvement in our data
sources. Though annual supplements (based on limited samples)
are now available for nearly all of the statistical products of the
Bureau of the Census, these are usually of very limited value
for small-area data purposes. Large-scale improvements in
sample size, collection methods, frequency of collection, and
offset time intervals may be warranted for the major censuses
now collected over five- and 10-year intervals. Noncommensurate
survey dates and serious updating problems also are involved in
major local data collection programs, such as transportation
studies, land-use planning inventories, and community renewal
programs. For many planning and analysis purposes, many kinds
of information should be made available monthly, especially for
monitoring the impact of short-range plans and programs.

5. Eliminating duplication and redundancy in data files. Successful
   coordination and integration of records will not only greatly
   decrease the time and effort necessary to make comparisons,
   correlation studies, and basic statistical analyses among related
   data sets, but also should eliminate much of the duplication and
   redundancy resulting from independent collection methods. Given
   a common referencing system, many agencies, including urban
   and regional planning agencies, are likely to find that needed but
   unavailable data will now be in acceptable format, permitting
   them to eliminate the collection and manipulation of less satisfactory surrogates. In general, each data item should be the
   responsibility of a single source. These improvements will also
   help to clarify the need for and scope of specially collected or
   nonadministrative data programs (in addition to the various federal census products).

6. Collecting new data. Urban and regional planners and analysts,
   in particular, are likely to find that some project or program
   impacts and levels of goal achievement (using the systems
   approach) cannot be evaluated using presently available data. New
   data may have to be collected, using appropriate sample survey
   and questionnaire techniques. In some cases, this data collection
   might be made a part of the administration of an ongoing or newly
   inaugurated public service program; in others, it might require
   the organization of a special survey staff—to determine, for
   example, citizen satisfaction with environmental-improvement
   programs, such as tree planting, park malls, street lighting,
   street cleaning and repair, neighborhood beautification, rodent
   and vermin control. Or a special survey might be desired to
   determine the recreation needs and preferences of low-income
   families, especially for children and elderly persons. To the
   extent possible, these specialized data sources should be made
   compatible with regularly updated data files, to permit maximum
   flexibility in subsequent analyses.

While these general categories of data improvement serve to
summarize much of the thrust behind general-purpose data system
development, the role of the planning agency in this process should
be outlined more clearly. In its attempts to structure its planning
operations more systematically, following the broad procedure outlined at the beginning of this chapter, the local planning agency should
first attempt to determine what its own continuing data needs will be.
Within each of the planning and analysis activities which the agency
conducts, what types of information are typically needed to identify
community objectives, to identify alternative programs, to predict
relative effectiveness levels, and to evaluate alternative programs?

In addition, what are the common or overlapping data needs of different local planning agencies (city, county, metropolitan, state, quasi-public)?

Given some feeling for anticipated planning data requirements, the local agency should then proceed to investigate (a) the availability of needed data from individual operating agencies and (b) the current status of interagency and intergovernmental cooperation in the development of some sort of coordinated, general-purpose information system. The process of acquiring or gaining access to needed information, as well as the process of effectively using that information, are, of course, complex undertakings, as other sections of the chapter have indicated. Individual circumstances will dictate which types of data might be made available through which of many possible cooperative arrangements. The degree to which centralized, interagency information systems have been locally developed will, however, significantly influence the relative ease with which planning information demands may be met. Local planning agencies should therefore vigorously support and promote the continuing development of area-wide data centers and multiple-purpose information systems.

NOTES

1. See Doris B. Holleb, Social and Economic Information for Urban Planning, vol. 1 (Chicago: Center for Urban Studies, University of Chicago, 1969), especially Chapter 5, "Functions and Requirements of Information in Planning," for further details on the relationship between the systems approach and urban information systems. See also Doris B. Holleb, "Social Statistics for Social Policy," in Planning 1968 (Chicago: American Society of Planning Officials, 1968); John K. Parker, "Decisions, Data Needs, and Rationality," in Threshold of Planning Information Systems (Chicago: American Society of Planning Officials, 1967); Melvin M. Webber, "The Roles of Intelligence Systems in Urban-Systems Planning," AIP Journal (November 1965).

2. For a general review and discussion of the parallel development of comprehensive metropolitan planning activities and general-purpose metropolitan information systems, the interrelationships between the two, and the need to have them conducted as separate activities (ideally with both under the aegis of a single, multimission metropolitan governmental council), see Willard B. Hansen, "Comprehensive Planning and General-Purpose Information Assistance for Metropolitan Regions," in Urban and Regional Information Systems: Federal Activities and Specialized Systems, John E. Rickert, ed. (Kent, Ohio: Kent State University, 1968).

3. Further details on these different types of governmental applications may be found in Public Automated Systems Services, Governmental ADP: The Practitioners Speak (Chicago: Public Administration Service, 1966); and in the monthly newsletter published by Public Automated Systems Service, Public Automation.

4. System Development Corporation, Urban and Regional Information Systems: Support for Planning in Metropolitan Areas (Washington, D.C.: Government Printing Office, 1968), Part IV, pp. 53-62. See also Glenn O. Johnson, "An Automated Data System: The Los Angeles Approach," in Proceedings of the Fourth Annual Conference on Urban Planning Information Systems and Programs (Berkeley, Calif.: Department of City and Regional Planning, University of California, 1966).

5. System Development Corporation, Support for Planning, Part IV, pp. 81-90; Robert A. Clark, "LOGIC: the Santa Clara County Government Information System and Its Relationship to the Planning Department," in Threshold of Planning Information Systems.

6. Robert Totschek, "An Outline of the Work Program Design for a Bay Region Planning Information Support Center," in Urban and Regional Information Systems: Service Systems for Cities, John E. Rickert, ed. (Kent, Ohio: Kent State University, 1969). See also System Development Corporation, Support for Planning, Part IV, pp. 27-38, for a description of the Bay Area Transportation Study Commission information system.

7. Samuel R. Norris, "California's San Gabriel Valley Municipal Data System: The First of Many?" Public Automation (October 1969).

8. In addition, significant new developments are currently under way in New York City, where the design of a Geographic Data Network has been inaugurated. Under this concept, individual agencies will continue to maintain their own data files independently, while a centralized, user-oriented capability for data interchange is provided. Central to the concept is the development of a Geographic Information System (GIST), designed to permit the assignment of geographic coordinates to the elements within a particular data set. Different data files can then be coordinated and compared according to the geographic location of each data item. See Robert Amsterdam, "The Concept of a Data Network and the Development of GIST," in Rickert, Service Systems for Cities; E. S. Savas, Robert Amsterdam, and Eric Brodheim, "Creation of a Geographic Information System," in Papers, Fourth Annual Symposium on the Application of Computers to the Problems of Urban Society (New York: Association for Computing Machinery, 1969); and E. S. Savas, "Heuristic and Opportunistic Incrementalism: the Road to Urban Information Systems," in Rickert, Federal Activities and Specialized Systems.

9. George C. Hemmens, "Survey of Planning Agency Experience with Urban Development Models, Data Processing, and Computers,"

in Urban Development Models, Special Report 97, George Hemmens, ed. (Washington, D.C.: Highway Research Board, 1968); George C. Hemmens, "Planning Agency Experience with Urban Development Models and Data Processing," AIP Journal (September 1968).

10. Clark D. Rogers and Claude D. Peters, "AIP Survey of Automated Information Systems for Urban Planning," draft (Information Systems Committee, American Institute of Planners, October 1967).

11. In addition, see Brian Barber, "Information Systems and Metropolitan Planning," in Urban and Regional Information Systems for Social Programs, John E. Rickert, ed. (Kent, Ohio: Kent State University, 1967), for a brief analysis of the interrelationships between five different types of metropolitan planning agencies (defined in terms of scope of activities) and 12 more detailed types of information-system usage or capability. In general, it is concluded that most typical data-system applications would be of value to each of the different levels of metropolitan planning.

12. These examples are taken from Manly Johnson and E. P. Alworth, eds., Metropolitan Data Center Project (Washington, D.C.: U.S. Housing and Home Finance Agency, 1966). See also Robert L. Wegner, "The Metropolitan Data Center: New Tool for Decision-Making," in Planning 1964 (Chicago: American Society of Planning Officials, 1964). This demonstration project resulted in the cooperative development of partial data systems, each aimed at a particular planning function, in five cities: Denver (comprehensive land-use inventory), Little Rock (school facility planning), Fort Worth (CBD planning), Tulsa (community renewal planning), and Wichita (capital-improvement programming).

13. Hemmens, "Survey of Planning Agency Experience."

14. George L. Farnsworth, "Current Developments in Dual Independent Map Encoding," in Rickert, Federal Activities and Specialized Systems.

15. Charles Barb, "Street Address Conversion System," in Rickert, Federal Activities and Specialized Systems; Robert B. Dial, "Street Address Conversion System," in Planning 1965 (Chicago: American Society of Planning Officials, 1965).

16. Laboratory for Computer Graphics and Spatial Analysis, User Reference Manual for Synagraphic Computer Mapping SYMAP, Version 5 (Cambridge, Mass.: Harvard University, 1968). See also Allan Schmidt, "The SYMAP Computer Mapping Program," in Rickert, Federal Activities and Specialized Systems.

17. Kendal H. Bishop and Steven C. Gibson, Mapping by 1401 Computer Using MAP 01, Publ. CP00-014-02 (Albany, N.Y.: Division of Transportation Planning and Programming, New York State Department of Public Works, 1966).

18. Farnsworth, "Map Encoding."

19. Both examples are taken from William H. Maxfield, "Computer Mapping of Census Aggregated Data: The New Haven Census Use Study Experience," in Rickert, Federal Activities and Specialized Systems. See also Donald F. Cooke, "Systems, Geocoding, and Mapping," in Rickert, Federal Activities and Specialized Systems; Donald F. Cooke and William H. Maxfield, "The Development of a Geographic Base File and Its Uses for Mapping," in Rickert, Social Programs.

20. U.S. Bureau of the Census, 1970 Census User Guide, second draft (Washington, D.C.: Government Printing Office, 1969); George McGimsey, "The 1970 Census: Changes and Innovations," AIP Journal (May 1970). See also William T. Fay, "The Geography of the 1970 Census: A Cooperative Effort," in Planning 1966 (Chicago: American Society of Planning Officials, 1966).

21. Caby C. Smith, "The New Haven Census Use Study: A General Description," in Rickert, Social Programs.

22. George L. Farnsworth, "Census Use Study," in Rickert, Service Systems for Cities.

23. George L. Farnsworth, "Current Developments in Dual Independent Map Encoding," in Rickert, Federal Activities and Specialized Systems; Heidi Cochran, "Address Matching," in Rickert, Federal Activities and Specialized Systems; Joseph Daly and Robert Voight, "The 1970 Census Address Coding Guide Improvement Program," in Rickert, Service Systems for Cities.

24. McGimsey, "The 1970 Census."

25. Bruce D. McDowell and Albert Mindlin, "A Local Based Metropolitan Planning Data System," in Rickert, Service Systems for Cities. See also J. C. Barrett, "Structuring Regional Data," ibid.

26. U.S. Department of Housing and Urban Development, Urban Renewal Administration, and U.S. Bureau of Public Roads, Standard Land Use Coding Manual (Washington, D.C.: Government Printing Office, 1965).

27. Robert D. Campbell and Hugh L. LeBlanc, An Information System for Urban Planning (Washington, D.C.: Government Printing Office, 1967).

28. Joan E. Jacoby, "DEWS: District Early Warning System for Neighborhood Deterioration," in Rickert, Social Programs; Joan E. Jacoby, "The Neighborhood Early Warning System: Design and Development," paper presented at the Third Annual Symposium on the Application of Computers to the Problems of Urban Society, Association for Computing Machinery, October 1968.

29. For a useful and thought provoking analysis of the general utility of urban information systems, see George Leyland, "Cost-Benefit Analysis of Urban Information Systems," in Rickert, Service

<u>Systems for Cities</u>. Leyland defines a series of eight broad data-
system alternatives (bibliographic reporting, social reporting, management information, computer modeling, data-series reporting,
program planning and budgeting, planning information, and research
information systems) and then compares them in terms of crude estimates of relative costs and benefits. Costs are defined in two parts:
start-up costs (distributed among some 20 major technical components) and other costs (composed of 15 different exogenous technical
features, as well as 27 different political/business elements). Benefits are defined in four parts: user/functional benefits (21 elements),
technical/operations benefits (23 elements), decision-making benefits
(20 elements), and political/organizational benefits (21 elements).
On the basis of these highly subjective and approximate comparisons,
program-planning and budgeting information systems are found to be
preferred, followed in order by social-reporting information systems
and planning information systems.

For a contrasting analysis of the costs and benefits of municipal
information systems, expressed in terms of expected return on
municipal investment, see Myron E. Weiner, "Cost-Benefit Ratio of
EDP: A Political Challenge," in <u>Threshold of Planning Information</u>
<u>Systems</u>. Return on investment is defined in terms of dollar savings
in governmental operating costs and potentials for sounder community
development. For a further discussion of the relationship of PPBS
and supporting information systems, see Richard A. Siegel, "A
Program Approach to Information Systems," <u>AIP Journal</u> (March 1968).

30. Edward F. R. Hearle and Raymond J. Mason, <u>A Data Proc-</u>
<u>essing System for State and Local Governments</u> (Englewood Cliffs,
N.J.: Prentice-Hall, 1963).

31. Ibid., pp. 61-72.

32. System Development Corporation, <u>Support for Planning</u>,
Part 1, pp. 41-44.

33. Ibid., pp. 45-46.

34. See ibid., Part 1, Ch. 9, "Data Base Organization," pp. 62-
67, for further discussion.

35. See Hearle and Mason, <u>State and Local Governments</u>, App. C,
"Equipment Evaluation and Selection," pp. 131-38, for a discussion
of some of the factors to consider in comparing different equipment
systems. Stress is on the importance of evaluating hardware options
in terms of their ability to perform a specific series of required or
desired operations.

36. System Development Corporation, <u>Support for Planning</u>,
Part 1, pp. 105-11.

37. Ibid., pp. 94-104.

38. Ibid., p. 40.

39. For a detailed review of the problems of information security, see System Development Corporation, Support for Planning, Part 1, Ch. 10, "Data Release Policy and Other Data Access Controls," pp. 68-83.

40. Similar arguments for greater coordination are presented by J. Richard Vincent, "Criteria for Linking Functional to Jurisdictional Systems," in Rickert, Social Programs, where functional information systems (intergovernmental usage for a single purpose, such as police administration or property assessment) and jurisdictional information systems (single governmental usage for a variety of departmental purposes, such as that achieved by many municipal and county systems) are described and compared. For a sobering examination of some of the political impediments to greater coordination, see Anthony Downs, "A Realistic Look at the Final Payoffs from Urban Data Systems," Public Administration Review (September 1967). Downs identifies a number of interagency or interdepartmental "power payoffs" that are likely to perpetuate highly piecemeal approaches to the adoption and use of automated urban information systems.

ABOUT THE AUTHOR

DARWIN G. STUART is a Principal Associate with Barton-Aschman Associates, Inc., transportation and urban planning consultants. He has directed a wide variety of research and planning studies throughout the country, for local, regional, state, and federal agencies.

Dr. Stuart has also served as a part-time faculty member in the planning programs of the University of Illinois, Urbana; San Diego State University; and the University of Southern California.

Dr. Stuart holds an A.B. degree from Dartmouth College, an M.U.P. from the University of Illinois, and M.S. and Ph.D. degrees from Northwestern University.

THE EFFECTS OF URBAN GROWTH: A Population
Impact Analysis
> Richard P. Appelbaum, Jennifer A. Bigelow,
> Henry P. Kramer, Harvey L. Molotch, and
> Paul Relis

THE POLITICAL REALITIES OF URBAN PLANNING
> Don T. Allensworth

URBAN GROWTH MANAGEMENT THROUGH
DEVELOPMENT TIMING
> David J. Brower, David W. Owens,
> Ronald Rosenberg, Ira Botvinick,
> and Michael Mandel

URBAN NONGROWTH: Planning for People
> Earl Finkler, William J. Toner,
> and Frank J. Popper

URBAN PROBLEMS AND PUBLIC POLICY CHOICES
> edited by Joel Bergsman
> and Howard L. Wiener